A Taste of Ohio History

Also by Debbie Nunley and Karen Jane Elliott

A Taste of Pennsylvania History
A Taste of Virginia History
A Taste of Maryland History

John F. Blair, Publisher
Winston-Salem, North Carolina

A Taste of Ohio History

SECOND EDITION

A Guide to Historic Eateries and Their Recipes

Debbie Nunley & Karen Jane Elliott

Published by John F. Blair, Publisher

*The paper in this book meets the guidelines
for permanence and durability of the Committee on Production
Guidelines for Book Longevity of the Council on Library Resources.*

ON THE FRONT COVER, CLOCKWISE FROM THE TOP—
The Clifton Mill in Clifton, Peerless Mill Inn in Miamisburg, and The Precinct in Cincinnati

Library of Congress Cataloging-in-Publication Data

Nunley, Debbie.
    A taste of Ohio history : a guide to historic eateries and their recipes / by Debbie Nunley and Karen Jane Elliott.— 2nd ed.
        p.   cm.
    Includes index.
    ISBN-13: 978-0-89587-341-5 (alk. paper)
    ISBN-10: 0-89587-341-9
1. Cookery. 2. Restaurants—Ohio—Guidebooks. 3. Historic buildings—Ohio. I. Elliott, Karen Jane, 1958- II. Title.

    TX714.N84 2007
    641.59771—dc22   2007005019

Design by Angela Harwood and Debra Long Hampton

To my daughter, Dori, whose infinite support, patience,
and understanding far exceed her years
Debbie

To my parents, John and Ann Lidiard, who taught me to be a strong,
independent woman, and who have been telling me to "write a book" for years
Karen

Contents

Restaurants Featured in *A Taste of Ohio History*

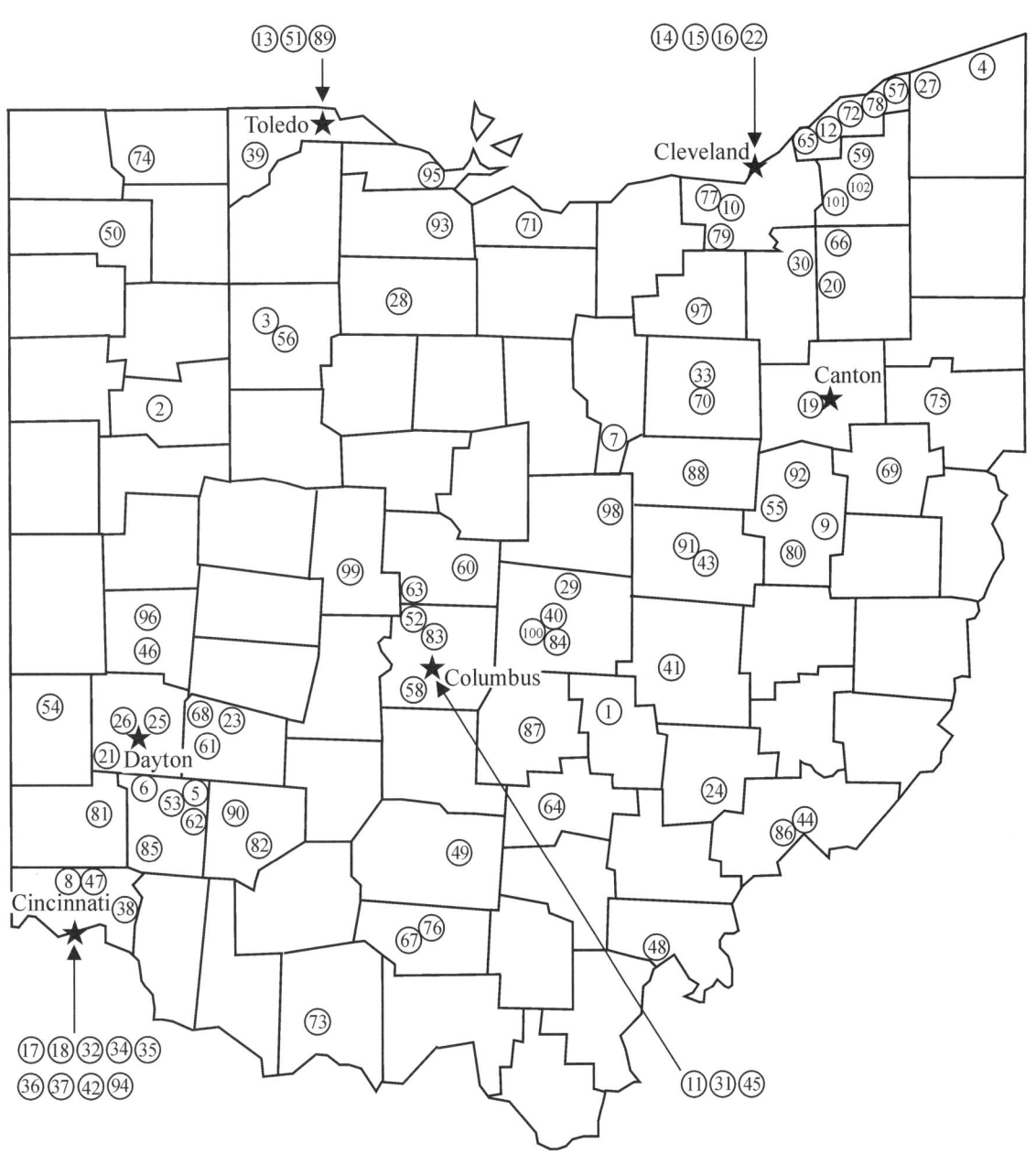

Preface

Our love of historic restaurants began who knows when. From earliest childhood memories, we both recall being fascinated by them. We began sharing the experience in 1993, shortly after we both moved to the northern suburbs of Pittsburgh. Going to historic restaurants was a method of getting to know yet another new area, after a series of moves. We were active volunteers at the elementary school our children attended, and word quickly got out that we had these wonderful luncheon adventures. Soon, we had a group of ladies who shared the joy of discovering wonderful relics. Over lunch, in an atmosphere steeped in history, these women became some of our dearest friends.

The restaurants that are of the most interest to us really fit into two categories. The first are longstanding inns, taverns, and the like that have been in business in the same locale for a significant period of time. In these, we look for historical integrity inside and out. In other words, we want them to look as if George Washington, Abe Lincoln, or some other famous personage might walk in any minute. The second type includes restaurants housed in historic buildings such as schools, churches, barns, and train stations. In these locales, the portion of the building that is old or original varies, as conversions from one use to another have necessitated some changes, and modern building codes have dictated others. The exteriors have changed very little, so each is quite recognizable as what it once was. Buildings that once served as stores have probably changed the most inside, although the long, narrow rooms are unmistakable. Since stores are defined more by the wares they've carried than their architectural features, this isn't surprising.

Our focus is on buildings that are more than one hundred years old, although on occasion we consider locations slightly younger than that if the history is of particular significance to the area. As we compile our initial list for consideration, we read absolutely everything we can. Typically, this starts with an Internet search for restaurants with their own web sites. Frequently, it also involves going through the yellow pages town by town, county by county, looking for names of restaurants that "sound historic." Because we try to represent each state thoroughly, we contact convention and visitors' bureaus and chambers of commerce for any literature they might have. This usually gives us additional information, as well as confirming our Internet resources. As we begin our travels, the gathering of information continues, as we pick up local fliers, seek personal recommendations, and drive the back roads in search of a "find."

During the research for the first edition of this book, we compiled a list of close to five hundred Ohio restaurants, knowing from experience that some of them wouldn't have maintained their historical features. Others would want to participate but would never quite get around to it. A few would think that sending us the recipes and history just wasn't worth the effort. The very few that choose not to participate for this reason always sadden us, because invariably they're fabulous

places full of interesting facts that we wish we could share. Alas, we can't begin to cover everything there is in three hundred pages anyway!

For this second edition, we began by contacting those restaurants that we'd included during our first Ohio go-round. Many were still as they had been when we did our initial research in 2000 and 2001. That's not surprising, since our focus is in historic locales, after all. Other establishments were still in business but had changed names, owners, chefs, décor, menus, and who knows what else. Those entries had to be updated to reflect their evolution. Unfortunately, there were restaurants that for a variety of reasons were no longer in business. So our quest began anew to replace those. First on the list were those eateries that we'd identified during our first-edition research that for one reason or another never got their information to us. If we wanted them then, we wanted them again. We then broadened our search to look for things we might have missed or places that had come to be since 2001.

Our goal is to be as thorough as possible in representing cuisine, price points, types of establishments, and historical information, while comprehensively and appropriately representing the cities and counties across the state. In more ways than one, our books truly are *A Taste of . . .*

Our favorite part of the research continues to be meeting and talking to the people involved with the restaurants. Their stories are intricately woven into the fascinating history of each locale. As always, there were certain aspects of local history we expected to learn, such as those involving prominent families and their lovely homes. We were thrilled to find Underground Railroad locations and to learn how significant Ohio was to the cause. Other stories took us quite by surprise, and we hope you find them equally enlightening.

As in the previous edition and all of our other books, we organized the restaurants into chapters based on what they have in common. The cohesive thread in each reflects a slice of Americana that still exists throughout the state. Thriving Main Streets, farmsteads, and log cabins all provided inspiration for chapters, as did the Underground Railroad. We've started the book with a chapter called "Main Street, USA," because in small towns across the heartland, what could be more appropriate? In this chapter, you'll find an establishment from the Underground Railroad. Helping slaves to freedom was so pervasive within this town that it was mainstream on Main Street!

Within each chapter, we have listed the eateries in the order visited. The one excep-tion is the travel chapter, "How Do I Get There from Here?" where we've arranged them by mode of conveyance, and within each mode by the order in which we visited. We've used pen-and-ink drawings to introduce each chapter. Each restaurant is represented by its own logo, giving the write-up its own unique heading.

Now that we've compiled five books in four different states, we continue to be amazed and thankful that so much history has been saved. Sometimes as we travel, we have difficulty telling exactly where we are as we drive past one mega store and chain establishment after another. While we accept that they serve a purpose and have a place in our economy and our lives, we lament the stories, history, and culture lost as independent businesses struggle to survive. We salute the warm, wonderful people throughout Ohio whom we've gotten to know, and hope that their stories, and this book, will in some way encourage others to take on the challenges and rewards of maintaining their local history.

Acknowledgments

I would like to extend my personal thanks to my neighbors Elody Krieger and Mona Marple for serving as my "research assistants" hither, thither, and yon.

Debbie

A Taste of
Ohio History

SECOND EDITION

CHAPTER 1
Main Street, USA

Clay Haus

Long the center of commerce and community activity throughout America, Main Street is not just a location but a term that has become synonymous with a down-home atmosphere. As society has changed, many Main Streets have struggled to survive. This chapter celebrates those establishments, and those cities, for which Main Street is still going strong!

Clay Haus

123 WEST MAIN STREET
SOMERSET, OH 43783
WWW.CLAYHAUS.COM
740-743-1326

Founder Betty Snider was a direct descendant of one of the voyagers on the *Mayflower*. Maybe that kind of lineage explains her love of history, artifacts, and old implements. She and her husband, Carl, opened Clay Haus in 1979 at Betty's insistence. Today, her son, Scott, and one of her grandsons run the business. The restaurant was named for her father, Irwin Clay Priest. The spelling of *Haus* honors this area of German settlement and her husband's Pennsylvania Dutch heritage.

As we browsed the old pictures along the walls, including many of family ancestors, we were particularly drawn to the one of the statue dedication in the town square. Ladies in their long dresses and fanciest hats and gentlemen in their best attire had gathered en masse for this civic celebration. Today, this area of Somerset, with a large flag flying over the likeness of Civil War general Philip Sheri-

dan, still looks almost identical to what is in that photo.

That square, just a block down the street from Clay Haus, used to be the hunting area for George Jackson. Clay Haus sits along what was once Zane Trace, the first major roadway through Ohio. At the time Jackson owned the building, the downstairs Keeping Room was at street level, but resurfacing through the years has raised the roadbed about five feet. It was in this room that George Jackson enjoyed a meal of venison and wild turkey that he'd caught while hunting with his cousin, President Andrew Jackson.

We were seated by the fireplace in the upstairs dining room. It was a treat after driving through the sleet on a January day. The cozy room had antique pictures and farm implements adorning the walls. Original random plank flooring, lace curtains, and a wedding-ring quilt all enhanced the quaint atmosphere.

The food was as comforting as the surroundings. Lunch choices include a BLT and a Barbecued Beef Sandwich. Side dishes such as German Potato Salad, Three Bean Salad, and Marinated Carrot Salad are all popular. Debbie chose a traditional plate lunch of Meat Loaf, Mashed Potatoes, and Green Beans, which really hit the spot. The Meat Loaf was a full inch thick, reminiscent of Grandma's. Karen also went traditional, enjoying a bowl of Bean Soup with a Pennsylvania Dutch flair—dumplings. It came with a wedge of Cornbread that had just been cooked in a large cast-iron skillet. With heartland cooking like this, we certainly weren't going to skip dessert. Karen's Cream Puff was full of whipped cream and topped with Chocolate Sauce. Debbie's Walnut Pie was a delicious kin to Pecan Pie.

We truly enjoyed chatting with the Sniders and learning about their life with the restaurant. We heard lots about their ghost, Mariah, whom Scott once saw waving at the kitchen door and Betty once mistook for one of her employees. Male ghosts have also been spotted, particularly on the stairs. As usual, we left without meeting any of them. Maybe next time.

GERMAN POTATO SALAD

6 large potatoes
½ pound (8 to 10 slices) bacon
½ cup chopped onions
1 cup vinegar
2 cups water
1 tablespoon salt
1 teaspoon pepper
1 cup brown sugar
1 to 2 tablespoons flour, if needed

Peel and slice potatoes. Boil in a large pot of water until soft but not mushy. Drain. Brown bacon and onions in skillet until bacon is crisp. (Don't worry if bacon gets dark; this enhances the flavor.) Combine vinegar and water and add to skillet. Add salt, pepper, and brown sugar. Bring to a boil to thicken. If you need to thicken the liquid further, combine flour with about 1 tablespoon water and stir into skillet. Put potato slices in a large bowl. Toss with salt and pepper if desired. Add hot dressing from skillet, stirring gently. Serve warm. Serves 8 to 10.

SAUERBRATEN

3- to 4-pound chuck roast
½ cup pearl onions
¾ cup chunked celery
¾ cup chunked carrots
½ cup vinegar
1 cup red wine
1 cup water
½ cup brown sugar
½ cup crushed gingersnaps
1 tablespoon salt
1 tablespoon peppercorns
½ tablespoon allspice
1 bay leaf
½ to 1 cup sour cream, as desired

Preheat oven to 350 degrees. Place chuck roast in a roasting pan. Put all remaining ingredients except sour cream in roaster with the roast. Cook 2 to 3 hours until roast is tender. Remove from oven. Take roast and vegetables out of broth. Stir sour cream into broth. If mixture is too thin, stir in additional crushed gingersnaps to thicken to a gravy consistency. Slice roast. Serve on a large platter with vegetables. Drizzle gravy over top; serve remaining gravy in a gravy boat. Serves 8 to 10.

Main Street Bistro

Casual Fine Dining

213-217 SOUTH MAIN STREET
LIMA, OH 45801
WWW.MAIN-STREET-BISTRO.COM
419-224-0473

No one is sure exactly when the first building was erected on lot 93 at 213 South Main Street. It is estimated that a modest house was constructed here between 1837 and 1847. By 1887, the Sanborn Fire Insurance maps showed a small dwelling. In 1888, Dr. Charles Metzger occupied the building. He had been a first lieutenant for the 125th Ohio Volunteer Infantry Regiment, which saw action in the Civil War. Now a successful physician and surgeon, he lived in 213 and set up his practice in 215. It was during his tenure that the building took its present form.

In 1907, Charles Metzger's wife, Clara, sold the property—which now consisted of 213, 215, and 217—to The Lima Home Baking Company. One of the new owners, a Mr. Frank Colucci, was a very successful businessman. An Italian immigrant, Colucci had started his career in the employment of the Baltimore & Ohio Railroad Company. He had moved progressively upward on a succession of railroad construction projects across the country. He was reputed to have an "excellent business capacity and judgement." Indeed, by the time he purchased the building outright in 1912, he was a stockholder and director of the American Bank of Lima. He also owned a real-estate company, which he operated out of his Main Street property.

Over the next seventy years, the three addresses that comprise the Main Street Bistro housed a hatchery, a music instrument store, a furniture store, a bar, apartments, and a used clothing store. The property looks much the same today as it did during the 1800s—a beautiful two-story brick building with a small turret at the center and tall sash windows on the second floor, surmounted by wrought-iron balustrades.

The inside of this Victorian building has been restored to much of its original splendor. Archways have been built into the exposed-brick walls to connect the three rooms on the first floor. The original plank floors are still there, as is the tiled entranceway to the bar area. Victorian chandeliers and wall sconces enhance the ambiance. The two dining rooms have a definite bistro flavor, with brown paper laid over white linen tablecloths.

On the day we visited, executive chef Alisa McPheron had prepared a selection of dishes for us to sample. We began with the Chicken Gumbo, which was spicy and delicious. The Crawfish Cakes were equally good, served with a side of Tomato Corn Relish. Debbie particularly enjoyed the Crispelli, a stuffed-crepe creation served with Roasted Red Pepper Cream Sauce. We also sampled

Gambari, which consisted of Pan-Roasted Prosciutto-Wrapped Shrimp together with Balsamic Caramelized Onions, and the Jumbo Deep-Fried Cheese Ravioli, both of which were good. Dessert is always Karen's favorite. Although the Tiramisu was wonderful, the Chocolate Truffle Cake won the day. Not too rich, it was definitely melt-in-the-mouth good.

CRAWFISH CAKES

1 small red onion, finely diced
½ green pepper, finely diced
½ yellow pepper, finely diced
1 pound crawfish tail meat, cooked and diced
¼ cup thick mayonnaise
1 small egg, beaten
1 tablespoon Old Bay seasoning
2 to 3 cups breadcrumbs
2 tablespoons vegetable oil
½ cup Lemon Cream Sauce (see next column)

In a medium skillet over medium heat, cook onions and peppers until onions are translucent. Place in a large bowl and set aside to cool. When cool, add crawfish, mayonnaise, and beaten egg and mix together thoroughly. Add seasoning and half the breadcrumbs and mix together. Slowly add enough breadcrumbs to bind mixture. Separate mixture into 8 equal balls. Form each into a patty and roll in remaining breadcrumbs to coat. Place patties in the refrigerator and chill for at least 30 minutes.

Heat oil in a skillet over medium heat. Sear patties and cook for 2 to 3 minutes on each side. Serve hot with Lemon Cream Sauce. Serves 4.

LEMON CREAM SAUCE

3 cups heavy cream
pinch of salt
pinch of pepper
2 teaspoons lemon zest
juice of ½ lemon
1 tablespoon chopped fresh parsley

Heat cream in a saucepan on high. Add salt, pepper, lemon zest, and juice. Cook until thickened. Finish with chopped parsley. Yields 2 cups.

ROSSILLI'S
CREATIVE AMERICAN & ITALIAN CUISINE
Boo's Lounge

217 SOUTH MAIN STREET
FINDLAY, OH 45840
419-423-5050

When we first visited Rossilli's, it was located one hundred feet north of its present location, in an entirely different historic building. At that time, chef Gary Rossilli was very generous in letting us sample, and the people at the tables nearby were somewhat affronted when three wait staff laden with plates and platters descended on us. We started with the Crab and Spinach Cannelloni in Lemon-Dill Sauce, which was fabulous. That was quickly followed by tasty portions of Smoked Chicken Ravioli, Focaccia, homemade Italian Sausage, Blackened Meat Loaf, and Wild Mushroom Pesto Bruschetta with fresh mozzarella. Talk about gastronomic delights! The Italian Sausage is still made from a family recipe, which Gary's dad developed and sold in his Cleveland grocery store. He used to travel to the restaurant to make it for Gary but finally decided that Gary was accomplished enough in the kitchen to make it for himself. The Meat Loaf, served with Garlic Mashed Potatoes and topped with Sherry Molasses Sauce, was the most popular item on the menu, and we could certainly see why.

Gary, his wife, Meg, and Meg's brother, Mike, own the restaurant. They're an enthu-

siastic bunch who were all doing very different things in 1994 when they decided to get into the restaurant business. Mike was in Florida working at a chain restaurant, Gary was a plumber, and Meg was working for a locksmith. The move into the restaurant world has been very successful for them, and in 2001 they purchased their own building. Constructed in 1875, it was originally J. B. Webers Saloon. Just two years later, it was so successful that food was added, turning it into J. B. Webers Saloon & Restaurant. However, many patrons of today remember it as the home of Bryant's Shoe Store, where their parents took them to buy shoes as children.

Debbie was elsewhere on the day that my husband, Gordon, and I visited to check out Rossilli's again. The building is long and thin with an ornate tin ceiling. Much of the wooden flooring is original, as are the exposed-brick walls. The bar area at the front of the building has a most unusual backbar. A lovely antique piece acquired at the restaurant's previous location, it was once used in the movie *The Unsinkable Molly Brown*. The porcelain inserts, woodwork beading, and other Victorian details are just delightful. Chef Gary proudly showed us around the dining room upstairs, known as Boo's Lounge. With its curved front window looking over Main Street, the location is just perfect for private dinner parties.

We settled at a table to the rear of the establishment and were thrilled with our lunch choices. The sushi-grade Sesame-Crusted Ahi Tuna served with Wasabi Mashed Potatoes and Asian Slaw was absolutely delicious, as was

Gordon's choice, the special of the day, Sesame Salmon. We couldn't resist trying a square of house-made Tiramisu. It was just as good as on the first visit! Gary is currently working on his new creations: West Coast Zas. These unique house-made pizzas are likely to be as successful with the people of Findlay as the restaurant itself.

ROASTED RED PEPPER VINAIGRETTE

3 large red peppers, roasted, peeled, and seeded
1 cup rice wine vinegar
1 tablespoon Dijon mustard
1 teaspoon dry mustard
2 cups olive oil
salt and freshly ground pepper to taste

In a blender, combine peppers, vinegar, and mustards. Purée. Put mixture into a bowl and slowly whisk in olive oil until mixture is emulsified. Add salt and pepper. Yields approximately 4 cups.

FLORENTINE MASHED POTATOES

5 pounds Yukon Gold or red-skin potatoes, skin on
16-ounce box frozen chopped spinach, thawed
1½ cups shredded mozzarella cheese
½ cup grated Parmesan cheese
4 sticks butter, cubed
⅓ cup heavy cream
salt and pepper to taste

Dice potatoes into medium-sized cubes. Place potatoes in a large pot and cover with at least 4 inches of cold water. Bring to a boil and cook until potatoes are tender but not falling apart. Drain and place in a mixing bowl. While potatoes are cooking, thoroughly squeeze all of the liquid from the spinach. Add half of the spinach to the potatoes, along with half of the cheeses, half of the butter, all of the cream, and salt and pepper. Combine using an electric mixer. Add remaining spinach, butter, and cheeses. Blend mixture until thoroughly combined. Serves 10 to 12.

CALAMATA OLIVE SPREAD

1 cup garlic cloves, peeled
1 tablespoon olive oil
2 cups calamata olives, pitted
¾ cup extra-virgin olive oil
½ cup sun-dried tomatoes, coarsely chopped

Preheat oven to 350 degrees. Place garlic cloves on a piece of foil and drizzle with 1 tablespoon olive oil. Close foil around garlic cloves and bake for 15 minutes until garlic is soft and golden. In a food processor, combine garlic and olives; continue to process while drizzling in extra-virgin olive oil. Remove mixture from processor, place in a small bowl, and stir in sun-dried tomatoes. Yields 3 cups.

CASA CAPELLI

GREAT FOOD
CHOICES
&
SPIRITS

4641 MAIN AVENUE
ASHTABULA, OH 44004
WWW.CASACAPELLI.COM
440-992-3700

In 1847, a petition was filed with the Ohio General Assembly at Columbus requesting authority to form a bank in Ashtabula. In due time, the petition was granted, and The Farmer's Bank of Ashtabula opened. The original offices were located above George Hubbard's hardware store, on the second floor of the wooden building directly across the street from the present bank. It's easy to imagine the excitement in the village when four horses pulling a huge coach along the dirt roads arrived with the first shipment of silver and gold bullion and bank notes. The Farmer's Bank operated as a state bank until the end of the Civil War. The shareholders petitioned for and were issued a national-bank charter in 1865.

The bank occupied several other buildings in town until 1904, when it moved to 4641 Main Avenue. Constructed just one year earlier, the building was an elegant home for the rapidly expanding bank. Ornate Corinthian columns stood on both sides of the main lobby, surmounted by a barrel ceiling with a gorgeous arched stained-glass skylight.

Over the ensuing decades, the bank stood at the forefront of convenience and comfort for both staff and customer alike. There are many newspaper articles about the comfort of the staff's chairs and the new Formica counters, reputed to be the finest of their kind. The two vaults featured the most up-to-date safety measures. Each required the pouring of sixty-one cubic yards of concrete, since the walls were to be eighteen inches thick and reinforced with steel bars. Each vault door was more than a foot thick, stood seven feet high, and weighed more than fourteen thousand pounds. As an added safety precaution, the bank directors insisted that a vault ventilation system be installed.

Today, visitors will discover that few changes have taken place. The walls are now painted a delicate lavender and are paneled with green marble, but the columns and barrel ceiling still exist. There are four enormous crystal-and-brass chandeliers overhead, two of which rotate. Guests may actually dine inside one of the bank vaults. Here and there amongst the profusion of fig trees and hanging plants are relics of the building's history. There are old deposit bags, checks, and even photographs and newspaper clippings to examine.

Oscar and Alexandra Tomasio are delightful. They encouraged us to sample many of the delicious items on the Italian-Mexican menu. The salad dressings and salsas are all homemade here. We tried the Mild Salsa with fresh-baked Tortilla Chips. It was very good indeed. Our families echoed this when we brought a couple of jars home with us. We also sampled the Langostinos Alexandra, the Marinara Calamari, and the Pollo de la Casa, all of which were tasty and beautifully presented. Karen, a huge Tiramisu fan, was very tempted by the Tiramisu with Kahlua but was persuaded to try the Apple Chimichanga instead. Served with a scoop of Vanilla Ice Cream and Caramel Syrup, it was fabulous. As the menu states, *"Mi Casa es su Casa."* Casa Capelli is most definitely a home away from home!

LANGOSTINOS ALEXANDRA

1 pound angel hair pasta
2 sticks butter, melted
1 cup lemon juice
3 tablespoons grated Parmesan cheese
1 tablespoon chopped fresh garlic
¼ teaspoon salt
⅛ teaspoon white pepper
24 ounces frozen langostinos
½ cup diced tomatoes
4 teaspoons chopped parsley
1 green onion, chopped
4 lemon wedges

Prepare pasta according to package directions. While pasta is cooking, place next 6 ingredients into a sealed container and shake well. Pour sauce into a large sauté pan and heat to medium. Add langostinos and bring to a simmer. Simmer about 5 minutes. Add tomatoes and parsley. Mix well. Serve immediately over pasta. Garnish with green onions and lemon wedges. Serves 4.

APPLE CHIMICHANGAS

4 12-inch flour tortillas
2 cups Apple Filling (see below)
4 scoops vanilla ice cream
6 tablespoons caramel sauce
1 to 2 tablespoons powdered sugar

In the center of each tortilla, place ½ cup Apple Filling. Fold one end in, then both sides; roll tightly. Deep-fry rolled tortillas 1 to 3 minutes until golden brown. Remove from oil. Serve with a scoop of ice cream. Decorate with caramel sauce and powdered sugar. Serves 4.

Apple Filling

2¼ pounds apple slices, frozen
1 stick butter
1½ cups sugar
1 tablespoon ground cinnamon
1 tablespoon lemon juice
¼ cup cold water
¼ cup flour

Place apples, butter, sugar, cinnamon, and lemon juice into a large pot and bring to a rolling boil. In a small container, mix together water and flour to make a slurry. Add slurry to apples and stir until thick. Lower heat and cover pot. Simmer for 5 to 8 minutes until apples are tender. Remove from heat and allow to cool. Yields 7 to 8 cups.

121 SOUTH MAIN STREET
WAYNESVILLE, OH 45068
WWW.WAYNESVILLESHOPS.COM
513-897-2333

Travelers to Waynesville in 1844 alighted at The Hammel House Inn, since it was the local office for the People's Stage Lines. At that time, the fare from Cincinnati to Waynesville was just $1.25. The inn's owner, Enoch Hammel, was popular with the locals, and this house of entertainment prospered under his tenure.

Hospitality has been a byword at this location since the original James Jennings Log Tavern was built on the site in 1799. The log structure was replaced in 1817 by the present frame part of the building. A brick addition was completed in 1822. There are many stories about famous people who stayed at the inn. President Martin Van Buren honored the inn with a visit, as did Vice President Richard Johnson in the 1820s. United States Supreme Court justice John McLean likely visited, since his brother, Nathaniel, was innkeeper from 1838 until 1841.

We enjoyed the story about William Mummer, a less distinguished visitor who came to the inn in 1866 and set up his photography business here. Mummer was a self-declared "spirit photographer," who claimed to be able to photograph spirits lurking on the premises. Business was brisk that summer until the day he developed a portrait of an elderly gentleman and a ghostly hand appeared on the gentleman's shoulder. Every photograph he took thereafter contained the ghostly hand. William was reputed to be so frightened by these apparitions that he fled the inn, never to return.

In 1901, William and Ollie Casey Gustin renovated the inn. They gave this country hotel an air of gentility and refinement. Advertising the "inviting and restful atmosphere" of The Hotel Gustin, the couple created a reputation that continues today under the ownership of Dale and Pam Bowman. After the Gustins' tenure, the structure became a boardinghouse, and then an apartment building in 1934. Ultimately, the hotel was restored in 1987 to bring it more in keeping with its original purpose. The main entrance with its harlequin-painted wooden floor and the shady porch that extends the full length of the building invite visitors to stay awhile and relax. There are no televisions or telephones here—just delightful guest rooms, each with a cozy four-poster bed, stenciled walls, and plank floors.

We enjoyed the colonial feel of the dining room, which is open most days for lunch. Plain white walls and candle sconces complement the exposed bricks and the large fireplace. The hunter-green swags at the windows are echoed in the leaf motif running around the top of the room. The Hammel House Inn is well known for its homemade soups and desserts, so we opted to each try a piece of the Coconut Cream Pie. Debbie has devoted a great many calories over the years to finding the perfect Coconut Cream Pie, and she declared that this was the very best she'd tasted in a long time!

CHICKEN QUICHE

2 cups shredded Swiss cheese
9-inch unbaked pie shell
1 cup shredded cheddar cheese
1 cup cooked chicken (may substitute broccoli or other ingredient of choice)
4 eggs, beaten
2 cups half-and-half
¼ teaspoon salt
¼ teaspoon white pepper
¼ teaspoon paprika
¼ teaspoon nutmeg

Preheat oven to 375 degrees. Place half of Swiss cheese in pie shell. Add cheddar, followed by rest of Swiss cheese. Place cooked chicken or other ingredient of choice on top and spread evenly. In a medium bowl, combine eggs, half-and-half, and seasonings. Pour egg mixture into pie shell. Bake for 1 hour. Serve warm. Serves 8.

SHIRLEY'S DILL TARTAR SAUCE

4 cups mayonnaise
½ cup dill relish
3 tablespoons finely grated onion
¼ teaspoon garlic powder

Mix ingredients together thoroughly and place in a sealed container in the refrigerator until needed. Yields 4½ cups.

The Brass Pig
Cafe & Gift Shop

245 SOUTH MAIN STREET
SPRINGBORO, OH 45066
937-748-2546

The Brass Pig Café was bustling the day we stopped in for lunch. The building was constructed by Jonathan Wright, founder of Springboro, in 1835 as M & J Wright General Merchandise. Today's open dining room—with plenty of space across the wooden floor for displaying merchandise—reflects that use.

Wright's sons, Mahlon and Josiah, operated the store from 1835 until sometime between 1885 and 1895. Dry goods were sold on the northern side of the store, while grocery transactions took place in the southern half. Eggs and butter were frequently bartered for other items. The Wrights offered excellent service, frequently traveling east by horseback or wagon to obtain special items for customers. One of the most interesting things they procured was for Mahlon's daughter, Mary. Women supposedly came from miles around to see the first sewing machine in Warren County and to marvel at the clothing she made with it.

The village of Springboro was reported to be the most active stop on the Under-ground Railroad. Records indicate that no runaways were ever captured while in the care of Springboro families. As a matter of fact, local history says that bounty men were once forced to turn back when practically the entire town came out to block their path and keep them from their appointed mission.

In the late 1800s, the Wrights sold the building to the Siegfrieds, who operated the store until 1930. After that, the Springboro Grange bought the building and used it for meetings until 1989. From that point until today, the old M & J has been used as an antique store, a gift shop, and a restaurant.

We sat at a table in what was once the grocery. Near the wide front windows, we gazed in amazement at the tiny white house across the street. Historical placards said that it and the larger home next door date to 1835. Much of historic Springboro—including The Brass Pig and the two homes—still stands. Black-and-white photos line the creamy walls of the dining room, depicting many scenes from the town's history. Black table coverings, a black mantelpiece, and a large Shaker-style black hutch add an elegant simplicity to the space. A peg rail runs the perimeter of the room, harking back to the days when it displayed new wares for sale. Other knickknacks of today are displayed in the large, deep-set windowsills, further echoing the building's former use.

We sipped Pink Lemonade as we scanned the menu. Karen quickly decided on the daily quiche selection, which was Quiche Lorraine. She vowed that it was quite good, particularly the crust. Debbie practically had to do *eenie*, *meenie, minie, moe* to choose between the Cashew Chicken Sandwich, which the restaurant recommended on wheat, and the Herbed Egg Salad Sandwich. Eventually, the Egg Salad won out, and it was delicious in its simplicity. Sometimes, you're just hungry for something reminiscent of childhood days on the family farm.

FRENCH BUTTER CRUST CHEESE QUICHE

French Butter Crust

2 sticks unsalted butter, frozen
5 tablespoons vegetable shortening
3 cups all-purpose flour
pinch of salt
pinch of sugar
3 tablespoons ice water

In a mixing bowl, grate the butter. Add next 4 ingredients. Using a fork or a pastry blender, combine until crumbly. Add ice water gradually, just until mixture comes together. Chill while preparing Egg Filling.

Egg Filling

4 eggs
2 cups half-and-half
¼ cup milk

pinch of salt
pinch of pepper
pinch of cayenne pepper
2 cups grated cheese (Swiss, cheddar, colby, or other favorite)

Preheat oven to 425 degrees. Combine eggs, half-and-half, milk, salt, pepper, and cayenne until well blended. Evenly divide French Butter Crust into 2 sections. Press each section into a quiche pan. Sprinkle cheese over each. Pour filling equally into quiche pans. Bake for 15 minutes. Reduce heat to 350 degrees and bake another 30 minutes. Serves 12.

Note: One cup diced ham, ½ cup chopped and steamed broccoli, and ¼ cup chopped mushrooms may be added to above filling. Another option is to add 1 cup crabmeat and 1 cup chopped spinach. These additional ingredients may be used together or individually, according to taste.

267 WEST MAIN STREET
LOUDONVILLE, OH 44842
WWW.THESOJOURNERCAFE.COM
419-994-0079

The Sojourner Café is a casual restaurant that is serious about its food. Owner John Barker describes the eatery as having "big-city food in quaint downtown Loudonville." I'd have to say that I agree. Karen was back in Pittsburgh the day I made my trek to this village of twenty-eight hundred people. The population swells to about ten thousand from May through the beautiful fall-foliage season. The area proudly proclaims itself to be the biggest and best canoeing site in the state, with at least eight canoe liveries in operation. Camping and other outdoor activities bring throngs, so the café is aptly named.

The foundation of the building may be traced back to the early part of the 1800s, when Sapp's Dry Goods Store operated here. That structure burned in 1847. Around the same time, Chapter 240 of the International Order of Odd Fellows was founded. The precise date is not known, but since the chapters are numbered chronologically, the inception date of this particular group was between 1838 and 1859. The Odd Fellows bought the old dry-goods building in 1860 to use as a meeting hall. At that time, the Odd Fellows had a specific architectural style for their lodges, so they added details to the Loudonville structure accordingly. Another fire in 1903 forced the building to undergo renovation and reconstruction again. Not all was destroyed, though. Some Odd Fellows memorabilia, including a jacket, was later found in the attic rafters.

Eventually, the building became a saloon and tavern. It has operated as such pretty much from that time until now, excluding a short stint as a tire store during the 1930s. Depending on the year, local residents could get a bite to eat at The Owl, The Corner Restaurant, or, as John put it, "The Brass Plate something." It seems that as the owners changed, the name varied slightly, from The Loudonville Brass Plate to The Brass Plate Café to other variations on the theme. Today, with a different name and an unusual menu, Sojourner Café stands on its own.

I had the special of the day, Ham and Bacon over Honey Raisin Walnut Bread, topped with Eggs and Hollandaise Sauce. It was an unusual twist on Eggs Benedict. The salad that preceded my entrée was a beautiful assortment of spring greens, red cabbage, sliced mushrooms, cucumbers, tomatoes, baby corn, and slivered almonds, topped with tasty, homemade, sugar-free Poppy Seed Dressing. The list of appetizers boasts many appealing choices, including Beef and Mushroom en Croute, Pineapple Casserole, and Teriyaki Green Beans, among a myriad of others. For folks like me who want to try it all, a sampler platter trio is available. Luncheon entrées range from Grilled Marsala Portabello to Chicken Pot Pie, proving that there is something delicious for everyone. For dinner, the restaurant is proud of its Black Angus Steaks and its plethora of satisfying seafood options, including one of my favorites, Coconut Shrimp. The guiding principle of Sojourner Café is this: "What good cheer we can give we give gladly." When tasty food is served up with a sentiment such as that, you just can't go wrong.

RASPBERRY WINE SAUCE

5 pounds red raspberries, cleaned and hulled
2 cups sugar
1 cup port wine
1 cup Moscato wine

Place all ingredients into a medium saucepan and bring to a boil. Reduce heat and simmer for 15 minutes, stirring occasionally. Liquids should be reduced by half to achieve correct thickness. Simmer for longer if necessary. Yields approximately 5 cups.

STROGANOFF

1½ quarts boiling water
1 tablespoon beef base
8 ounces mushrooms, sliced
5 shallots, sliced
1 stick butter
2 tablespoons minced garlic
3 pounds stew meat
1 cup Cabernet Sauvignon
1 cup roux
2 tablespoons Hungarian paprika
1½ cups sour cream
16-ounce package egg noodles, cooked
    according to package directions

Place water and beef base in a large pot. Bring to a boil. Sauté mushrooms and shallots in butter and garlic until tender. Set vegetables aside. In the same skillet, sauté beef. Stir in wine. When beef is browned, add vegetables and meat to boiling water. Pour into a large container. Stir in roux a little at a time to thicken to desired consistency. Stir in paprika. Let mixture cool slightly. Stir in sour cream. Serve over noodles. Serves 8 to 10.

CHAPTER 2

How Do I Get There from Here?

Schmidt's Restaurant and Sausage Haus

Transportation during the early years of this country proved a great challenge.
Many long and arduous journeys took place on foot, on horseback, or in
some type of rough conveyance. Each of the restaurants featured in the following
pages had some part in getting people from one place to another. Livery stables,
trolley repair depots, train stations—all played a part in making the task
of getting from here to there just a little bit easier.

Iron Horse Inn
Restaurant

40 VILLAGE SQUARE
GLENDALE, OH 45246
WWW.IRONHORSEINN.COM
513-771-4787

The hamlet that became Glendale started in the 1840s as a railroad labor camp. The settlement was clustered on property deeded to John C. Symmes in 1792 and was situated around the Cincinnati, Hamilton & Dayton Railroad right of way. George Crawford and Henry Clark had a different vision for the property. In 1851, they purchased six hundred acres for residential development, establishing the first known planned subdivision community in America.

In 1853, Bracker Tavern was constructed for community refreshment. When Prohibition came to pass in 1918, the tavern became more of a restaurant, although slot machines and liquor, conveniently hidden in the foundation, were available in the back room of the wood-frame structure. Not being able to openly serve liquor wasn't all bad for this establishment. During that same time, it also supplied food for inmates at the local jail. Its reputation for good food became so widely known that hobos frequently chose to be locked up rather than to move along,

just so they could have a meal prepared by the tavern.

As Glendale developed into a true suburb of Cincinnati, professional men and their families moved to the area. Many of these gentlemen were Proctor & Gamble executives who would catch the train to work; that train departed just outside the tavern. The rail line ran right past the Ivorydale Plant, where Ivory Soap was made, making these men some of the first local commuters. The lovely Victorian homes just down the street speak to their success.

Eventually, a daughter of the Bracker family and her husband, Robert Heine, took over the saloon. They installed a soda fountain and sold ice cream and penny candy—quite a change from the back-room Prohibition days! They also served hot soup and sandwiches. In 1962, Bracker Tavern was purchased by a group of investors, who changed the name to the Iron Horse Inn to honor the 1856 steam engine. The restaurant was sold again in 1971 and again in 1984. The latter transaction brought the Iron Horse Inn to Dewey and Betty Huff, who established a tradition of having nationally known jazz artists perform during Sunday brunch. The jazz continues today, with live music four nights a week.

Current owners Edward, William, Robert, and Henry Sawyer are brothers with a long family tradition in Glendale. In June 1994, they purchased the inn and began its restoration and renovation. Today, the downstairs dining room is painted a rich red, aptly reflecting the bold creations on the menu. Starters such as Duck Sausage in Cabernet

Demi-Glace and Limoncello Smoked Salmon with Fennel Slaw are among the inn's creations. Sassafras Barbecued Pork Chops and Filet Mignon topped with Smoked Duck Breast and Gorgonzola Cheese are sure to attract diners' notice.

One customer recently paid the proprietors quite a compliment, as a northbound train slowed to a stop on the tracks just outside the inn. The engineer climbed down and went inside, demonstrating that he didn't want to miss an opportunity to dine at the Iron Horse Inn.

TASSO-ESCOLAR STEW

1 cup diced onions
½ cup diced celery
½ cup diced carrots
¼ cup olive oil
1 cup diced tasso ham
2 cups diced potatoes
1 cup canned tomatoes, diced
1 bay leaf
4 cups fish stock
1 pound escolar
pinch of cayenne
salt and pepper to taste
lemon slices or wedges, if desired
chopped Italian parsley, if desired

In a large pot, sauté onions, celery, and carrots in olive oil. Add ham, potatoes, and tomatoes. Add bay leaf and stock. Simmer until potatoes are tender. Add escolar, cayenne, and salt and pepper. Heat through and serve immediately. Garnish with lemon and parsley. Serves 6 as an appetizer or 3 as an entrée.

SHRIMP GRITS

8 cups water, salted
2 cups instant grits
fresh cracked black pepper to taste
2 cups small shrimp, peeled and deveined
½ stick butter
1 cup shredded cheddar cheese

Bring water to a boil. Stir in grits and pepper. Cover and reduce heat to simmer. Cook 3 to 4 minutes. Add shrimp and butter. Cook about 4 minutes until shrimp are done. Garnish with cheddar. Serves 12.

LAVENDER SYRUP

1 tablespoon lavender blossom
½ cup sugar
½ cup water
1 teaspoon light rum
½ cup Parfait Amore liqueur
1 tablespoon lemon juice

Put all ingredients in a small saucepan and reduce by half; this will take about 3 minutes. Strain and let cool. Yields approximately ¾ cup. Syrup may be enjoyed over ice cream or pound cake. Or it may be mixed with vanilla ice cream for an interesting shake, or added to sugar cookie mix to make Lavender Cookies.

402 CENTER STREET
DENNISON, OH 44621
WWW.DENNISONDEPOT.ORG
740-922-9485

This location was once a Salvation Army canteen that served 13 percent of American military personnel during World War II, operating from March 1942 to April 1946. This made the Dennison Depot the third-largest canteen in the United States. Coming from eight counties, working day and night, 3,957 women volunteered here during that time, passing out approximately 2 million sandwiches, 1.5 million cookies, and similar quantities of milk, coffee, and other selections. A quote from an unknown soldier reads, "When you are headed to war, homesick, afraid, you have no money, and are very hungry—receiving free food from friendly people in a hometown that is very much like your home you left—it was like a dream come true." Soldiers traveling through Dennison on the National Defense Railway Route were so appreciative of the effort that they fondly nicknamed the town Dreamville.

Today, pictures of the volunteers and of men lining up for meals are proudly displayed on the premises. Murals of a variety of railroad scenes have been painted on two of the walls. A wide range of railroad crossing signs, railroad insignias, rail pictures, and other railroad items fills the space along the expansive walls.

It's as difficult to take in the myriad menu choices as it is to look at all of the décor. Appetizer selections range from Nachos to Shrimp Cocktails, with the lightly breaded Kosher Pickle Spears getting our vote. Several soups, salads, and sandwiches are available, appealing to a wide range of palates. The Black and Blue Burger—pepper-encrusted char-broiled beef topped with Blue Cheese Sauce—sounds delicious and filling. Entrées run the gamut from Cottage Pie, reflective of proprietor Sandy Armitt's English heritage, to New York Strip Steak or Scrod Almondine, creations of chef and co-proprietor Michael Smith. Be sure to save room for The Caboose, a crisp shell coated with cinnamon and sugar and filled with vanilla ice cream, caramel, chocolate, whipped cream, nuts, and a cherry.

The train station was built of brick and sandstone in 1873. At one time, it housed the Western Union telegraph office and saw as many as twenty-two trains per day pass by. Situated halfway between Pittsburgh and Columbus, the depot was once a stopover point for trains called the Spirit of St. Louis and the Jeffersonian. Doris Day, Dwight Eisenhower, Glenn Miller, and Harry Truman are but a few of the famous people who passed through this terminal. As we walked around the exterior, we admired the decorative stained-glass upper windows. Karen smiled, saying that it reminded her very much of the English stations she'd used as a child.

Scheduled for demolition, the building was saved by local citizens in the early 1980s. Today, the depot is again a vital part of the community, closely linked to many events in town. In addition to the restaurant, it houses a gift shop, a railroad museum, and the Keystone Theater. Excursion trains follow the historic Panhandle Route of the Pennsylvania Railroad, now called the Columbus & Ohio River Railroad. Fall foliage trips, a murder mystery evening, a holiday train ride, or a simple dinner at the old canteen now known as Trax Diner may prove to be just your ticket.

PEANUT BUTTER CREAM PIE

8-ounce package cream cheese, room
   temperature
1 cup sugar
1 cup peanut butter
1 tablespoon butter
1 tablespoon vanilla
9-inch prepared graham cracker piecrust
whipped cream for garnish

In a mixing bowl, combine cream cheese, sugar, peanut butter, butter, and vanilla. Mix until smooth. Spread evenly in piecrust. Refrigerate for 1 hour. Top with whipped cream. Slice and serve. Serves 6 to 8.

COTTAGE PIE

2 pounds stew meat, cubed
8 cups beef gravy
4 carrots, peeled and sliced ¼ inch thick
4 celery stalks, sliced ¼ inch thick
1 Spanish onion, chopped
2 pounds potatoes, cooked
¼ to ½ cup milk
½ stick butter

In a pot or a large saucepan, simmer beef in gravy on low heat for approximately 30 minutes until tender. Add carrots, celery, and onions. Cook approximately 15 minutes until carrots are soft. While carrots are cooking, make mashed potatoes with the cooked potatoes, milk, and butter. Ladle beef mixture into individual bowls and top with mashed potatoes. Place under broiler to lightly brown potatoes. Serves 4.

30 DEPOT STREET
BEREA, OH 44017
440-234-1144

When the depot that now houses The Station Restaurant was built in 1876, it replaced a dingy, dilapidated building that was an eyesore to the community and a disappointment to passengers. Conversely, the new building—made of local stone, roofed with slate, and adorned with a twelve-foot-wide veranda—was a great source of pride. A forty-five-foot tower and flagstaff and a platform extending two hundred feet in either direction along the rails ornamented the front of the building. The interior saw to the creature comforts that the previous building had overlooked. The oak moldings were designed to create an attractive contrast to the tinted pine walls and ceiling. Today, both the interior and the exterior are remarkably similar to the days of old.

We enjoyed looking at the memorabilia displayed on the wall. A valise and old suitcases are artfully arranged in the dining room to the left of the entrance. A piece of wood signed by several men hangs in the bar area.

Dated 1876, it was found during recent renovations. A framed copy of an old telegraph is just around the corner. Several collages of tickets to Elyria, Cincinnati, Medina, Delaware, and other destinations can be found throughout the restaurant. The framed obituary of railroad man Casey Jones also makes interesting reading. Just outside the restaurant is the Berea Pullman, a restored 1927 Pullman dining car outfitted for private dining for parties of up to twenty-seven.

It was quite chilly the day we visited, so both of us opted for a bowl of The Station's homemade soup. Karen ordered the Chicken Gumbo, while Debbie selected the Beef Noodle. Both were served piping hot and full of delicious morsels. The Quiche, served with a Popover fresh out of the oven, looked scrumptious as it was delivered to a table nearby. Another menu item that appealed to our palates was the Turkey Pita Grill, consisting of turkey, bacon, and Monterey Jack cheese grilled on pita bread, then topped with Horseradish–Sour Cream Sauce. We also eyed the San Francisco Beef Sandwich, served open-faced on pumpernickel bread and topped with Mushroom Wine Sauce and colby cheese. In a mood for beef, we discussed the Steak Madagascar, a six-ounce fillet served with mushrooms and Green Peppercorn Sauce.

Save room for dessert, as The Station has selections ranging from Fruit Crumble to Bananas Foster. The Boule de Neige is a dark chocolate creation laced with Grand Marnier and topped with whipped cream. Yum. The Black Forest Coupe—a scoop of Black Cherry Ice Cream nestled in a Chocolate Cup, then surrounded by Raspberry Sauce and whipped cream—was a temptation hard to pass up.

The restaurant was busy during our lunchtime visit. Just as we were finishing our meal, we heard an unmistakable rumbling outside, reminding us that although freight and passenger trains no longer stop here, The Station Restaurant keeps the hustle and bustle of this depot alive.

HERBED CHICKEN PAILLARD

6 boneless chicken breasts
1 cup olive oil
¼ cup finely chopped fresh parsley
3 tablespoons frozen or fresh chives
1 tablespoon fresh basil
1 tablespoon thyme
1 tablespoon grated fresh lemon rind
1½ teaspoons salt
1 teaspoon pepper
12 thin lemon slices

Gently pound chicken breasts until about ¼ inch thin. In a shallow dish, mix together remaining ingredients except lemon slices to make a marinade. Lay chicken in marinade for at least 30 minutes; it is necessary that the marinade penetrates the breasts for flavor. Char-broil on high heat on 1 side just long enough to mark. Turn and finish cooking about 3 minutes, just long enough to cook through. Garnish with fresh lemon slices. Serves 6.

CHOCOLATE WALNUT PIE

3 large eggs
1½ cups sugar
¾ stick butter
2 teaspoons vanilla
¾ cup flour
1½ cups mini chocolate chips
1½ cups chopped walnuts, toasted
1 unbaked 9-inch piecrust
vanilla ice cream, if desired

Preheat oven to 350 degrees. Lightly beat eggs. Add sugar, butter, and vanilla. Blend well. Gradually add flour, mixing thoroughly. Stir in chocolate chips and walnuts. Pour mixture into piecrust and place on center rack of oven. Bake for approximately 50 minutes, until a knife inserted in center comes out clean. Cool to room temperature. Serve with scoops of vanilla ice cream, if desired. Serves 6 to 8.

SCHMIDT'S RESTAURANT
UND SAUSAGE HOUSE
240 EAST KOSSUTH STREET
COLUMBUS, OH 43206
WWW.SCHMIDTHAUS.COM
614-444-6808

Family is important to Geoff Schmidt, as was obvious when he showed us the family portraits and other memorabilia on the wall. He is most proud of his father's paintings, which hang alongside works of local German Village artists. The family has run the business since 1886. Geoff's brothers and sisters are all still involved in some aspect of the operation. The founder, John Fred Schmidt, left Germany at the age of seventeen and settled in Columbus. In partnership with several others, he formed the Columbus Meat Packing Company. After several years, J. Fred Schmidt sold his share and formed a new partnership, establishing another meat-packing house on East Kossuth Street, in the area known today as German Village. The business grew until the 1960s, when the influx of chain grocery stores and large packing operations forced the Schmidts to close shop. It was either that or sacrifice the quality of their product.

As a business alternative, the family decided in 1967 to open a small retail meat store in an old livery stable built in the 1890s. They processed and packed the meat in the back and offered sandwiches and cold drinks to the customers while their orders were being filled. After only two weeks, the restaurant was already in need of expansion, as customers came in just to eat. The heavy wooden door speaks to the family's heritage—a large wooden lard paddle has been used as the door handle! Inside, smooth wood floors, stall-like booths, and old brick walls tell of the building's past, as do the bright red stable doors in the room that houses the daily buffet.

Rather than spend our calorie allotment at the German Autobahn Buffet, we opted for the Chicken and Spatzel Salad for Debbie and the German-Style Meat Loaf for Karen. Both were yummy. Unable to completely behave when such excellent German desserts were available, we decided to share a German Cream Puff filled with Mocha-Almond Cream. It was light and delicious—a lovely way to end an enjoyable meal.

Many of the recipes on Schmidt's menu today are courtesy of the original waitresses, who still wear traditional German costumes. Longevity is common here. Several of the wait staff have been working at the restaurant for more than thirty years!

Fortunately, a fire in 1983 that burned the entire upstairs of the restaurant did not destroy the structure. Undaunted, the Schmidt family immediately began restoration—and tried to figure out how to keep the restaurant open during the reconstruction. Fortunately, it was late spring and early summer, and the

Schmidts were able to set up a big tent outside, creating a *biergarten* atmosphere. Once the business details were attended to, the family turned its attention to creating something positive out of a difficult situation. Realizing that others had suffered more than they had as the result of fires, the family donated the first proceeds of the tent restaurant to the Children's Burn Unit in Columbus. We think that pretty well sums up what the Schmidts and their restaurant are all about—service to the community.

SCHMIDT'S SWEETKRAUT

20-ounce can sauerkraut
¼ cup canola oil
¼ cup apple cider vinegar
½ cup sugar
1½ cups finely chopped celery
1 cup finely chopped onion
⅓ cup finely chopped green pepper

Drain sauerkraut and set aside. In a separate bowl, combine oil, vinegar, and sugar. Mix well with a wire whisk until uniform in color. Add celery, onions, and peppers to mixture. Continue to whisk until liquid becomes a light green. Add sauerkraut and mix well by hand. Refrigerate overnight. Serve chilled. Yields 6 cups.

PEACH PIE

2 egg yolks
1 cup sugar, divided
1½ tablespoons milk
2 sticks margarine, softened
3 cups flour
30-ounce can peach halves, drained
1 tablespoon tapioca
¼ teaspoon cinnamon

In a medium bowl, mix egg yolks, ¾ cup sugar, and milk until blended. Add margarine and mix until blended. Add flour and mix slowly until all flour is moistened. Refrigerate dough for at least 4 hours; refrigerating overnight works best.

Preheat oven to 375 degrees. Divide dough into 5 equal parts. Using 3 parts of the dough, roll out to ⅛-inch thickness and lay in a 9-inch pie pan. Press dough into bottom and around edges. Remove excess dough. Poke holes in the bottom with a fork. Bake crust 10 to 12 minutes until light brown.

Dice peaches and place in a large bowl. In a small bowl, mix tapioca, cinnamon, and remaining sugar. Add mixture to peaches and blend by hand. Place peach filling in piecrust. Roll out remaining 2 parts of dough to ⅛-inch thickness and cut into 1-inch strips. Lay strips across the top, evenly spaced in a crisscross pattern. Bake for 50 minutes until crust is golden brown. Set aside to cool. Cut and serve. Serves 8.

4057 ERIE STREET
WILLOUGHBY, OH 44094
WWW.WILLOUGHBYBREWING.COM
440-975-0202

This enormous red brick building was originally a railway-car repair depot for the Cleveland-to-Ashtabula interurban rail line. Now over a hundred years old, it also holds a claim to fame as Lake County's first brewpub since Prohibition. The only obvious additions to the carefully preserved structure are the huge Palladian windows along the length of the building. Inside, the warehouse-like quality of the building has been retained. Visitors can still look up and see the large steel beams that once held the overhead cranes necessary for the repair shop.

A great deal of care has been taken with the décor of this beautiful building. Overhead are large, dangling light fixtures that help to draw the eye to the small train track that circles the central area of the dining room. Beer advertisements from days gone by have been carefully painted onto the interior brickwork. The brewery proudly displays a photograph of its founder, T. J. Reagan, with Bob Taft during the governor's visit to the brewery in 1998. Other equally historic pictures of the surrounding area can be found around the room, including an aerial view of the old street that clearly shows how little has changed in the past hundred years.

The brewery operations are visible behind the bar at one end of the building. The shiny stainless-steel and copper tanks add a charm of their own. Watching the staff at work creates a definite need to taste the various brews created here. Karen was interested to note that, of the six samples of beer in the Brewhouse Sampler, two are of English heritage. The Lost Nation Pale Ale is a sharp beer rich in hops that was originally brewed to survive the long voyage from Britain to India for Her Majesty's troops. Visitors interested in unusual beers should try the Railway Razz, made with red and black raspberries. It was the Silver Medal winner at the 1999 Great American Beer Festival.

Like the beer, the food is excellent. We started with a sampling of the three soups on the menu that day. The Potato and Cheddar Ale, the New England Chowder, and the French Onion Soup were all piping hot and garnished with homemade croutons. We found the menu choices to be unusual and creative, particularly the Three Cheese Beer Fondue. We sampled the Swiss, Gruyère, and Gouda cheeses—baked with Willoughby Pale Ale—by dipping a large selection of fresh vegetables and breads. Karen's favorite dish was the Southwestern Pub Pizza, which consisted of grilled chicken, black beans, Roasted Corn Salsa, cheddar and Asadero cheeses, tasso ham, and Sweet Chile Sauce. It was absolutely delicious. The service was prompt and attentive, even during that very crowded Wednesday lunchtime.

Don't forget to save room for the Grand Finale, a Special Reserve Root Beer float. The old-fashioned root beer is created on the premises, brewed with honey and root extracts. The float also features rich Vanilla Ice Cream and a Chocolate Cigar. You're going to love it!

CHARDONNAY MUSSELS TOMATO

2 pounds mussels
¼ cup pesto
½ cup white wine
1 cup cream
salt and pepper to taste
2 lemon wedges for garnish
freshly chopped parsley for garnish
6 crostini

Cook mussels, pesto, and wine in a skillet over medium heat. Cover to allow mussels to open. When mussels open, remove from skillet and place equally on 2 serving plates. Add cream to skillet and reduce until slightly thickened. Pour over mussels. Season with salt and pepper and garnish with lemon and parsley. Serve with 3 crostini per plate. Serves 2 as an appetizer.

SPINACH CON QUESO

2 tablespoons margarine
½ cup diced onion
2 tablespoons diced jalapeño pepper
¾ cup white sauce
¾ cup heavy cream
2 teaspoons diced scallions
¾ teaspoon Worcestershire sauce
⅓ teaspoon Tabasco sauce
salt and pepper to taste
1¼ pounds Pepper Jack cheese, coarsely grated
½ pound frozen spinach, drained and chopped

Melt margarine in a skillet. Sauté onions and jalapeños for 3 minutes until onions are translucent. Add white sauce and cream and bring to a simmer. Add remaining ingredients and stir well until cheese is melted. Transfer to a serving dish. Serve with tortilla chips or crostini. Serves 6 to 8 as an appetizer.

953 PHILLIPS AVENUE
TOLEDO, OH 43612
WWW.MANCYS.COM
419-476-4154

It was a raw, wet day when I visited, so it didn't take me long to decide on my order. I needed to warm up, so I opted for the New England Clam Chowder, positively recommended by one of Mancy's staff members. She did not steer me wrong. I also enjoyed the Spinach Salad with Button Mushrooms, topped with roasted pecans and warm Bacon Dressing. The two items made a nice luncheon combination.

As its name suggests, Mancy's is well known for its steaks. Strip, Fillet, Porterhouse, T-Bone, and Rib-Eye cuts all appear on the menu. Any of the steaks may be ordered with Cajun spice, cracked black peppercorns, or fresh garlic. Bearnaise, Hollandaise, or Bordelaise sauces may be added, as may sautéed mushrooms or sweet onions. The Tournedos Oscar is considered one of the house specialties, but the New York Strip with Toasted Walnut Blue Cheese Sauce also caught my eye.

Gus Mancy and his cousin Nicholas Graham founded the Ideal Restaurant in 1921. They converted an old Oldsmobile carriage dealership on Phillips Avenue into an eatery. Located at the end of the trolley line, it was a convenient spot for customers, and business grew. As its popularity expanded, the restaurant became known for its Tiffany lamps, chandeliers, and stained and leaded glass, as well as its quality menu.

Then, in 1973, the original Mancy's suffered a devastating fire. The only thing that remained was the scorched wooden statue of a clown. Still smiling, he stands repainted in the entryway of Mancy's today.

In rebuilding from the ashes, the owners paid great attention to re-creating and preserving the memory and feel of the restaurant. Much of the glass throughout Mancy's once graced elegant homes, offices, and churches in the area. The entrance was garnered from a Historic West End residence on Collingwood Boulevard that at one time was home to the Toledo Art Club. Other glass panels from the same stately home were used as dividers in one corner of the dining room. Astounding examples of beveled and leaded glass rescued from old Toledo homes have been incorporated in other areas of the restaurant.

The fourteen stained-glass panels were discovered by someone whose hobby was decorative window glass. They came from a small church in Michigan and now form the foyer ceiling at Mancy's. The old Penn Central railroad station in downtown Detroit provided the railroad benches from which the dining booths were crafted. Although both bars in the restaurant were made around 1900 by a firm located in Toledo, they were obtained from very different locales—one came from West Virginia and one from Michigan. The stained-glass depiction of Rip Van Winkle came from an even more unlikely source, a Chicago speakeasy once owned by Al Capone. Karen wasn't with me to experience all these interesting finds, and trying to describe them over the phone was just impossible. Mancy's is one of those places you just have to see for yourself.

FRENCH ONION SOUP

2 tablespoons beef base or 8 bouillon cubes
8 cups water
1 tablespoon brown sugar
1½ teaspoons white wine
1 large onion, sliced
2 tablespoons butter
16 large croutons
16 slices mozzarella cheese
1½ cups shredded Parmesan cheese

Combine first 4 ingredients in a large pot and bring to a boil. Sauté onions in butter until a light golden brown. Mix onions into soup mixture. Place 2 croutons in bottom of each of 8 cups or soup bowls. Ladle soup into cups. Top each with 2 slices of mozzarella and sprinkle with Parmesan. Brown under a broiler until bubbly. Serves 8.

OYSTERS ROCKEFELLER

1 cup spinach, rinsed and drained
¼ medium red onion
5 strips bacon, crisply fried
⅜ teaspoon white pepper
½ teaspoon Tabasco sauce
¾ cup heavy cream
2 egg yolks
1 cup breadcrumbs
3 tablespoons white wine
1 tablespoon lemon juice
⅜ teaspoon cayenne pepper
½ teaspoon minced garlic
36 oysters on the half shell
¾ cup hollandaise sauce

In a food processor, finely chop spinach, onions, and bacon. Mix together with next 9 ingredients in a large bowl. Place 1 tablespoon of mixture on top of each oyster. Brown under a broiler for approximately 4 minutes. Spoon 1 teaspoon of hollandaise over each oyster. Brown 30 seconds and serve. Serves 6 as an appetizer.

11401 BELLFLOWER ROAD
CLEVELAND, OH 44106
WWW.THATPLACE.ORG
216-231-4469

To start with the Lobster Bisque or the Chilled Raspberry Soup? Such are the choices that guests have to make when dining at That Place on Bellflower. Choosing among entrées like Roasted Duckling with Grand Marnier, Chicken Champagne and the house specialty, Veal Sweetbreads, is just as difficult. Had we been having a full meal, Karen vowed that the Veal and Leek Strudel would have been her choice. Debbie might have chosen the Crispy Parsley Trout Hunan. Since we were there about two in the afternoon, we opted for a dessert before continuing on our way. Because we couldn't decide among Cheesecake, Torta Ciccolata, Sweet Potato Pie, and the four Ice Cream Truffle selections, we asked our server, Marko, for his recommendation. He emphatically replied, "Torta Ciccolata!" Our arms don't need to be twisted too hard to order a chocolate-and-raspberry combination, so we quickly placed one order. We then asked him to recommend a second dessert, and he replied, "Torta Ciccolata!" We'd found a fellow chocoholic. In the end, we ordered the Piña Colada Truffle, a refreshing combination of vanilla ice cream, coconut, and Pineapple Sauce.

The restaurant was once the stable and carriage house of a large estate. Marvelous horse heads are displayed on three sides of the older of the two buildings. Original brick floors, posts, and beams further enhance the ambiance. We were seated at a small table overlooking the lovely courtyard. During warm-weather months, it's a popular place to grab a late bite to eat after nearby cultural activities. Our favorite room is at one end of the restaurant. It encompasses the original fireplace and really gives a feel for the building's past use.

The modern artwork displayed throughout is in such stark contrast to the structures and their past that it works perfectly. The majority of the paintings are in black and white; most are contemporary nudes. Many of these are the work of Joseph Glasco, a prominent Texas artist.

The carriage house made the transition to restaurant during the original hippie days of the late 1960s and early 1970s. However, the chef did not serve up granola and tofu. At one time, this was a hamburger joint, then a pizza parlor, until Isabella Chesler and her son, David, purchased it. The original That Place on Bellflower menu was upscale continental. A few of those dishes have remained, such as Filet Mignon in Bearnaise Sauce and Beef Wellington. Now, there's a much more international flair, including flavors of Cuba and the Pacific Rim. If that doesn't fit your palate or your budget, never fear—order a "That Place" Burger As You Like It and Fries.

With its location near Cleveland's cultural district and medical mecca, this restaurant has something for everyone.

VEAL AND LEEK STRUDEL

1 pound ground veal
1 cup coarsely chopped leek
1 egg
1 teaspoon salt
½ teaspoon white pepper
½ teaspoon nutmeg
1 sheet puff pastry
1 egg yolk
Béchamel Sauce (see below)

Preheat oven to 400 degrees. Brown veal over low heat. In a large bowl, mix veal with leeks, egg, salt, pepper, and nutmeg. Place puff pastry on a baking sheet. Form veal mixture into a loaf shape on top of pastry. Wrap pastry around veal mixture to completely enclose it. Seal edges with a little water. Bake for 45 minutes. Brush top of strudel with a little egg yolk. Place back in oven for 15 minutes until top is browned. Slice and serve with Béchamel Sauce. Serves 4.

BÉCHAMEL SAUCE

½ stick butter
¼ cup flour
1 cup milk
1 cup heavy cream
1 teaspoon chicken bouillon granules

½ teaspoon nutmeg
salt and pepper to taste

Melt butter over low heat, then add flour, whisking constantly until mixture is completely smooth. Using a wire whisk, slowly add milk, cream, and bouillon. Add nutmeg and heat until thickened. Add salt and pepper. Yields about 1½ cups.

VEGETARIAN COUNTRY-STYLE SPAGHETTI

1 pound spaghetti
1 tablespoon oil
1 cup plum tomatoes, chopped
1 cup green olives, sliced
½ cup chopped red onion
¼ cup chopped Poblano peppers
4 cloves garlic, crushed
½ pound feta cheese, crumbled
1 cup dry vermouth
½ teaspoon saffron
3 tablespoons cracked black pepper
3 eggs, beaten

Cook spaghetti al dente. Rinse, drain, and set aside. Heat oil in a large sauté pan. Add tomatoes, olives, onions, peppers, and garlic. Sauté approximately 1 minute. Add feta, vermouth, and saffron and sauté another 2 to 3 minutes. Add spaghetti and black pepper. Cook uncovered for 5 minutes. Add eggs and toss quickly. Remove from heat and place in serving bowls. Garnish with additional black pepper if desired. Serves 4 to 6.

2025 UNIVERSITY HOSPITAL DRIVE
CLEVELAND, OH 44106
WWW.CLUBISABELLA.COM
216-229-1177

At the turn of the twentieth century, this section of Euclid Avenue—indeed, this area of Cleveland—was abundant with lovely Victorian homes of wealthy and successful families. Today, Major's Club Isabella stands as a lonely reminder of those times. When it was constructed, the building was the carriage house for the Douby family estate. Records indicate that Mr. Nathan Douby was the first businessman to run the May Company retail stores here in Cleveland. After the mansion was torn down, the carriage house was donated to an order of nuns, who used it as their nunnery. Around the time of Prohibition, the structure did a real about-face, becoming a speakeasy. It's rumored that Bob Hope once performed here during its heyday.

Today, the small structure is surrounded by concrete giants. Major's Club Isabella sits just outside the main entrance of University Hospitals. Its proximity to Case Western also encourages students and faculty to frequent

the restaurant. As one local reviewer put it, from "local docs to post-docs," they're all here. In addition, the establishment is close to the Cleveland Museum of Art, the Cleveland Historical Society, the Cleveland Museum of Natural History, and Severance Hall, home of the Cleveland Orchestra, so it also has a following in the community's cultural sector.

The restaurant's ambiance is casual; it is a perfect place to kick back and relax. The live jazz that can be enjoyed almost any night of the week further adds to the mellow atmosphere. The original stable doors open from the main dining room onto patio seating in a garden-like setting, where tables are nestled near ivy-covered walls. This was quite popular the day we visited, with several tables of guests lingering in the warm sunshine.

Inside, interesting dividers sit in several locations. Their top halves are constructed from leaded-glass squares, while the bottom halves are typical of common stall dividers. A splash of color is provided by large paper flowers twined above the simple bar. Potted palms placed throughout soften the angular lines of the very open main dining room. The original posts and beams are still intact, as is the narrow wooden-slat ceiling. Offsetting the rustic feel of the carriage house is an eclectic mix of contemporary portrait paintings.

The menu is appropriately simple, yet offers a variety that includes something for everyone. The Russian Salmon Salad Sandwich, served on pumpernickel bread with a side dish of Potato Salad, was a popular choice with Debbie, as was the Almond-Crusted Chicken Strips. The Triangle Duck Cakes, served with

Mint Hollandaise Sauce, caught Karen's eye. And those were just the lunch choices. For dinner, the menu tends more toward an Italian influence. Choices include Calamari Fritti, Mussels Basilico, and Spaghetti à la Frutti di Mare.

As we left, we waved to the chef, visible behind a large picture window set into a brick archway in one wall of the building. It provided an interesting contrast—an individual plying his trade in a century-old structure, able to look out over the hustle and bustle related to medical technology and the modern world.

BOMBALOTTI

2 cups penne pasta
1 cup Italian sausage
½ cup sliced button mushrooms
½ cup fresh peas
½ teaspoon chopped fresh garlic
1 tablespoon olive oil
salt and pepper to taste
1 cup heavy cream
½ cup chicken stock
¼ to ½ cup Parmesan cheese

Cook penne according to package directions. Drain and set aside. In a sauté pan, sauté sausage, mushrooms, peas, and garlic in olive oil. Drain excess oil. Season sausage mixture with salt and pepper. Add cream and chicken stock. Simmer 5 to 8 minutes until sauce thickens. Add pasta and toss to mix. Top with Parmesan and serve. Serves 2 generously.

SHRIMP PROVENÇALE

10 large shrimp, peeled and deveined
1 tablespoon chopped fresh garlic
1 tablespoon olive oil
½ cup white wine
½ cup tomato juice
½ teaspoon chopped fresh basil
½ teaspoon crushed red pepper
1 cup chopped tomatoes
salt and pepper to taste
2 slices French bread

In a sauté pan, sear shrimp and garlic in olive oil. Add wine and tomato juice. Add basil and red pepper. Allow to cook down approximately 4 to 5 minutes. Add tomatoes and season with salt and pepper. Pour over French bread. Serves 2 as an appetizer.

CHAPTER 3

You Know Who

The Precinct

According to the dictionary, synonyms for the word *famous* include *renowned, illustrious, celebrated, distinguished,* and *eminent.* The definitions and connotations of these words pretty well sum up the focus of this chapter. Within these pages are establishments that have been frequented by folks from many walks of life with one thing in common—they're all famous. We don't need to tell you exactly because . . . you know who!

GREAT LAKES
BREWING CO.
CLEVELAND, OHIO

2516 MARKET AVENUE
CLEVELAND, OH 44113
WWW.GREATLAKESBREWING.COM
216-771-4404

McClean's Feed & Seed Co. and the Market Tavern were established circa 1865. The tavern became a popular spot for tradesmen and Cleveland's legal and civil-service professionals. One of its most famous patrons was Eliot Ness, who first gained fame as the leader of Chicago's Untouchables, the renowned Prohibition agents. Ness is credited with reining in Al Capone's gang. After those successes, he came to Cleveland, which was teeming with organized crime and government corruption during that time. Following a favorable tenure as Cleveland's director of public safety, he ran unsuccessfully for mayor. Today, a picture of Ness hangs on the wall of Great Lakes Brewing Co., and one of the beers served here bears his name.

The barroom retains much of its nineteenth-century charm, with its simple booth seating and its lovely tiger mahogany bar, which is riddled with bullet holes attributed to an exchange between Eliot Ness and an unknown assailant. The rooms on the second story above the bar figured in the life of another famous individual. Today, that space is used as banquet rooms. At one time, however, it served as the law offices where a young clerk named John D. Rockefeller got his start before moving onward and upward to found Standard Oil.

Great Lakes Brewing Co. opened for business on September 6, 1988, becoming the first microbrewery in the state of Ohio, and the first brewery to open since Prohibition. Although the buildings at 2516 Market Avenue had never been a brewery, tradition was nearby. German immigrant Leonard Schlather established Schlather Brewing Company in 1878 on the corner of Carroll Avenue where Dave's Supermarket now stands. The brick structure across the street from Great Lakes Brewing Co. was once the horse stables for the Schlather operation. In March 1998, Great Lakes Brewing Co. expanded its operations, incorporating the horse stables into its new state-of-the-art brewing plant.

The restaurant was quite busy the day we visited. The sidewalk dining area, the main dining room (located in the old feed store), and the bar area were all full. A wait for a table would have been more than twenty minutes, which our tight schedule didn't allow. Instead, we hoisted ourselves onto barstools and enjoyed the ambiance à la Mr. Ness. In addition to the amber lager called Eliot Ness, the brews for the day were Dortmunder Gold, Burning River Pale Ale, Edmund Fitzgerald Porter, and Westside Wheat Ale. An extensive list of Pub Exclusive Brews and several seasonal beers were also available.

We chose to share the Barbecued Brewery Shrimp, skewered and served on a bed of tasty Onion Straws, and the Walleye Bites, delicious bits of Lake Erie walleye battered, fried, and served with Cocktail Sauce and spicy Creole Sauce. On another visit, we might choose the Cajun Chicken Barley Salad, the Taproom Tortellini Salad, or the Apple Pork Tenderloin Salad, all of which sounded wonderfully unique. There are plenty of selections to suit every appetite, but don't miss the Walleye Bites. They're habit forming!

PRETZEL AND CONFETTI CHICKEN

1 cup grated Parmesan cheese
2 cups pretzel crumbs
5 boneless chicken breasts
2 tablespoons oil
Mustard Ale Sauce (see next column)
Confetti Vegetable Relish (see next column)

Preheat oven to 350 degrees. Mix together Parmesan and pretzel crumbs. Dredge chicken breasts in pretzel mixture. Heat oil in a large sauté pan and brown chicken on both sides. Remove from pan, place in a baking dish, and put in oven for approximately 20 minutes.

To serve, place a chicken breast on each of 5 plates. Drizzle Mustard Ale Sauce on top of or under chicken, then sprinkle chilled Confetti Vegetable Relish over top. Serves 5.

MUSTARD ALE SAUCE

¾ cup ale
⅔ cup water
½ teaspoon chicken base
½ teaspoon thyme
½ teaspoon cumin
¼ teaspoon white pepper
2 cups heavy cream
2 tablespoons Dijon mustard
2 tablespoons whole-grain mustard

Combine ale, water, chicken base, thyme, cumin, and white pepper in a large saucepan. Reduce by half. Add cream. Reduce again until thickened to sauce consistency. Add mustards. Yields approximately 2 cups.

CONFETTI VEGETABLE RELISH

½ red pepper, seeded
½ yellow pepper, seeded
½ cucumber, seeded
1 tablespoon minced red onion
½ cup olive oil
juice of 1½ limes
⅜ teaspoon cumin
¼ teaspoon white pepper

Finely dice vegetables and mix together with remaining ingredients. Chill until served. Yields approximately 1 cup.

THE FORUM GRILL AT

The Vernon Manor Hotel

400 OAK STREET
CINCINNATI, OH 45219
WWW.VERNON-MANOR.COM
513-281-3300

Since the early 1900s, The Vernon Manor Hotel has maintained a stately presence in Cincinnati's Pill Hill district, not too far from the University of Cincinnati. It was built as a retreat for wealthy Cincinnati residents, although with today's modern conveyances, its location two and a half miles from downtown makes that hard to comprehend. It was here that people came to escape from the busy downtown Riverfront district and to enjoy wonderful service and a fabulous view.

The hotel was designed to emulate the style and character of Hatfield House, the ancestral home of the earls of Percy in Hertfordshire, England. The forward-thinking architect included the most modern conveniences, including fireproof floors and refrigerators in every room. His blueprints included large guest rooms, a variety of suites, wide corridors, and gardens with wonderful oak trees. This spaciousness attracted long-term guests and many permanent residents. Their presence helped The Vernon Manor Hotel to weather the tough times that many elite hotels of the era were unable to endure. The establishment was also fortunate to have wealthy owners during the 1950s and 1960s who liberally entertained their influential friends here. Thus, The Vernon Manor has emerged as the oldest continuously operating hotel in Cincinnati.

Through the years, notable personalities such as Mikhail Baryshnikov, Bob Dylan, Liza Minnelli, Kevin Bacon, Keanu Reeves, Tiger Woods, several presidents, and many, many others have come to enjoy this haven. The Beatles stayed here when on tour and now have one of the suites named and decorated in their honor. There are 119 guest rooms in this impressive facility. In addition, the hotel was center stage for the 1988 Oscar-winning movie *Rain Man*, starring Dustin Hoffman and Tom Cruise. Although he was referring to something else, the address that Hoffman's character frequently uttered, "400 Oak Street, Cincinnati, Ohio," is actually that of The Vernon Manor Hotel.

During our breakfast in The Forum Grill, the service was friendly and attentive, and we quickly felt at home. We were seated in a corner of the dining room, next to the fireplace. A coat of arms hung over the stone mantel, creating a bit of castle ambiance. Wood paneling and hunter and burgundy accents enhanced the décor. The menu here offers a wide array of selections, from sandwiches to steaks and chops. The grill offers the Friday-night Seafood Festival and one of the most renowned Sunday brunches in the city. We hope this Cincinnati tradition will continue to thrive for years to come.

CHICKEN APRICOT

4 8-ounce boneless, skinless chicken breasts
4-ounce package chopped spinach
¾ cup shredded mozzarella cheese
⅓ cup cottage cheese
salt and pepper to taste
3 tablespoons olive oil, divided
1 teaspoon chopped ginger
4-ounce jar apricot preserves

Preheat oven to 350 degrees. Place a chicken breast between 2 sheets of plastic wrap and pound with a mallet until uniform in thickness. Repeat with remaining 3 breasts. Mix together spinach, mozzarella, cottage cheese, and salt and pepper in a bowl. Divide mixture into 4 equal portions. Place 1 portion in the center of each breast. Fold breast to cover mixture. In a saucepan, heat 1 tablespoon of the olive oil over medium heat. Add ginger and stir about 30 seconds until it softens. Add apricot preserves and stir. Reduce heat to simmer, stirring occasionally. Reserve for later use. Heat remaining 2 tablespoons olive oil in a heavy ovenproof skillet until it just begins to smoke. Carefully place chicken in pan. Sear chicken on both sides. Place skillet in oven and cook about 20 minutes until internal temperature reaches 175 degrees. During the last 5 minutes, baste chicken with apricot glaze, reserving a little to drizzle over chicken when served. Serves 4.

ROASTED CORN AND BLACK BEAN RELISH

6 ears fresh corn or 12-ounce bag frozen
  corn
olive oil
1 fresh jalapeño pepper
2 teaspoons cumin
2 teaspoons coriander
6 Roma tomatoes
1 bunch cilantro, stems removed
12-ounce can black beans, drained and
  rinsed

Preheat oven to 375 degrees. Shuck corn, remove silk, rinse, and cut from cob. In a medium bowl, drizzle a little olive oil over corn and whole jalapeño. Add cumin and coriander. Spread corn and jalapeño on a cookie sheet. Place sheet in oven and stir occasionally. Roast until corn dries and browns slightly and jalapeño blisters. Remove from oven and cool. Slice tomatoes in half and squeeze out seeds. Remove cores and dice tomatoes. Place in a bowl. Chop cilantro and add to tomatoes. Slice jalapeño in half and remove seeds and outer skin. Dice jalapeño and add to tomatoes. Add corn and beans and mix well. Cover and refrigerate until needed. Yields 3 cups.

THE PRECINCT
SINCE 1981
Good Food · Good · Fun · Good Friends

311 DELTA AVENUE
CINCINNATI, OH 45226
WWW.JEFFRUBY.COM
513-321-5454

Police Patrol House No. 6 was designed and constructed by Samuel P. Hannaford and Sons in 1901. Designed in the Romanesque style, the distinctive brick building has remained unchanged. Among its unique features are a corner turret, arched windows, a winged gable dormer, and a corbeled chimney. The architecture is truly outstanding, as would be expected from the firm that designed the Cincinnati Music Hall, Cincinnati City Hall, and Cincinnati General Hospital.

Back in the early 1900s, horses pulled patrol wagons. Police equipment was carried in the wagons, as were medical supplies sometimes. When this patrol service was instituted, it made Cincinnati only the second city in the nation to have its streets patrolled by policemen. Visitors can still see the old station sign. They can also see where the huge double doors used to open to let the horses into the stable. Remodeled by entrepreneur Jeff Ruby in 1981, the stable has now become the main dining room.

We entered the building via the lobby,

which was once the office area for the two-man shifts. At the far end of the room was a small bar with a leaded-glass surround. We sat in the corner turret and sipped our drinks while admiring the many artifacts, which included a large number of black-and-white photographs of police officers. Regulars consider this to be a mecca for top-quality American cuisine, as is witnessed by the numerous photos of exceptionally famous guests. Visitors might bump into anyone from Tom Selleck to Liza Minnelli, or even Sparky Anderson or Johnny Bench.

Entering the dining room, we walked past the life-sized poster of a policeman on the original brick wall. The room is elegantly furnished with white table linens and ornate Victorian bowl-style chandeliers and lamps. The lighting is muted and the service impeccable. Ably assisted by our server, Zach, we decided to sample the appetizers. Freshly baked Bread arrived first, accompanied by Hazelnut, Pear, Parmesan, and Gorgonzola Butter. We sampled the Crab Cakes with Creole Mustard Sauce, the Mixed Mushroom Garlic Toast, the Crisp Fried Frog Legs, the Alaskan King Crab Legs, and the Tiger Shrimp, served with The Precinct's Fresh Horseradish Cocktail Sauce. All of the appetizers were superb.

Our entrée, Steak Diane, was prepared table-side while we savored the Asparagus and Green Bean Salad, served with Maytag blue cheese and a dressing of bacon and hazelnuts. Both the steaks and salads were excellent, and we agreed that dessert was now out of the question. We should have known better. Our table was barely cleared when dessert arrived. We shared an enormous helping of Jeff's Grandmother's Cheesecake, served in a pool of Raspberry Coulis, and Karen's favorite, Bananas Foster. The bananas had been flambéed in a banana liqueur together with walnuts and cinnamon. It was a truly delectable concoction. What a tremendous combination—an exceptional meal in luxurious surroundings. You can't ask for better than that!

PRECINCT CRAB CAKES

2 pounds lump crabmeat, drained and
   picked
¼ cup chopped sweet onion
¼ cup chopped red onion
2 eggs
pinch of dry mustard
pinch of nutmeg
1 cup breadcrumbs, divided
2 tablespoons mayonnaise
salt to taste
white pepper to taste
cayenne to taste
1 tablespoon olive oil
1 tablespoon butter
Crab Cake Sauce (see next column)

Gently toss together crabmeat, sweet onions, red onions, eggs, mustard, nutmeg, and 2 tablespoons of the breadcrumbs. Reserve remaining breadcrumbs for dredging. Add mayonnaise, salt, white pepper, and cayenne to crabmeat mixture, being careful not

to overseason. Form into 4-ounce balls and refrigerate for 1 hour.

Preheat oven to 450 degrees. To cook, lightly dredge crab balls in remaining breadcrumbs, pressing lightly to flatten slightly. Place cakes in a preheated nonstick skillet with olive oil and butter. Cook for 2 minutes on each side at medium-high heat. Place in oven for 2 to 3 minutes. Pour Crab Cake Sauce over cakes and serve immediately. Serves 4.

CRAB CAKE SAUCE

½ cup heavy cream
2 tablespoons sherry wine (not cooking
   sherry)
4 tablespoons Creole mustard (coarse
   mustard or Dijon mustard may be
   substituted)
2 tablespoons butter
salt and pepper to taste

Stir cream, wine, and mustard into a hot skillet. Bring mixture to a boil. Reduce heat and cook until reduced by half. Add butter and season with salt and pepper. Yields ½ cup.

Since 1902
Bender's Tavern

137 COURT AVENUE SW
CANTON, OH 44702
WWW.BENDERSRESTAURANT.COM
330-453-8424

Bender's Tavern advertises itself as the place "where fine food and the best of service have been nationally famous." The slogan is right—this is a place that is serious about food, having celebrated its hundredth anniversary in 2002. There are four dining rooms and a taproom in which you can enjoy the very extensive selection of items. The menus change daily, and there are never fewer than nine or ten seafood specials. Karen selected the Char-Broiled Tasmanian Salmon with Tomato Caper Relish, Bender Fries, and Coleslaw, while Debbie opted for the Baked Mushroom–Chicken Noodle Casserole. Both choices were delicious. The Bender Fries, which are a kind of scalloped-potato hash browns, were unusual and so good that we were forced to have a second helping. Bender's serves a selection of pies and cheesecakes for dessert, but its specialty is the Bender's Sundae, served with homemade Peanut Chocolate Sauce.

We sat and chatted with Jerry Jacob, the current owner. He showed us one of his old postcards of the taproom from 1902. Very little has changed since then. The brown and white hexagonal tiles are all still there, as is the ornate tin tile ceiling. The large bar is still in use, only now it is surmounted by an enormous blue marlin. The unbelievably intricate mural surrounding the taproom is impressive. Painted in 1907 by an itinerant Dutchman in exchange for room and board, and based on illustrated chapter headings from a German book, it used to contain German quotations and satirical quips that have unfortunately long since been painted out.

Sadly, a fire in 1988 destroyed the upstairs banquet rooms—and also the murals on those walls. However, guests can still enjoy the priceless marble and the tiger oak paneling in the four remaining dining rooms, each more ornate than the last. Jerry chatted about his childhood. He recalled visiting Bender's when ladies and gentlemen entered through separate doorways into different dining rooms. We were in the main dining room, which had once been for gentlemen only. Ladies were occasionally allowed, but only if escorted, and rarely even then. If a gentleman visited Bender's with his wife or family, he was expected to eat in the ladies' dining room. Back then, a couple of the favorite menu items were Sardine Sandwiches and Peanut Butter and Bacon Sandwiches.

Many famous people have visited Bender's over the years. Newspaper articles tell of guests such as Billy Graham, Tom Poston, and Joel Rose. Football celebrities have included Jim Thorpe, Lou Groza, and Brian

Piccolo. Karen would have been thrilled to meet Olympic swimmer Johnny Weissmuller, best known for playing Tarzan.

It was a delightful meal. Clearly, the clientele shared our appreciation of "Canton's oldest and finest restaurant and tavern." As we stepped back outside to Court Avenue and placed our feet on the well-worn front step, we reflected on the thousands of people who had walked this path before us.

YELLOW PICKEREL CAMP KAGEL–STYLE

salt and pepper to taste
½ teaspoon paprika
2 yellow pickerel, heads and tails removed, deboned
2 tablespoons flour
¼ lemon, cut in half
2 tablespoons finely chopped fresh parsley

Preheat oven to 400 degrees. Sprinkle salt and pepper and paprika over fish. Roll fish in flour and place flesh side down in a buttered ovenproof skillet. Brown fish over medium heat for about 2 minutes, then turn fish over and place skillet in oven for 15 minutes. Remove fish from skillet. Squeeze lemon pieces into skillet, add half of parsley to the drippings, and sauté for 1 minute. Arrange pickerel on 2 plates and pour drippings over top. Sprinkle with remaining parsley and serve immediately. Serves 2.

BENDER'S TURTLE SOUP

½ cup oil
1 cup diced carrots
1 cup diced celery
2 medium onions, diced
3 medium cloves garlic, finely chopped
⅓ cup flour
7 cups fish stock
1 tablespoon pickling spices
1 cup tomato paste
½ teaspoon thyme
½ teaspoon basil
¼ teaspoon black pepper
¾ teaspoon salt
1 tablespoon parsley flakes
¼ teaspoon dill
¼ teaspoon MSG, if desired
⅓ teaspoon rosemary
½ teaspoon sugar
2½ pounds turtle meat, diced
½ cup sherry
2 tablespoons lemon juice

Heat oil in a large stockpot and sauté carrots, celery, and onions. Add garlic and continue to cook. Gradually stir in flour. Whisk in stock a little at a time until well blended. Add rest of ingredients except turtle meat, sherry, and lemon juice. Simmer for 2 hours, stirring occasionally. Ten minutes before serving, add final 3 ingredients. Continue to cook, stirring frequently to break up turtle meat. Serves 8 to 10.

FRANKLIN AVENUE AND
WEST MAIN STREET
KENT, OH 44240
WWW.PUFFERBELLYLTD.COM
330-673-1771

There is no mistaking this brick building for anything other than a train station. Built in 1875, it has an interesting story to tell. It seems that during the time George Hinds was stationmaster, a circus was in town. Now, this wasn't uncommon, nor was it rare for circus personnel to try to finagle lower fares or free rides to their next destination. One day, the circus master, unsuccessful in his negotiations with Mr. Hinds, absconded with the ticket money, leaving his performers stranded. It was in this circumstance that the stationmaster came across a shivering boy dressed in a flamboyant shirt, puffing on a stogie. "My good man," the boy began, "I'll give you eight dollars for my fare to New York now and pay the rest after the show." Mr. Hinds declined, stating that the circus master had already been turned down. But seeing how pitiful the boy was, Hinds's generosity eventually got the better of him, and he gave the boy the rest of the fare, along with an additional ten dollars.

The boy shed tears of joy and promised to return the loan. It was some years later when Mr. Hinds received an envelope addressed to him that contained tickets to a local traveling show. Upon arriving, he was ushered backstage, where he recognized a more mature version of the boy he'd helped. "Why, Whitey Dunkenfield!" Mr. Hinds exclaimed. "I don't go by Whitey anymore," the young man replied. "I'm known as W. C. Fields. Here's the ten dollars you loaned me and ten dollars more for interest."

We thoroughly enjoyed the story, as well as the décor. Framed telegrams told the stories of people who missed trains and caught wrong trains, which brought us visions of comic situations, the stuff of which early motion pictures were made. Also framed and displayed along the walls were many, many photographs and pictures related to rail history. A full-sized carriage that may once have conveyed a local citizen to the station hung above one section of the restaurant, and an old luggage cart laden with baggage was suspended nearby.

Since our visit was on a Sunday, we took advantage of the buffet, which included salads, quiche, omelets, waffles, several entrées, and many dessert choices. Debbie enjoyed the Chive Potato Salad and the Barbecued Beef. Karen's favorite was the Sweet and Sour Chicken. The regular menu features sandwiches such as a Spicy Black Bean Burger and a Cashew Chicken Croissant. Thin-Crust Pizzas are quite popular, as are the Barbecued Jamaican Shrimp and the Thai Shrimp Pasta.

It is said that W. C. Fields delighted in

telling of his experience at the Kent station. The tale has even been credited with starting the tradition of traveling performers honoring the harried stationmasters of the world. Today, in Kent, it's hats off to chef and general manager Kevin Long and his staff as they welcome travelers from near and far.

HERB-CRUSTED SALMON

¼ cup dried basil
2 tablespoons dried thyme
2 tablespoons dried oregano
1 teaspoon rosemary, crumbled
½ teaspoon coarsely ground pepper
½ cup flour
1¼ teaspoons salt
5 8-ounce salmon fillets
2 tablespoons olive oil, divided

Preheat oven to 375 degrees. With a mortar and pestle, blend all ingredients except salmon and olive oil until mixture is very fine. Dredge salmon on both sides in herb mixture. Coat a baking pan with 1 tablespoon of the olive oil. Place salmon in pan. Brush top of each fillet lightly with remaining olive oil. Bake in oven for 8 to 10 minutes until salmon is cooked through but not overdone. Serves 5.

MARGARITA PIE

1 stick margarine
1¼ cups finely crushed salted pretzels
½ cup granulated sugar
14-ounce can sweetened condensed milk
2 tablespoons lime juice
2 tablespoons tequila
2 tablespoons triple sec
1 drop green food coloring
2 cups whipping cream

Generously grease a 9-inch metal pie pan. In a medium saucepan, melt margarine over low heat. Remove from heat and stir in pretzels and sugar until well blended. Press mixture firmly over bottom and up sides of pie pan, forming a rim above edge of pan. Place in freezer to firm while making filling.

Mix sweetened condensed milk, lime juice, tequila, triple sec, and food coloring, being careful to measure accurately, as too much liquid will keep the filling from becoming firm. In another bowl, beat whipping cream with an electric mixer until peaks form when beaters are lifted. Gradually fold condensed milk mixture into whipped cream, mixing gently but well. Pour into crust.

Freeze uncovered at least 8 hours. Wrap airtight and return to freezer until ready to serve. Serves 6 to 8.

THE florentine RESTAURANT

21 WEST MARKET STREET
GERMANTOWN, OH 45327
937-855-7759

Chef Brandon Clausing certainly has a wide range of menu items to manage. Entrées range from favorites such as Pork Chops, Fried Shrimp, and Swiss Steak to Teriyaki Sirloin, Chicken Marsala, and the ever-popular Beer-Battered Orange Roughy. That was almost the selection I made, before I spied Lasagna on the list of specials. Served with a side salad and Garlic Bread, it was a more-than-ample portion. Karen had a hard time believing that I had no room for dessert, even though the restaurant is known for its homemade pies, including my favorite, Coconut Cream.

Germantown was settled in 1804 by families from Pennsylvania. Philip Gunckel, the only English speaker among them, led the group. Gunckel filed the first plat for the village on October 4, 1814. The town was laid out in eight blocks, each 330 feet square, divided by a diagonal alley with a central open space. This created a spider-web alleyway system rarely seen in the United States. As buildings were erected, their fronts sat close to the street, while space for horses and buggies was provided in the rear, satisfying the German penchant for uncluttered streets.

Gunckel built The Florentine Hotel two years later. It is considered the second-oldest inn in Ohio. It was later sold to William Schaeffer. During the Civil War, ownership passed to William Leighty, and the establishment became known as the Leighty House. Since it was a stop on the stagecoach route, many famous Americans stayed at the hotel. Henry Clay and Clement Vallandingham, a noted Southern sympathizer, are both said to have addressed crowds from the structure's second-story balcony.

That ornate iron balcony, fabricated at the ironworks in the Oregon District of nearby Dayton, still stands today. In fact, the entire structure looks almost identical to its earlier days. The barn-red clapboard exterior trimmed in taupe looks like something you'd find on the set of an old Western. I kept expecting Marshal Dillon and Miss Kitty to come walking out the door.

Inside, much remains the same as well. To the left is the bar area, highlighted by an incredible backbar. Crafted in Europe, it made its way to a New Orleans soda fountain before being purchased by a local doctor. The piece is so large that workers had to cut out the second floor above it to fit it in. Three sections of stained glass enhance the woodwork and give the backbar unique beauty.

In contrast to the stylized woodwork of the backbar is the visible post-and-beam construction of the inn. Made from old-forest red oak, the beams are something to behold. Owner Martin Hale marvels at the beams' age, wondering, as old as the inn is, how much older were those trees? I admired the photo of the inn just across from my table. In front were a horse and buggy, the traction-line engine, and an automobile. The photo, taken just after the turn of the twentieth century, depicts the inn's span of time. Automobiles have changed, and the other modes of transportation are all but gone. The inn, however, has withstood the passage of time.

SPICY BLACK BEAN SOUP

3 cups black beans, rinsed and strained
1 large tomato, finely diced
1 large onion, finely diced
½ cup chopped green onions
1 cup chopped jalapeño peppers
1 large red pepper, seeded and chopped
1 ham hock
8 cups chicken stock
½ stick butter
¼ cup flour
1 tablespoon seasoned salt
1 teaspoon pepper
tortilla strips, if desired
sour cream, if desired
sliced green onions, if desired

Place beans, tomatoes, onions, jalapeños, red pepper, and ham hock in a large pot. Add enough chicken stock to cover the ingredients. Bring to a boil. Reduce heat and simmer for 30 minutes. In a small pan, melt butter. Whisk in flour to make a roux. Set aside. Strain bean mixture, reserving liquid and 1 cup of beans. Purée remaining bean mixture.

Add purée to reserved liquid. Stir in remaining 1 cup of beans. Bring to a boil, whisking constantly. Reduce heat. Whisk in roux a little at a time until desired thickness is achieved. Add seasoned salt and pepper. Garnish with tortilla strips, sour cream, or green onions. Serves 8.

PAN-FRIED TILAPIA WITH CUCUMBER DILL SAUCE

1 large cucumber, peeled, seeded, and finely diced
1 small onion, diced
1 teaspoon white vinegar
1 teaspoon lemon juice
½ teaspoon garlic powder
¼ teaspoon white pepper
1 tablespoon dill
3 cups sour cream
¼ cup flour
salt and pepper to taste
2 tablespoons butter or olive oil
4 6-ounce tilapia fillets

Preheat oven to 350 degrees. Stir together cucumber and onions in a mixing bowl. Add vinegar, lemon juice, garlic powder, white pepper, and dill. Stir to mix. Fold in sour cream to finish sauce. Mix together flour and salt and pepper in a flat container. Heat butter or olive oil in a large sauté pan. Dredge tilapia fillets in flour and place face down in sauté pan. Flip fish when golden brown. Place in a baking dish to finish in oven for 5 to 9 minutes. Plate fillets and top with sauce. Serves 4.

8905 LAKE AVENUE
CLEVELAND, OH 44102
WWW.DONSLIGHTHOUSE.COM
216-961-6700

Both the Bronzed Salmon Salad and the Blackened Tenderloin Salad were quite popular with lunch guests the day that we visited. The salmon salad was concocted of spinach, grape tomatoes, and carrots, garnished with potato straws, and then tossed in Honey Mustard Dressing. The tenderloin variety also utilizes spinach, combined with tomatoes, red onions, Gorgonzola cheese, and warm Bacon Shallot Vinaigrette. The Seafood Chowder and the Mussels Pernod that we sampled to start the meal were excellent, and certainly point to why Don's Lighthouse Grille is known for its seafood. The Crab Cakes are always a hit, too, particularly with the Apricot Hot and Sour Sauce that accompanies them.

For dinner, the Lobster Fettuccine is consistently popular. The Great Lakes Walleye, crusted in pretzels and served with Mustard Aioli, sounded so scrumptious we were tempted to return for a second meal later in the day.

Otto Poschke had the building con-

structed in 1928. Early in the 1900s, Otto was a streetcar conductor on the old St. Clair run. In 1911, he married Elma, and the pair opened a ten-by-ten-foot barbecue shack north of Lake Avenue, where they sold soft drinks, taffy, peanuts, popcorn, hot dogs, hamburgers, and barbecue to sunbathers and beachgoers. By the 1920s, the Poschkes had several locations along the shoreline but wanted to consolidate. Otto also wanted to shake the frequent comments that went something like this: "Aren't you the owner of the little barbecue place?"

To counter that persona, Otto contracted to build a restaurant, specifying that it be constructed in the style of an elegant library or art museum. To the tune of $250,000, the new Poschke's was erected in the Renaissance Pastiche style. The first floor was an elaborate version of the old barbecue shacks. The mezzanine had a soda fountain and an area where many society parties were held. The third floor was family space, complete with a glass-ceilinged solarium, marble floors, and a fountain.

The exterior of the building today is almost identical to what it was during Otto's time. The large arched windows and French doors bathe the interior of the dining room in light, softening its somewhat formal décor. Murals of Cleveland scenes span the walls, connecting diners with other area treasures. We were intrigued by the curved copper accents throughout the dining room and were surprised to discover that they're actually quite heavy, weighing in combination half a ton!

We always like stories of who has visited restaurants, and our favorite one at Don's relates to Gary Burghoff, well known for his character Radar O'Reilly in the TV series "M*A*S*H". Apparently, Gary was visiting one day and was recognized by his server. The quick-thinking server ran across the street and purchased a Grape Nehi soda, a beverage of which Radar spoke fondly on the show. Mr. Burghoff got quite a chuckle over the stunt and has returned again and again. You should, too.

CRAB DIP

2 8-ounce packages cream cheese, softened
2 tablespoons horseradish
1 tablespoon lemon juice
1 teaspoon Tabasco sauce
½ tablespoon finely chopped fresh parsley
1 teaspoon garlic powder
⅓ cup chopped scallions
⅓ cup Asiago cheese
12 ounces crab claw meat

In a medium bowl, beat cream cheese until soft and creamy. Add horseradish, lemon juice, Tabasco, parsley, and garlic powder. Mix well to combine. Fold in scallions and Asiago. When ingredients are well incorporated, fold in crab claw meat. Serve with crackers or bread. Serves 4 as an appetizer.

LOBSTER ROLLS

2 tablespoons sesame oil
1 head savory cabbage, finely chopped
1 red onion, finely chopped
2 cups grated carrots
2 tablespoons garlic, chopped
2 tablespoons Thai chili garlic sauce
2 tablespoons cornstarch, divided
1 tablespoon water
32 spring roll skins
1 pound lobster meat

In a large skillet, heat sesame oil and sauté cabbage, onions, carrots, and garlic until tender. Drain off remaining oil. Add chili garlic sauce and toss well to combine. Set aside to cool. In a small bowl, mix together 1 tablespoon cornstarch and water to make a slurry. In the center of 1 spring roll wrapper, place 2 tablespoons vegetable mixture and 1 tablespoon lobster meat. Roll up tightly and seal using cornstarch slurry. Wrap roll a second time with an additional spring roll skin and seal with cornstarch slurry. Repeat until all ingredients have been used. Dust completed rolls lightly with remaining cornstarch to keep from sticking together. Refrigerate until ready to fry. Preheat oil in deep-fat fryer to 350 degrees. Cook small batches of lobster rolls until pale golden, turning several times to ensure that all sides are cooked. Each batch should take about 2 minutes to cook. Remove from fryer and place on paper towels to drain. Yields 16 rolls.

CHAPTER 4

Just Millin' Around

Jay's Restaurant

In *Titus Andronicus*, Shakespeare penned, "More water glideth by the mill than wots the miller of." Early communities frequently developed along water sources for just that reason. After the general store, the mill was one of the businesses most essential to settlers. Gristmills ground farmers' crops into various food products. And the presence of a gristmill encouraged further settlement. Lumbermills soon followed, supplying lumber for construction. Some of the mills featured here are still in operation, and all satisfy the needs of modern citizens by serving up good meals.

75 WATER STREET
CLIFTON, OH 45316
WWW.CLIFTONMILL.COM
937-767-5501

There used to be almost a hundred thousand mills operating in this country. Now, fewer than fifty are still in their original condition. Antonio Satariano Sr. and Jr. take great pride in being the owners of one of the oldest of those remaining few. They share a passion for preserving history, which led them to return their mill from a state of disrepair in 1988 to its original purpose. Under their supervision, the original grinding stones were reinstalled and a replica of the original waterwheel was constructed. They repaired floors and walls and even added a covered porch from which to view the waterfall that drops to the Little Miami River.

We sat in the Millrace Restaurant, one of the two dining rooms in The Clifton Mill. The view from atop the gorge is spectacular, even more so in winter, when every inch of the mill and the gorge below is covered with 2.5 million lights. The restaurant is located in the old storage and storefront part of the building. It is full of interesting photographs of the village of Clifton, mill memorabilia (including a fabulous collection of old flour bags), and wooden tables and chairs. It is easy to be transported back in time. The cooking is home-style. Whole-grain breads, pies, and cookies are baked daily.

Built in 1802 and originally named after its owner, Owen Davis, this is one of the largest water-powered gristmills still in operation. The old Davis Mill was owned and operated by many different families over the years as it quietly provided a backdrop to history itself. The whole village is historic. The Old Stagecoach Inn—a stop on the Accommodation Line—is opposite the mill. The stagecoach ran from Springfield to Cincinnati. At that time, the village of Clifton was well known for its clay soil and freshwater springs. During the rainy season, boggy roads were common, making stagecoach operation difficult at best. It did not surprise us to learn that in 1836, Clifton was the site of Ohio's first recorded stagecoach accident, which took place on the northern side of the village.

We visited at breakfast time to sample the famous Pancakes, made from grain ground on the premises. Opting for the Millrace Breakfast Combo—which includes Buttermilk, Cornmeal, and Buckwheat pancakes, served with a side of Sausage—we chatted with Antonio Jr. as we ate. He told us that the mill endeavors to support the local community in its purchases for the restaurant. To that end, it buys ostrich from a local ostrich farm. Hogs raised at another local farm are used in the mill's Whole-Hog Sausages—and jolly delicious they are, too!

There is much history to see here, both at the mill and in the village. We knew we would have to return another day for a more leisurely walk down to the narrows, where famous Indian scout Cornelius Darnell is supposed to have leapt over the gorge to escape pursuing braves. In the meantime, supporting local farmers with every mouthful, we settled down to clean our plates!

ARTISTS' SUGAR MAPLE THREE-LAYER CORNBREAD

1 cup cornmeal
½ cup whole hard wheat bread flour
½ cup white flour
2 teaspoons baking powder
½ teaspoon sea salt
1 brown egg, well beaten
¼ to ½ cup molasses or honey
¼ cup vegetable oil
3 cups milk or buttermilk

Preheat oven to 350 degrees. In a large bowl, mix together all dry ingredients. In a medium bowl, combine all wet ingredients. Pour wet ingredients into the large bowl and combine thoroughly with dry ingredients; mixture will be very liquid. Grease a 9-by-9-inch pan and pour in batter. Bake for approximately 50 minutes. Serves 10 to 12.

APPLE FARM BREAD

2 packages dry yeast
½ cup lukewarm water
1½ teaspoons salt
1 tablespoon pasteurized honey
1 tablespoon maple syrup
⅓ cup vegetable shortening, softened
½ teaspoon cinnamon
1⅔ cups hot water
1¼ cups applesauce (not chunky)
⅔ cup powdered milk
5 cups all-purpose flour
2 cups whole-wheat flour

In a small bowl, dissolve yeast in lukewarm water. Set aside to activate. In a large mixing bowl, combine salt, honey, syrup, shortening, cinnamon, and hot water. Mix thoroughly. Gradually stir in applesauce, then powdered milk. Add dissolved yeast and mix well. Stir in flours a cup at a time until dough is stiff but not tacky.

Lightly flour a breadboard and knead dough for at least 10 minutes. Place dough in a lightly greased bowl and cover with a moist cloth. Put bowl in a warm place and let dough rise for approximately 1 hour until it doubles in size.

Preheat oven to 400 degrees. Uncover and punch dough down. Cut dough in half and place each half in a lightly greased 9-by-5-inch loaf pan. Let pans stand for 30 minutes to allow dough to rise again. Bake for 45 minutes. Yields 2 loaves.

STOCKPORT MILL INN

1995 BROADWAY AVENUE
STOCKPORT, OH 43787
WWW.STOCKPORTMILL.COM
740-559-2822

The only remaining hand-operated lock system in the United States is here on the Muskingum River in Stockport. The influence of Lock #6 has been felt both in the community and in the Stockport Mill Inn. The mill's original twin Leffel turbines powered both the mill and the village streetlights in the 1920s. During our initial visit, we were shown the papers certifying government approval for the mill to again generate its own power. What's old is now new again.

The day we visited, we shared the dining room with the Hook family, descendants of Captain Isaac Newton Hook, a Muskingum riverboat pilot. He died in 1906, the year the current mill was built. But he was around to see the first mill here, built in 1842 and then rebuilt in 1849 after a fire destroyed the original. After operating for fifty-four years, the rebuilt structure also burned down.

When the Dover brothers put up the current building in 1906, a young lad by the name of Fred James declared it to be "plen-

ty sturdy." Its sturdiness passed muster, as it withstood not only the 1913 flood but all subsequent floods as well. It remains the only surviving mill on the Muskingum River. Fred James and Ray Devitt eventually bought the mill and then sold it to the Farm Bureau. In 1979, the operation was taken over by Robert and Jack Grove. During their tenure, the mill was involved in many 4-H projects. This venture lasted for almost twenty years, until the doors closed in 1997. They didn't stay that way for long.

In August 1998, Laura and Randy Smith were on a motorcycle ride, pursuing Randy's hobby of collecting antique autos. What they ended up with was an antique mill instead. During the renovation, the couple used as much of the mill and its machinery as possible. The original flooring, hand-hewn beams, gears, and grain bins were left exposed. Rather than being painted or stained, one wall is covered with slate tiles once used as roofing. Each of the lovely guest rooms upstairs is named for a significant part of the area's past, highlighting the connections between the mill's history and Stockport's legacy.

As we sat at a table with a picturesque view of the river and the locks, we were very glad the Smiths had taken that fateful motorcycle ride, and additionally glad that Dottie Singer is currently at the helm and is continuing to maintain what began more than one hundred years ago. The current menu features New York Strip Steak, Baby Back Ribs, and Southwestern Chicken. The freshest locally produced ingredients are used in season. Homemade breads, pies, and desserts are served. The popular Sunday buffet features Oven-Fried Chicken, homemade Noodles, Beef Pot Roast, and warm Fruit Cobbler. Wanting to linger awhile longer after a fulfilling meal, we decided to share dessert, hoping to catch a glimpse of one of the American bald eagles that have nested near the mill.

MUSKINGUM RIVER BROWNIES

1 box German chocolate cake mix
⅔ cup evaporated milk, divided
¾ cup melted margarine
1 cup pecans, chopped
14-ounce package Kraft caramels
12-ounce package chocolate chips

Preheat oven to 350 degrees. Combine cake mix, ⅓ cup evaporated milk, margarine, and nuts. Pat half of mixture into a 9-by-13-inch pan. Bake for 6 to 8 minutes. Combine caramels and remaining ⅓ cup evaporated milk in a saucepan on low heat. Cook until melted and smooth. Remove from heat. Sprinkle partially baked brownies with chocolate chips. Pour caramel mixture slowly over chips. Drop remaining cake mixture over top. Bake an additional 15 to 20 minutes. Serves 8 to 10.

MORGAN COUNTY CAVIAR

15-ounce can shoepeg corn
15-ounce can yellow corn niblets
15-ounce can black-eyed peas
15-ounce can black beans
15-ounce can black olives
4-ounce can jalapeño peppers (optional)
4-ounce can diced green chile peppers
1 medium tomato, diced
4 green onions with tops, thinly sliced
1 medium green pepper, diced
1 teaspoon minced garlic
1 cup Italian dressing

Drain canned ingredients while chopping vegetables. Add chopped vegetables and garlic to drained canned ingredients. Drizzle with Italian dressing and toss. May be refrigerated for 5 to 7 days. Serve as a dip with tortilla chops or in lettuce cups as a salad course. Yields 6 cups.

225 EAST SIXTH STREET
DAYTON, OH 45402
WWW.JAYS.COM
937-222-2892

When we arrived at Jay's at seven-thirty on a Thursday evening, it was packed. Those waiting assured us that it was definitely worth the delay. How very true that was. Jay's Restaurant was unveiled in 1976 and quickly became renowned for its wine list and its seafood. The wine list reads like poetry, and Karen enjoyed perusing it thoroughly. It is so comprehensive that it even has several pages at the front explaining the different types of wine, for those unsure of exactly what they should select. There are also maps with descriptions of various wine regions, all there for customers' education. On Fridays and Saturdays, bottles of wine are available for sale from the restaurant. Five different bottles are opened each of those days for customers to sample and purchase. The approach reflects owner Jay Haverstick's passion for excellent wine.

This excellence is reflected in the seafood as well. Seven or eight selections are available baked, char-grilled, or blackened. Monkfish, Tuna, Swordfish, Salmon, Halibut, Scrod, and

Lake Erie Walleye were among the choices the night we dined. For landlubbers, there are chicken and steak options, but Jay's and seafood really are synonymous. We opted for the Crab Cakes, which were fabulous. They had tiny bits of red cabbage and red pepper mixed in, which added an interesting texture and just a bit of flavor. The cakes were served with Remoulade Sauce and Asian Vinaigrette. Debbie preferred the rich ginger flavor of the Asian sauce, although both were excellent. For dessert, Karen was tempted by the Chocolate Coffee Torte, but we ended up sharing a piece of Jay's famous Lemon Sour Cream Pie. Both of us delighted in the light, not-too-sweet finish to our meal.

Jay's Restaurant is located in the Joseph Kratochwill Dayton Corn and Grist Mill, built in the 1850s on the bank of the Miami-Erie Canal. At one time, this mill provided Dayton and much of the Midwest with the Snow Flakes and New Process brands of flour, which were well known for their outstanding purity and fineness. The latter half of the 1900s was a prosperous time for Dayton's Oregon District. Commercial and residential development here left an architectural legacy unparalleled in the city. Visitors to the district—which is Dayton's oldest neighborhood—can still see the mansions of the wealthy standing among the simpler homes of laborers and craftsmen.

The interior of the restaurant is appealing in its simplicity. The brick walls of the old mill stand fairly unadorned. The beautiful light fixtures are of the time period of the mill's construction, and the railings were saved from the Old Xenia Hotel. In one corner of the room is an enormous fifty-four-hundred-pound Honduran mahogany backbar. It was commissioned for the opening of the Pony House Restaurant, an establishment where John Dillinger was a regular and where Buffalo Bill Cody is said to have ridden his horse right up to the bar! The bar serves a slightly more refined clientele today, but Jay's is popular with just about everyone, so you never know whom you might see!

SEARED TUNA

2 4-ounce Ahi tuna steaks
2 tablespoons wasabi paste
¼ cup black sesame seeds
2 tablespoons canola oil
2 cups seaweed salad or other greens of
 choice
2 radishes, thinly sliced
½ cup Sweet Chili-Soy Ginger Sauce (see
 next column)
handful of fried won tons

Coat tuna steaks with wasabi paste, then dredge in black sesame seeds. Heat oil in a large sauté pan. Sear tuna on each side for 2 minutes. Place steaks on a cutting board and thinly slice. Divide salad greens and place in center of 2 plates. Fan each tuna steak around greens. Place radishes around tuna. Top tuna with Sweet Chili-Soy Ginger Sauce. Place fried won tons on top of greens. Serves 2.

SWEET CHILI-SOY GINGER SAUCE

1 cup light soy sauce
½ cup sweet chili sauce
2 teaspoons freshly grated ginger
1 tablespoon honey

Place all ingredients into a small bowl and whisk together to blend. Place in a sealed container in refrigerator for at least 1 hour to allow flavors to combine. Yields approximately 2 cups.

PEERLESS MILL INN
319 SOUTH SECOND STREET
MIAMISBURG, OH 45342
WWW.PEERLESSMILLINN.NET
937-866-5968

Once a water-powered lumbermill on the bank of the Miami-Erie Canal, this charming inn is an ideal choice whether you're dining with a large group of friends or seeking a romantic dinner for two. The rustic hand-hewn timbers and enormous beams of dark wood give the six dining rooms and tavern a cozy, intimate feel. The large wood-burning fireplaces in most of the rooms and the flagstone floors enhance the historic ambiance, as do the wrought-iron chandeliers and the pewter chargers. Floral tablecloths and the assorted pieces of artwork adorning the walls lend a touch of warmth.

A favorite gathering place for the townsfolk, it was fairly full on the day we visited. The menu selections all looked good, from the Seafood Casserole Gratinée to the Lemon Pepper Marinated Roast Pork Loin. We opted for the Peerless Mill Inn's signature Seven-Layer Mill Salad and a homemade loaf of Bread. Debbie enjoyed her Veal Piccata with Lemon Cilantro Butter, while Karen savored the Roast Duckling with Cranberry Orange Glaze. The homemade desserts all sounded as wonderful as the entrées. Hot Peach Crisp à la Mode topped Karen's list, with Black Bottom Pecan Pie running a close second. It was a leisurely meal orchestrated by an attentive staff. We had plenty of time to investigate the small wooden curio boxes around the room, each filled with antique glassware and china.

Built in 1828, the lumbermill sat side by side with a gristmill. The Miami-Erie Canal had just been built, and the mills—locally known as the Great Peerless Mills—made a substantial contribution to the local economy. Named for the Miami tribe of Indians, who once roamed the local hills, Miamisburg was a growing village and a small but important center for cultivating tobacco. Wheel and carriage factories, binderies, and paper making were among the local industries.

The sawmill was powered by a large overshot waterwheel turned by the waters of the canal. Giant logs were dragged in from nearby woodlands and turned into beams and planks. Over the next seventy years, a city built from the products of the sawmill grew. The gristmill also prospered, wagons continuously passing through to pick up meal or flour. In 1938, the gristmill closed its doors for the last time, and the building was destroyed. Visitors now park their cars on what was once the site of that picturesque structure. The lumbermill was converted into a restaurant called the Peerless Pantry. That prosperous business was eventually renamed the Peerless Mill Inn. Today, the inn is proud to be called a living part of the history of Miamisburg.

TOURNEDOS DUMAS

1 cup chopped onions
2¼ cups cream
1 tablespoon butter
1 tablespoon flour
salt and pepper to taste
4 4-ounce beef fillets
4 toast rounds
4 slices ham
2 ounces Gruyère cheese, grated

In a medium pan, simmer onions in cream. In a second pan, melt butter and stir in flour. Cook over medium heat for 1 minute. Add onion mixture and cook until thickened. Add salt and pepper.

Broil or pan-fry fillets to desired doneness. Place on toast rounds and top with onion sauce, ham, and cheese. Place under broiler for about 30 seconds until cheese is melted. Serves 2.

APPLE DUMPLING CAKE

1½ cups oil
2 cups sugar
3 eggs
2 teaspoons vanilla
3 cups flour
1 teaspoon salt
1 teaspoon baking soda
1 teaspoon cinnamon
3 cups diced apples, skin on
1 cup nuts
1 cup brown sugar
1 stick butter, softened
¼ cup milk

Preheat oven to 350 degrees. In a large bowl, combine oil, sugar, eggs, and vanilla. Add flour, salt, baking soda, and cinnamon and stir to combine. Add apples and nuts. Stir mixture well and pour into a Bundt pan or an 8-by-12-inch cake pan. Bake for 1 hour.

In a small bowl, combine brown sugar, butter, and milk. Pour mixture over top of cake as soon as it is removed from oven. Let set for at least 1½ hours before removing cake from pan. Serves 12.

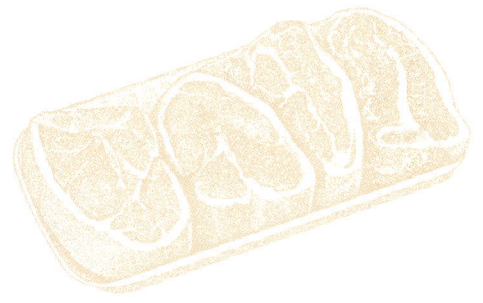

OLD MILL WINERY

403 SOUTH BROADWAY
GENEVA, OH 44041
WWW.THEOLDMILLWINERY.COM
440-466-5560

As you drive on State Route 534, you can't miss the freshly painted barn-red buildings highlighted in crisp white trim that comprise the Old Mill Winery. We arrived after a long day on the road, so the casual, laid-back atmosphere was quite welcome. Tables for four provided ample seating throughout the spacious interior of this old feed mill. The original wooden floor echoed with a warm resonance as guests moseyed up to the bar to get a drink or order a bite to eat.

We opted for one of the Wednesday-night specials, steamed Peel-and-Eat Shrimp, served in a basket with Red Potatoes, Corn on the Cob, and Garlic Bread. As our food was being prepared, we wandered through the interior, looking at the antique cash registers, stoves, trunks, and wooden buckets. We even discovered the Christmas bell that helped dress the holiday windows at Macy's Department Store in downtown Cleveland during the early 1900s.

The J. E. Goodrich family started a milling business in this building sometime in the early 1860s. The plastered and wallpapered rooms on three floors at the back of the structure probably functioned as the Goodrich residence. During the early 1900s, the mill was owned by George Brown, and then by Farmer's Supply Corporation. In 1937, General Mills took over the operation, using the mill to turn out ingredients for its wide array of products. All in all, the mill supplied the needs of the area for almost one hundred years.

At the time the mill was constructed, Ohio led the nation in the production of wines. Mr. and Mrs. Richard Kinkopf converted the mill into a winery in 1980, recapturing a piece of Ohio's history. Paul Cantwell and Alan and Joanne Schnider became subsequent owners. The Schniders bought the business to provide money for a unique spiritual concept they call their "Faith Foundation." The Old Mill Winery has sixteen wines on its list, including Geneva Blanc, a fruity, semisweet wine excellent for Sangria Coolers, and Grindstone White, a sweet dessert wine made from popular native Niagara grapes and similar in flavor to French Sauternes. In addition, the mill produces and bottles altar wines for church consumption in the Cleveland and Akron Catholic Diocese. A real highlight for the establishment came when Mrs. Schnider had the opportunity to offer a bottle of Old Mill wine to the pope!

Many people ask how the Old Mill Winery can offer home-style meals at such bargain prices. Whether you go on Tuesday for

Soup Night, visit on Thursday for Pasta Night, or order off the menu, the price is definitely right. The Schniders' philosophy is to "tempt them with food and keep them with wine and great entertainment." Everything from Irish folk music to classic rock can be heard. Sunday is the night when local performers (sometimes after a glass or two of wine) are encouraged to take center stage. But any night of the week, fun is on the menu!

MEAT LOAF

2 pounds freshly ground sirloin
2 pounds freshly ground pork
2 cups fresh breadcrumbs
1 large green pepper, finely diced
1 large red pepper, finely diced
2 cups marinara sauce
2 teaspoons pepper
2 teaspoons granulated garlic
1 tablespoon chopped fresh parsley
½ cup sweet red wine
4 large eggs
1 large onion, finely diced

Preheat oven to 350 degrees. Mix together all ingredients in a large bowl, kneading until thoroughly blended. Form into 4 small loaves and place in a shallow baking pan. Bake for 45 minutes to 1 hour until centers are 155 degrees. Serves 10 to 12.

CHAMBOURGIN DRESSING

½ cup sugar
1½ cups oil
½ cup Chambourgin wine or other dry red wine
1 cup balsamic vinegar
1 teaspoon granulated garlic
1 teaspoon pepper
½ teaspoon basil
1 tablespoon salt

Combine all ingredients with a whisk in a large bowl. Store in an airtight container in the refrigerator. Yields approximately 3 cups.

ALFREDO SAUCE

2 cups heavy cream
½ cup Chablis
1 teaspoon chopped fresh basil
1 teaspoon chopped garlic
1 teaspoon chopped fresh parsley
1 cup grated Romano cheese
salt to taste
3 egg yolks

In a medium saucepan, heat heavy cream slowly. Do not boil. Gradually add next 6 ingredients, whisking well. When cheese is just about completely melted, slowly whisk in egg yolks. Yields approximately 4 cups.

255 RIVERSIDE DRIVE
TIFFIN, OH 44883
WWW.DINEPIONEERMILL.COM
419-448-0100

The Sandusky River, source of power for the Pioneer Mill, is one of only a handful of rivers in the world to flow northward. We were seated in the main dining room, called the Millstone Room, at a table overlooking the water. The large, deep-set windows provided an ample view of the property and the river. Intrigued by the items adorning the walls, we wandered, as we are prone to do. Our most interesting discovery was the "swing sifter," a type of elevator in which small buckets were attached to a four-inch-wide cotton belt. The belt stretched from the basement to the third floor. The small containers on the belt would pick up grain and carry it upward, where it would be ground into flour, bran, or middling. We also enjoyed the printed quotations and bits of information about the mill's history displayed throughout the building. Two large metal drive wheels located in the basement were put in place shortly before the mill closed in 1951. The electricity generated by one of those wheels is enough to supply pow-

er for heat for the entire winter to the house across the street from the mill. During a power outage, the restaurant can obtain enough juice from the other wheel to continue operating. The metal wheels replaced the wooden handcrafted drive wheels that supplied the power for most of the mill's history. Today, the wooden wheels are displayed throughout the restaurant. Many are now in service as unique chandeliers.

Josiah Hedges, founder of the town of Tiffin, built the mill. Begun in 1822, construction of the frame building and the raceway took two years to complete. When fire destroyed much of this flour mill and gristmill in 1875, it was rebuilt using brick. But that was not to be the only disaster facing the mill. In 1913, the town of Tiffin was devastated by a flood. As the waters receded, a two-acre island comprised of debris, primarily bricks and stones, was formed beside the mill. Today, bits and pieces of brick can still be seen on the island. In 1937, a disastrous fire swept through the building. Charring is visible on many of the heavy wooden posts and beams that still support the structure.

On the day we visited, the luncheon buffet was a popular choice with many diners. It featured Tomato Bisque and Broccoli Cheddar Soup, several salads, Liver and Onions, Sliced Beef, and several dessert choices. Debbie's Broiled Walleye Sandwich was made with fish straight from the Great Lakes. Karen chose to experience the other end of the country for her lunch, ordering the Texiana Salad. It consisted of a chicken breast basted in Barbecue Sauce and seasoned with Cajun spices, served over a bed of greens, all of which was topped with shredded cheese, crisp bacon, and onion slices. Prime Rib is the house specialty for dinner, and we can't think of a more fitting environment in which to enjoy it.

PRIME RIB AND FETA SPUDS

4 ounces prime rib, cooked
4 potatoes, baked
¼ cup sliced mushrooms
¼ cup diced onions
⅓ cup feta cheese

Cut prime rib into small cubes. Cut potatoes in half and scoop out insides, reserving skins. Place insides in a medium bowl and add prime rib and rest of ingredients. Stir together. Divide mixture into 8 portions and mound inside the 8 potato skins. Place under broiler for about 30 seconds until golden brown. Serve immediately. Serves 4 as an appetizer.

PIONEER SIGNATURE CUT

4 8-ounce Delmonico steaks
2 tablespoons butter
1 cup chopped onions
8 ounces mushrooms, sliced
1 teaspoon Magic Spice
1 teaspoon garlic salt
1 cup Worcestershire sauce
1 cup soy sauce
1 tablespoon red wine vinegar
8 slices provolone cheese

Char-grill steaks to desired doneness. While meat is cooking, melt butter in a large skillet. Add onions, mushrooms, and all spices and liquids to pan. Cook until vegetables are soft and liquid is reduced by a third. Put steaks on plates. Pour ¼ of mushroom mixture over each steak and top with 2 slices of cheese. Place under broiler for 30 seconds to melt cheese. Serve immediately. Serves 4.

Ye Olde Mill
Home of
Velvet Ice Cream

11324 MOUNT VERNON ROAD
UTICA, OH 43080
WWW.VELVETICECREAM.COM
740-892-3921

The tradition of making Velvet Ice Cream began in 1914 when Grandpa Joe Dager set sail for America as a fifteen-year-old Lebanese immigrant. Seeking the good life, he found his future in ice cream. His belief in hard work and the dedication involved in creating and maintaining a quality product have been passed down through four subsequent generations of the Dager family. They've evolved from making hand-cranked vanilla ice cream to churning out more than 6 million gallons of ice cream per year in more than fifty varieties. What hasn't changed is the use of the freshest cream and finest ingredients available.

The gristmill on the property is frequently the focus of much attention, since it houses the ice-cream parlor. Built in 1817 by James King, the original mill was destroyed by fire ten years later. After it was rebuilt, another fire roared through the structure in 1865. The third building to rise above the stone foundation was known as McNaughten Mill. Its gray

slate roof had the words "Cash for Wheat" and the year "1817" spelled out in black. Milling operations ceased in 1907, and the structure changed hands multiple times.

Bought by Jake and Minnie Spillman in 1930, the property was given the name Ye Olde Mill by its new owners. They put in a miniature golf course and a dance club, where couples paid a dime to dance to the tunes of Kenny Stewart and his orchestra. Ox-roast dinners, at a cost of fifty cents, were another popular event. Rollerskating became popular in 1934. Since the skating took place on the second floor and refreshments were offered on the first, guests became quite good at maneuvering up and down the stairs with their skates still on! Jake Spillman ran a tight ship at the rink, so parents were comfortable in letting their children attend, knowing they were safe and well supervised. Eventually, the activity became so popular that a new rink was built complete with its own electric organ. It was such a destination that skaters dressed up to attend. The girls wore special skating outfits, and the men sported their best white flannel trousers.

The twenty acres encompassing Ye Olde Mill and the home of Velvet Ice Cream are still a picturesque setting full of family fun. Guests can start their visit at the museum, which tells the story of ice cream from Roman times through the present day. Antique ice-cream-making equipment is on display, intermingled with fun facts and historical information. Many visitors to this site choose to take advantage of the picnic area, nature trails, playground, and petting zoo. Some enjoy the shade in the grove of buckeye trees, while others idle in the sun on the banks of the peaceful lake. Always popular is the tour where folks can watch Velvet Ice Cream being made.

Ye Olde Mill is open spring, summer, and fall, with a huge ice-cream festival each year over Memorial Day weekend. In addition, Velvet Ice Cream is available in retail locations throughout Ohio, Indiana, Kentucky, and West Virginia. Along with my neighbor Mona Marple, I enjoyed my visit and my ample Banana Split. Other guests were relishing a meal, munching on sandwiches and salads. It's a great destination for old-fashioned fun that Karen and her family will be sure to enjoy when they visit.

GRIST MILLER

¼ cup first choice of ice-cream topping, divided
1 scoop each of 3 different ice-cream flavors
2 tablespoons second choice of ice-cream topping
2 tablespoons cashews
½ banana
whipped cream
1 tablespoon crushed nuts
1 maraschino cherry
1 pretzel rod

Ladle 2 tablespoons of your first choice of ice-cream topping into the bottom of a soda glass. Spoon 1 scoop of ice cream into glass.

Place remaining amount of first topping over ice cream. Continue with second scoop of ice cream. Spoon second choice of topping over ice cream. Add cashews. Add third scoop of ice cream. Cut banana into 5 round wheels and place around the side of the glass. Top with whipped cream, crushed nuts, cherry, and pretzel. Serves 1.

FEED BIN

14 scoops of ice cream (several flavors)
¼ cup chocolate ice-cream topping
¼ cup cherry ice-cream topping
¼ cup marshmallow ice-cream topping
2 bananas, cut into wheels
whipped cream
½ cup crushed nuts
4 maraschino cherries
8 pretzel rods

Spoon 7 ice-cream scoops into each of 2 ice-cream trays. Top ice cream with equal amounts of chocolate, cherry, and marshmallow toppings. Distribute bananas over each tray. Top with whipped cream, nuts, and cherries and garnish with pretzel rods. Serves 4 to 6. Note: Ye Olde Mill serves this by setting trays in a wooden feed bin.

36 EAST STREETSBORO STREET
HUDSON, OH 44236
WWW.TURNERSMILL.COM
330-655-2949

I was told that I couldn't go wrong with the seafood. Since I'd never sampled it, I chose the Opah, which has a flavor and meatiness somewhere between tuna and sea bass. My spice-rubbed variety, served with Saffron Rice and fresh Green Beans, was wonderful. I'd started with Corn Chowder, full of corn right off the cob. What followed was a delightful salad of Bibb lettuce, plums, pecans, and blue cheese, tossed ever so lightly in Balsamic Vinaigrette made on site. For dessert, I was sorely tempted by the Caramelized Plum Napoleon but chose the White and Dark Chocolate Bombe, a creamy Bavarian Mousse coated in a wisp of crisp chocolate. The concoction literally melted in my mouth.

Other diners enjoyed the popular Char-Grilled Trout with Oyster Mushrooms, accompanied by Tasso Ham and Fingerling Potato Hash, and the Beef Tenderloin, served with Cauliflower Gratin and Tomato Pie. The menu at Turner's Mill changes seasonally to take advantage of nature's bounty, and the of-

ferings of summer were deliciously present during my visit.

The atmosphere here is subdued and comfortable. I dined on the enclosed porch, where the large windows are treated with grapevines wound sparingly with tiny lights, giving the room a homey touch. There are two other dining rooms on the main floor, one of which is the Fireside Room. The tavern downstairs is every bit as cozy as the upstairs dining rooms. Booths line the massive stone foundation walls, and single white tapers in pewter candlesticks blink atop linen-covered tables, just as they do in the other dining areas.

This large red brick building, listed on the National Register of Historic Places, was built in 1852 by a group of businessmen who started a steam mill to house the Hudson Planing and Lumber Company. Twenty years later, Jacob Miner acquired the structure and refitted it to mill grain.

In 1891, Ernest Fillius took ownership and again changed the product line. In addition to hay and grain, he began to make flour, selling the well-known Perfection, Crown, and Crystal brands. The mill was sold in 1923 but continued operations under the moniker of the Hudson Milling Company.

Charles Turner, the man for whom the restaurant is named, took over in 1933 and continued to make flour. Eventually, his son C. Francis Turner assumed the reins and continued operating the mill until 1969. That legacy and longevity are carried on today by Brad Buchanan, proprietor of The Inn at Turner's Mill. It's certainly something of which David

Hudson, founder of the town and the great-great-great-granduncle of Francis Turner, could be proud!

ROAST CHICKEN

3- to 4-pound whole chicken, giblets
   reserved
4 sprigs rosemary
2 tablespoons wild flower honey
½ cup Dijon mustard
juice and zest of 1 lemon
salt and pepper to taste
½ cup canola oil
1 cup white wine
4 cups chicken stock
2 tablespoons cornstarch
2 tablespoons water

Rinse the chicken cavity. Pat dry. In a blender, combine the next five ingredients. Blend until well combined. With blender running, add oil in a steady stream to emulsify. Place chicken in a large plastic bag and add marinade. Seal top and allow to marinate in refrigerator for 2 to 6 hours.

Preheat oven to 450 degrees. Remove chicken from marinade and wipe off excess. Season with salt and pepper. Truss chicken and place on a rack in a roasting pan along with the giblets. Roast, basting frequently. Allow 20 minutes per pound, cooking to a thigh temperature of 165 degrees. Remove from oven and rest for 15 minutes. Reserve pan drippings for sauce. Heat roasting pan on stovetop. Add wine to deglaze pan. Add chicken stock and reduce until well flavored. In a small container, mix together cornstarch and water. Add slurry to chicken stock in small quantities until desired thickness is reached. Adjust seasonings. If desired, mince giblets and pull meat from neck bones to garnish sauce. Serves 4.

BAVARIAN MOUSSE

1 sheet gelatin
1 cup water
½ cup chopped white chocolate
½ cup chopped bittersweet chocolate
2⅓ cups heavy cream, divided
3 egg yolks
6 tablespoons sugar

Bloom gelatin in water and set aside. Melt white chocolate and bittersweet chocolate separately in double boilers. In a large saucepan, heat 1 cup heavy cream almost to boil. In a bowl, whisk together egg yolks and sugar to ribbon stage. Add hot cream a little at a time and return mixture to saucepan, whisking constantly until a temperature of 185 to 190 degrees is reached. Remove from heat. Squeeze water out of gelatin and add gelatin to saucepan, stirring until completely dissolved. Pour half of mixture into white chocolate and half into dark chocolate. Stir each until combined. Whip remaining cream to soft peaks. Fold half into white chocolate and the other half into dark chocolate. Fill individual molds about halfway with dark chocolate, then fill with white chocolate. Refrigerate to set. Serves 8.

CHAPTER 5

All Around the Town

Granville Inn

As settlements grew, farming was still the main source of income in Ohio, but labor did diversify. In each town, it was necessary to have churches, schools, banks, and other businesses to meet the needs of the growing population. This chapter features restaurants with cuisines and ambiance as varied as the businesses that once occupied their locations. From gentlemen's clubs to the jail, there's something for everyone.

Refectory
RESTAURANT

1092 BETHEL ROAD
COLUMBUS, OH 43220
WWW.THEREFECTORY.CITYSEARCH.COM
614-451-9774

As we prepared to take our first bite of dessert, the background music eased its way into the strains of "My Favorite Things" from *The Sound of Music.* How appropriate! Karen's Apple Tart with Rosemary was phenomenal, and Debbie's Chocolate Pistachio Torte was equally satisfying. The final course was truly the "icing on the cake" in a totally wonderful dinner. We both started with soup, tasting the Butternut Squash Velvet Soup and the Creamy Asparagus. That was followed by an entrée of Salmon, served with Truffled Potatoes Napoleon, and an entrée of Swordfish Tournedos. Everything was absolutely delicious, and the ambiance was every bit as enjoyable.

The Refectory Restaurant is housed in what was once Bethel United Methodist Church. The congregation began in 1842 in a defunct distillery. A barn at the corner of Francisco and Kenny roads housed the worshipers until 1858. Eventually, noise from the nearby train tracks forced the church to move so sermons could be heard. It was relocated next to the Perry Township schoolhouse, which was remodeled and eventually used as a Sunday school. Only for the last thirty years have the two structures been connected. In 1966, the church family felt it had outgrown the structure and made a decision to relocate once again. December 1971 saw the completion of a new church and the sale of the old building to a group of individuals interested in starting a restaurant. When they signed the deed that created The Olde Church-House, an interesting clause was written into it stating that the building could never again be used as a church. But thanks to the stained-glass windows, the high beam ceilings, the candlelight, and the servers dressed in monklike garb, the serenity of the building continued to be felt. The wait staff no longer wears robes, dressing in formal attire instead. The restaurant evolved from The Olde Church-House into The Refectory in 1980.

We were seated in the main dining room, which was once the sanctuary. We would have been equally happy to sit in the bistro, located in the old schoolhouse, where diners enjoy a special three-course prix fixe menu. On the night we visited, the choices were starters of Lobster Terrine or Creamy Asparagus Soup, entrées of Monkfish Stew or Beef Tenderloin Fricassee, and desserts of Chocolate Bread Pudding or Vanilla Crème Brûlée.

Such gastronomic delights are the creations of chef Richard Blondin, a native of Lyon, France, and a protege of chef Paul Bocuse. Among the clientele for Blondin's memorable meals are old parishioners. Choir members and Sunday-school graduates happily stroll through the hallways and reminisce.

One former pastor has celebrated several wedding anniversaries in the very place where he once presided over his congregation.

BUTTERNUT SQUASH SOUP

1 medium-sized leek
1½-pound butternut squash
2 tablespoons unsalted butter
¼ cup chopped onion
2 tablespoons minced celery
3 cups whole milk
salt and freshly ground pepper to taste
2 tablespoons chopped fresh chives

Trim leek at both ends, leaving 2 to 3 inches of light green stalk. Slice lengthwise, pull the layers apart, and rinse thoroughly. Chop into ½-inch-thick slices, rinse again, and drain. Peel squash, then cut in half and remove seeds by scraping with a soup spoon. Cut squash into ½-inch cubes. Heat butter in a large saucepan. Sauté leeks, onions, and celery over medium heat for about 8 minutes. Add squash and sauté another 4 minutes. Add milk and bring to a simmer. Cook uncovered for 30 minutes. Let mixture cool slightly, then purée in 2 or 3 batches in a blender or a food processor until very smooth. Add salt and pepper. Return mixture to saucepan and keep warm. Ladle into bowls and garnish with fresh chives. Serves 6 to 8.

WARM APPLE TARTS WITH ROSEMARY

1¼ sheets frozen puff pastry
5 Golden Delicious apples
⅓ cup plus 4 tablespoons sugar, divided
1 stick unsalted butter, divided
½ teaspoon finely chopped fresh rosemary
3 tablespoons powdered sugar, sifted
4 unblemished mint sprigs

Thaw pastry and roll it out to ½-inch thickness on a floured surface. Cut out four 5-inch rounds. Transfer to a baking sheet lined with parchment or wax paper and refrigerate for at least 35 minutes. Peel, core, and finely dice 1 apple. Place apple in a small saucepan with ⅓ cup sugar and half the butter. Cook over low heat until apple is very soft and sugar is dissolved to make a spreadable compote. Set aside to cool.

Preheat oven to 350 degrees. Cut four 6-inch squares of parchment paper. Arrange squares on a baking sheet and sprinkle 2 tablespoons sugar evenly over sheets. Place chilled pastry rounds on top of sugar and prick dough with a fork. Spread 1 tablespoon of cooled apple compote over each pastry round. Sprinkle rosemary evenly over compote. Peel, core, and thinly slice remaining apples. Fan out slices in a circular pattern on top of tarts. Melt remaining butter; using a pastry brush, coat tops of tarts carefully with butter. Sprinkle remaining 2 tablespoons sugar over tarts. Bake for 18 minutes until apples turn a light golden brown. Serve hot, dusted with powdered sugar and garnished with mint sprigs. Serves 4.

302 EAST UNIVERSITY AVENUE
CINCINNATI, OH 45219
WWW.MECKLENBURGS.NET
513-221-5353

Mecklenburg Gardens has been a Cincinnati tradition since 1865. It was originally named Mount Auburn Garden Restaurant and Billiard Saloon under owner John Neeb, who created a prominent gathering place for German immigrants and singing societies. The grape arbor outside the front door became a *biergarten* where famous sopranos and baritones gathered to entertain their countrymen. In 1881, headwaiter Louis Mecklenburg purchased the restaurant. He was determined to teach his fellow immigrants about American traditions, and thus the fictional town of Kloppenburg was created. Mecklenburg's restaurant was the "town hall," and mock elections were held to teach the locals about the American political process. It is said that Kloppenburg was named after the noise that patrons made when banging their empty beer steins on the tables to indicate their need for a refill.

Over the next fifty years, Louis Mecklenburg and eventually his son Carl continued to host the rich and famous, as well as their regulars. Local rumor states that during Prohibition, the Mecklenburg family informed faithful customers about the availability of strong libations by the northward or southward direction of the ship placed over the bar. If you sit at the bar today and check out the unbelievable collection of German beers, you will spot a replica of that ship on the back wall.

The restaurant has passed through many hands, both German and non-German. However, in the 1960s, as the public's desire for fine dining declined, there was no longer a call for German favorites such as Hasenpfeffer (a country-style rabbit dish) or Mrs. Mecklenburg's famous Kartoffeln (potato pancakes) or, indeed, steins of German lager. Despite the hard times, the historic building survived through a variety of cuisines until the current owners, the Harten family, initiated the rebirth of this symbol of German heritage.

We sat in the charming main dining room, which was once the old grill room. Guests can still see parts of the old chimney, and the antique oven still stands in the center of the far wall. The room is surrounded by hand-hewn paneled walls. A hand-painted grapevine winds its way around the room, which overlooks the fully restored *biergarten* and the street beyond. In one corner, glass-fronted shelving abounds with steins.

The extensive menu offers a full range of German favorites and American creations. Debbie chose the Mecklenburg Sampler and thoroughly enjoyed its many appetizers, including Potato Pancakes, Crab Cakes, and Sauerkraut Balls. Karen chose the Chicken

Strudel, which consisted of chicken, spinach, and feta cheese in a light Cream Sauce, wrapped in puff pastry. It was an unusual and extremely good dish. The servings were large, so we decided to have a slice of the Apple Cinnamon Strudel to go. We lasted about an hour before we broke down and devoured the strudel and the carton of Caramel Sauce that came with it. It was definitely the best strudel either of us had ever tasted.

CHICKEN SCHNITZEL

6 4- to 6-ounce chicken breasts
½ cup flour
2 eggs, beaten
1 cup breadcrumbs
¼ cup oil
Dunkelwizen Sauce (see next column)

Pound chicken breasts until ¼ inch thick. Dredge chicken in flour, then dip in eggs, then dredge in breadcrumbs. Heat oil in a skillet and pan-sear chicken for 5 minutes on each side. Place chicken on plates and pour Dunkelwizen Sauce over top. Serve immediately. Serves 6.

DUNKELWIZEN SAUCE

¾ cup white wine
½ cup beer
2 cubes chicken bouillon
¼ cup lemon juice
⅔ cup capers
3 14-ounce cans artichoke hearts, quartered
4 sticks butter

In a medium saucepan, combine all ingredients except butter. Stir together over medium-low heat. Remove pan from heat. Cut butter into small chunks and add to pan. Stir until creamy. If sauce is thin, add more butter. Keep sauce at room temperature when serving over chicken. Yields approximately 4 cups.

**215 NORTH WALNUT STREET
WOOSTER, OH 44691
330-262-3333**

The first jail to be constructed in Wayne County was made of timber and had walls twenty-six feet in length. It was completed in August 1817. Twenty-two years later, a second solid, dungeon-like building was erected. It came to be known as "the Stone Jail." It burned during the Civil War, on December 18, 1863. Its replacement was built in the early 1870s on the northwest corner of North Walnut and North streets. Wayne County historian Benjamin Douglas described it as "one of the finest edifices of its kind in the state." He went on to say that "it was constructed of brick, stone, and iron at a great cost." The actual sum is not known, but an 1899 addition cost taxpayers fifteen thousand dollars.

Guests access the restaurant through an upstairs entrance, where attractive banquet rooms have been fashioned from what was once the sheriff's living quarters. Just off the hallway, down a steep flight of steps, and between thick brick walls is the Olde Jaol Brewing Company. The restaurant prides itself on presenting a limited menu focused on consis-

tent excellence. However, I'm sure the choices are more varied than they were for "guests" more than 130 years ago. My meal was certainly more upscale than the bread and water some prisoners must have received, although I did dine in one of the cells.

The unique structure and its excellent food create a first-rate dining experience. From the moment I entered, I tried to count the brick archways in an attempt to ascertain how many prisoners may have been housed here. Looking around the particular cell in which I was seated, I could easily imagine one man existing in the space, but I wondered how crowded it actually got, particularly since the entire jail was much roomier than I'd expected. Subtle lighting and occasional barred doorways completed the ambiance. Old photos of faculty members from nearby Wooster University and a vintage photograph of the jail provided further perspective.

Although I arrived before five o'clock, guests were already seated at several tables, taking advantage of the "Early Parole Dinners," the Olde Jaol's rendition of early-bird specials. The choices that particular evening were Chicken Piccata, Prime Rib, Salmon, Orange Roughy, and Beef Bourguignonne. I opted to order from the regular menu, choosing the Sirloin, an extremely tender cut of certified Black Angus beef garnished with deliciously thin, crispy Onion Rings and served with Garlic Red-Skinned Mashed Potatoes. At the suggestion of the staff, I also enjoyed a serving of Upside Down Apple Cinnamon Walnut Pie, accompanied by Vanilla Ice Cream. I was sorry that Karen wasn't there to dig into it with me.

Guests wanting a more casual atmosphere can stop by the Olde Jaol Tavern, once the carriage house for the jail. There, the menu includes Bail Burgers, Steak Escape Sandwiches, and other choices such as the Sticky Fingers Basket of Chicken Fingers and the Call Out the Dogs Basket, consisting of a Chili Dog topped with onions and cheddar cheese. If I were sentenced to the Olde Jaol Brewing Company, I'd never seek parole!

JAOL HOUSE CHICKEN

2 4-ounce chicken breasts
½ cup sliced mushrooms
½ cup demi-glace
2 2-ounce slices Canadian bacon
2 slices Monterey Jack cheese

Place chicken breasts in a broiler pan and broil for 10 minutes, turning halfway through. While chicken is broiling, sauté mushrooms in demi-glace. Reduce heat to warm and set aside. Top chicken with Canadian bacon and cheese. Return to broiler until cheese is melted. To serve, make an oval of mushroom sauce on each of 2 plates and top with a chicken breast. Serves 2.

CHEDDAR AND ALE SOUP

2 tablespoons vegetable oil
4 slices bacon, diced
½ onion, diced
2 stalks celery, diced
2 carrots, peeled and diced
6 cups milk
2 15-ounce cans cheese sauce
1 heaping tablespoon chicken bouillon granules
2 teaspoons basil
2 to 3 capfuls Worcestershire sauce
2 to 3 shakes Tabasco sauce
1 heaping tablespoon Lawry's salt
2 teaspoons pepper
1 cup beer
¼ cup cornstarch
¼ cup water

Heat oil in a large pot and sauté bacon and vegetables until cooked. Add milk and cheese sauce, stirring until well combined. Add bouillon, basil, Worcestershire, Tabasco, Lawry's, and pepper. Bring to a simmer. Add beer. Stir together cornstarch and water in a small bowl to make a slurry. Thicken soup by adding 1 to 2 tablespoons slurry at a time until it reaches desired consistency. Serves 8.

210 EAST EIGHTH STREET
CINCINNATI, OH 45202
WWW.ARNOLDSBARANDGRILL.COM
513-421-6234

Arnold's has an unimposing facade with gray paint peeling off the red bricks underneath. The only exterior change since 1848 was the removal of the wrought-iron balustrade surrounding the first floor. Reputed to be Cincinnati's oldest tavern in continuous operation, Arnold's Bar & Grill serves fine, made-from-scratch meals in an atmosphere redolent of the past.

There are several dining areas on the ground floor, each with a character of its own. We entered the bar area through what used to be the door for gentlemen only. This part of the building housed a barbershop until Simon Arnold opened his saloon in 1861. A simple wooden backbar runs almost the whole length of the room. The tables are gaily covered with red and white gingham tablecloths. Visitors are watched over by a voluptuous temptress depicted in stained glass over the entrance.

We sat at one of the booths in the second dining area (which used to be a feed store) and looked at the myriad photographs of Victorian ladies. The walls and floors here are attractively shabby. The old linoleum has

been worn away in many places to reveal the original wooden floor below. Throughout the establishment, an eclectic collection of curios, antiques, and old photographs catches the eye. Ronda Androski, the proprietor, told us that the most popular place to eat is the covered courtyard, bounded on two sides by brick walls. Guests sit at the small wooden tables and listen to some of the best folk and bluegrass music to be found.

When the Arnold family moved to Cincinnati, the five brothers and their wives and children all lived above the bar on the second and third floors of the building. For ninety-eight years, they prospered by operating Arnold's. During Prohibition, most of the family moved out of the building to allow dining rooms on the second floor. Elmer Arnold, a descendant of the original brothers, remained on the third floor. It is rumored that he used the bathtub on the second floor to brew illegal gin. The bathtub is still there—but unfortunately, the gin is not!

Before deciding what to eat, we consulted our helpful waitress, Debi, who makes all the desserts in her spare time. She encouraged us to choose the Greek Spaghetti Deluxe, a house specialty. It certainly lived up to its reputation. The spaghetti is lightly tossed in butter, olive oil, and Garlic Sauce and topped with olives, bacon, and tomatoes, a totally delicious combination. The menu offers a large selection of sandwiches, salads, and burgers, as well as many pasta choices. The Muffaleta Sandwich—with capacola, salami, provolone, mozzarella, tomato, and lettuce, dressed in Three-Olive Relish—caught our eye. We also noticed that a number of the salads may be ordered over fettuccine, an unusual twist to an old favorite. We completed our meal with a slice of Chocolate Opera. This dessert's filling is created from Opera Creams, made right here in Cincinnati. It was a slice of heaven on earth.

CRÈME BRÛLÉE

4 egg yolks
4 tablespoons sugar
pinch of salt
2 cups heavy cream
4 tablespoons brown sugar

Preheat oven to 350 degrees. Beat egg yolks in a medium bowl until slightly thickened. Add sugar and salt and beat to combine. In a medium saucepan, heat cream to a simmer. Pour hot cream into egg-yolk mixture and beat well to combine. Pour mixture into custard cups. Place cups in a deep baking pan and fill with water halfway up cups. Bake for 60 minutes, until a knife inserted in cups comes out clean. Set aside to cool, then place in refrigerator to chill.

Just before serving, sprinkle with brown sugar and caramelize with a kitchen torch. Serve immediately. Serves 4.

ARNOLD'S FAMOUS CORNBREAD

2 cups flour
2 cups buttermilk
4 eggs
2 cups cornmeal
½ cup honey
2 tablespoons baking powder
¾ cup oil

Preheat oven to 375 degrees. In a large bowl, combine all ingredients except oil. Add oil and mix again to combine. Pour into a deep 11-by-13-inch baking dish. Bake for at least 30 minutes, until inserted toothpick comes out clean. Serve warm. Serves 12.

ARTICHOKE-STUFFED MUSHROOMS

8-ounce can artichokes, drained and chopped
¼ cup mayonnaise
½ teaspoon minced garlic
2 tablespoons grated Romano cheese
4 large portabello mushrooms, stemmed and scraped

Preheat oven to 350 degrees. In a medium bowl, mix together artichokes, mayonnaise, garlic, and Romano. Mound ¼ of mixture in center of each mushroom. Bake for 10 to 15 minutes until golden brown. Serves 4 as an appetizer.

Teller's

OF HYDE PARK

2710 ERIE AVENUE
CINCINNATI, OH 45208
WWW.TELLERSOFHYDEPARK.COM
513-321-4717

The original settlers of this area were weary Revolutionary War veterans entitled to buy land at $1.50 per acre. A deed signed by President George Washington included what is now Hyde Park in the Miami Purchase land grant of more than three hundred thousand acres, acquired by John C. Symmes. Mr. Symmes deeded a large tract to Isaac Ferris. The transaction was dated 1798, but Ferris's residence in the area is documented prior to that date, when he helped found Columbia Baptist Church in 1790. It was purportedly the first Protestant church in the Northwest Territory.

The area remained fairly rural until 1892, when a syndicate of citizens purchased almost all of the property in the triangle bounded by Edwards Road, Observatory Road, and Madison Pike. The vision of James Mooney, Colonel A. S. Berry, T. B. Youtsey, John Zumstein, Wallace Birch, and Charles H. and John Kilgour was to create an elite suburb, one of many around the nation made possible by the expansion of electric streetcar lines.

As successful professionals and their families moved to the area, the Madison Road Improvement Association was formed. The Hyde Park Business Club grew out of that organization. Its five hundred–plus members sought fire protection, a branch library, and improved streets with incandescent lighting, among other things. The first village meeting, with Louis E. Ziegle presiding, was held after the election of officials in 1896 in the space eventually occupied by the Hyde Park Savings Bank. It was also in that building that the first city council was organized.

Not only did Mr. Ziegle serve as the first president of the Hyde Park Business Club, he was also the president of the Hyde Park Savings Bank. The bank continued in operation until 1971. At the time of its closing, it was part of the Fifth Third Bank. After that, the bank space was converted into the Left Bank, an arcade of upscale boutiques. During the transition, a fifteen-by-forty-five-foot skylight that had been covered during Fifth Third's tenure was unveiled. Today, that skylight floods the interior of Teller's of Hyde Park with sunlight. Healthy-looking philodendrons hang nearby. The restaurant uses what is left of the Hyde Park Savings Bank in interesting ways. An old safe serves as the reception desk; bar-style seating on the main floor utilizes the iron-barred teller windows; and the vault is used as a cozy seating area.

We dined on the upper balcony, likely the office space from yesteryear. Karen chose one of the day's specials, the Caramelized Onion and Potato Frittata with Gorgonzola Cheese. Debbie, in an Eastern mood, paused over the Cantonese Chicken Salad before finally deciding to sample the Thai Chicken Pizza. The menu and atmosphere obviously appeal to a wide range, as we dined near tables of senior citizens as well as families with young children. The restaurant is an interesting mix of old and new, and we're certainly glad that we had the opportunity to cash in.

HYDE PARK CHOPS WITH MAYTAG BLUE CHEESE SAUCE

1 cup port wine
½ cup heavy cream
1 slice bacon, finely diced
1 shallot, diced
1 tablespoon flour
½ cup Maytag blue cheese
½ cup veal demi-glace or reduction
2 10-ounce bone-in pork chops, butterflied
salt and pepper to taste

Pour port into a medium saucepan. Place on stove over medium-high heat. Simmer until reduced by half. Add cream and reduce again by half. Sauté bacon in a skillet until fat is rendered. Add shallots and cook until caramelized. Add flour to skillet to create a roux. Whisk roux into the reduction and stir until well blended. Add blue cheese and demi-glace. Cook pork chops on a grill for 4 to 5 minutes per side. Season with salt and pepper. To serve, spoon sauce over pork chops. Serves 2.

GOAT CHEESE–STUFFED SHRIMP

10 shrimp, 16-20 count, tails on
2 tablespoons olive oil
½ cup goat cheese
1 tablespoon plus 1 teaspoon minced cilantro
2 teaspoons minced garlic
Tomato Coulis (see below)

Preheat oven to 400 degrees. Butterfly the shrimp. Place shrimp on a baking sheet and brush with olive oil. Combine goat cheese, cilantro, and garlic and place evenly on shrimp. Bake for approximately 8 minutes. To serve, pool Tomato Coulis in center of 2 plates. Arrange shrimp, tails outward, around coulis. Serves 2.

TOMATO COULIS

2 cups diced Roma tomatoes
2 tablespoons olive oil
2 teaspoons chopped cilantro
juice of 2 limes
2 teaspoons sugar
2 teaspoons crushed red pepper

Sauté tomatoes in olive oil over medium heat until they break down. Add remaining ingredients and cook to heat through. Place in a blender or a food processor and purée. Yields approximately 1 cup.

812 RACE STREET
CINCINNATI, OH 45202
WWW.THEPHX.COM
513-721-8901

Cincinnati's finest example of Italian Renaissance architecture was built in 1893 as The Phoenix Club, the first Jewish businessmen's organization in this area of the country. The architect was Samuel Hannaford, well known for Cincinnati landmarks such as city hall, St. George Church, and what is today The Cincinnatian Hotel. Nothing was spared in The Phoenix Club's interior details. Cherubs, filigree, and scrollwork adorn much of the woodwork. All of the marble, imported from Germany, is original. The grand staircase, made of white marble, is one of the finest examples of its kind in North America. Lovely arched stained-glass panels are situated above the curving staircase, adding further elegance to the entrance.

The Phoenix Club was purchased as a sports annex in 1911 by the members of the Cincinnati Club, just around the corner. A full-length lap pool and a bowling alley were located in the basement. The Archway Ballroom, on the second floor, became the Billiards Room, holding approximately twenty-five pool tables. On the third floor, the Grand Ballroom with its thirty-three-foot ceiling became a basketball court with a balcony for spectators on three sides.

After ninety years as a private club, the building was closed in 1983 when interest in such clubs declined. It was sold, boarded up, and left untouched for three years. In 1986, it was sold again, this time to owners interested in helping The Phoenix rise again to its original beauty. The restoration took two years to complete. One of the difficulties was the stained-glass windows in the Archway Ballroom. Sometime between 1984 and 1986, they were stolen—dismantled and carried away without anyone's noticing. The person suspected of the theft was ultimately charged and tried for his misdeed. During the trial, some unknown individual placed the missing windows in the hallway of the courthouse. The case was then dropped, and the windows were returned to their rightful place. Only a few pieces were not recovered. Their replacements are recognizable by their darker shade of brown. It seems that modern technology couldn't reproduce the original color.

Dinner is served in the former Reading Room, now called the President's Room. The huge, hand-carved breakfront was built entirely on site and spans the width of the room. The Phoenix's starters, listed on the menu as "First Plates," include a pleasant combination of traditional favorites such as Jumbo Shrimp, served creatively with Tomato Cocktail Sorbet, and a Crab Cake accompanied by Bacon, Leek, and Potato Salad. The Smoked Salmon and Grilled Asparagus in a homemade Lasagna Noodle was too good to pass up. Our

"Second Plate" choices were Shrimp Tempura and Roast Amish Chicken with asparagus and Crimini Risotto. The service was excellent, the atmosphere opulent, and the food sumptuous. It was like Cinderella going to the ball without having to worry about pumpkins or glass slippers.

ROAST ARTICHOKES

3 small artichokes
juice of 1 lemon
½ cup olive oil, divided
3 cloves garlic, minced
1 cup white wine
1 cup water

Peel the hard green outer leaves off the artichokes, leaving the tender greens intact. Trim stems with a paring knife, reaching the tender yellow area. Using a spoon, scoop the choke out of the center, leaving the soft, smooth surface. Rub gently with lemon juice to slow down the oxidation process. Heat ¼ cup of the olive oil in a medium saucepan. Place garlic in the pan with the artichokes and lightly sauté, bulb sides down. Cover with wine, water, and rest of olive oil. Cook covered until tender. Drain. Serve or chill and reserve until needed. Serves 1 as an appetizer.

TOMATO COCKTAIL SORBET

3 Roma tomatoes, peeled, seeded, and finely diced
1 shallot bulb, minced
1 clove garlic, minced
½ cup grated horseradish
juice of ½ lemon
pinch of cayenne pepper
salt and pepper to taste

Mix together all ingredients. Freeze in ice-cube trays. Remove from freezer a few minutes before serving. Serves 5.

NEW ENGLAND CRAB CAKES

8 ounces jumbo lump crabmeat
8 ounces crab claw meat
2 teaspoons Dijon mustard
½ cup mayonnaise
¼ cup chopped chives
¼ cup chopped parsley
pinch of cayenne pepper
salt and pepper to taste
1 cup dried breadcrumbs
1 tablespoon olive oil

Mix together all ingredients except breadcrumbs and olive oil. Chill for 4 to 6 hours. Preheat oven to 400 degrees. Form mixture into 4 cakes. Roll in breadcrumbs until fully coated. Heat oil in a pan and sear crab cakes. Bake for 10 to 15 minutes until cooked through. Serves 4 as an appetizer or 2 as an entrée.

6892 CLOUGH PIKE
CINCINNATI, OH 45244
WWW.CLOUGHCROSSINGS.COM
513-624-7800

Flora Hess opened her first restaurant on Beechmont Hill in 1925. At that time, she and her staff raised, slaughtered, and prepared all the meats served there. In 1943, she bought the old Clough Pike School from Mount Washington American Legion Post 484 and moved her tavern to this location. "Miss Flo," as she was called, was a devout Catholic who enjoyed people. Each year, she entertained the graduating class from nearby St. Gregory's. In 1983, when Flora Hess was forced to retire due to failing health, she was the oldest active businesswoman in Hamilton and Clermont counties, as well as the oldest woman in Ohio holding a state liquor license. The tavern passed to her great-nephew Charles Sutter. A long succession of pubs and taverns has since occupied the site.

Gary Sammons decided to take the old school building in a new direction when he opened Clough Crossings in 1997. The two-story brick structure is attractively painted in cream and white, while the interior of the restaurant is suited for casual or fine dining.

The walls are simply decorated with framed black-and-white photos of earlier events and scenes from around Anderson Township, named for the area's surveyor, John Clough Anderson. Two old school desks intertwined with flowers decorate the center of the room.

At one end of the room is a remarkable bookcase that served as the backbar in this location when Miss Flo was operating her tavern. The piece, hand-carved in Germany, was one of a matched pair owned by Charles Wolff. Before libraries were provided by the township, most wealthy residents endeavored to create their own. Mr. Wolff owned one of the most extensive collections of books in the area. At the time his palatial residence was built in 1858, he also owned the old Stephen Davis–Stephen Corbly Home. On the land surrounding that home, he constructed a special building to house his rare books, which included an impressive variety of rare Bibles. The bookcase at Clough Crossings and its mate were used to display a portion of Mr. Wolff's fine collection.

We were seated at the opposite end of the room from this lovely piece of furniture, and so could easily admire its craftsmanship. There was also much to look at on the menu, including many tidbits of history, among them an 1898 program from "Cluff" Principal School. We were so engrossed in the history that it took awhile for us to order. The Almond-Crusted Salmon, served in Ginger Saffron Sauce, is one of the most popular entrées, as is the Cajun Seafood Fettuccine. Debbie was in the mood for a light meal, so she selected the Creamy Turkey Vegetable Soup and a side salad. The soup was deliciously full of bite-sized pieces of turkey and assorted vegetables. Karen chose the Tarragon Pork Chop, topped with Horseradish Sour Cream and attractively served with Wild Rice and Sautéed Vegetables. It was certainly not the type of meal either of us was ever served in the school cafeteria!

ALMOND-CRUSTED SALMON

¾ cup sliced almonds
2 6- to 7-ounce salmon fillets
½ cup flour
1 egg, slightly beaten
2 tablespoons oil
Ginger Saffron Sauce (see next column)

Preheat oven to 350 degrees. Place almonds in a single layer on a baking sheet and lightly toast for 2 minutes. Do not over-brown. Allow to cool. Lightly crush almonds by placing in a sandwich bag, sealing, then squeezing between hands. Pour into a shallow container.

Dredge salmon in flour, dip in egg wash, then roll in crushed almonds. Heat oil in an ovenproof skillet over medium heat. Sauté salmon in pan until almonds start to brown. Bake in skillet in oven for 3 to 4 minutes on each side. Remove salmon from pan, set aside, and keep warm.

Using the same pan, make Ginger Saffron Sauce. When sauce is done, pour ½ cup sauce into center of each of 2 plates. Place salmon in center over sauce and serve. Note: The chef suggests serving this dish with rice and fresh vegetables. Serves 2.

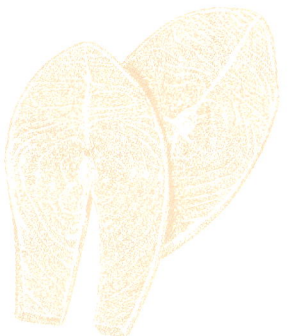

GINGER SAFFRON SAUCE

¼ red bell pepper, finely diced
1 teaspoon minced garlic
1 teaspoon finely diced shallots
1 teaspoon minced fresh ginger
½ cup white wine
pinch of fresh saffron
1 cup heavy cream

Sauté peppers, garlic, shallots, and ginger until tender. Add wine to deglaze pan. Reduce by half. Stir in saffron. Add cream and bring to a simmer. Do not boil. Continue cooking until sauce is reduced and thick enough to coat the back of a spoon. Yields 1 cup.

THE SCHOOLHOUSE RESTAURANT
Camp Dennison, Ohio

8031 GLENDALE-MILFORD ROAD
CAMP DENNISON, OH 45111
513-831-5753

How many children do you know who would voluntarily go to school on a Sunday evening? There were quite a few at Camp Dennison School the night we visited. In 1962, when Don and Phyllis Miller converted the school building into a family restaurant, Phyllis's vision was to provide an establishment where children were welcome. If our experience is any indication, she has certainly met her goal. Octogenarians dined with their children, grandchildren, and great-grandchildren at many of the round tables throughout the old classroom.

The cursive alphabet still runs atop the chalkboard, but instead of seeing lessons printed on the board, guests can find the menu for the evening. The entrées here include Schoolhouse Chicken (which Karen ordered), Country Fried Steak, Ham, Fried Shrimp, Baked Salmon, Prime Rib, Top Round Roast, Meat Loaf (which Debbie enjoyed), and Chicken Livers, among others. The side

dishes are served family-style atop lazy Susans in the center of the gingham-covered tables. Before our dinners arrived, we enjoyed Coleslaw, a salad tossed with delicious Sweet French House Dressing, and Corn Fritters, served piping hot. Bowls of Green Beans, Mashed Potatoes, and Stewed Tomatoes arrived along with our Schoolhouse Chicken and Meat Loaf. The Stewed Tomatoes, not typically a favorite of either of us, were so flavorful that we had a second helping. Sadly, neither of us had room to enjoy the homemade pies or cobblers for dessert.

The dining room is remarkably like the classrooms in which both of us were educated. Large windows softened by blue-and-white gingham curtains fill the exterior wall. Pictures of Abraham Lincoln, who once visited the school, abound, as do likenesses of George Washington and other presidential personages. A potbelly stove sits against the opposite wall. The high shelf that runs around the room holds tinware, cast-iron cooking utensils, and other paraphernalia.

The school was built in 1863 and is thought to have been the first two-story school in the Midwest. It was named for the Union camp nearby, which was used for the recruitment and training of more than thirty thousand Northern soldiers during the Civil War. It also served as a hospital for the wounded when needed. One of the few military actions—and the only known death—north of the Ohio River occurred in Camp Dennison. John Hunt Morgan and his Confederate raiders burned government wagons, resulting in the death of Daniel McCook, who was riding with Union troops as a volunteer.

An old picture of the building shows that the structure has changed very little. Guests can even sit at old desks while they wait for a table to become available, since reservations are not accepted. Many families choose to feed the goats and the geese housed at the back of the property. Still others while away the time gamboling around the school grounds, just as children more than 140 years ago must have done. Some things never change!

BAKED CRUMB COD

6 saltine crackers
3 tablespoons grated Parmesan cheese
4 6-ounce Icelandic cod fillets
2 tablespoons butter, melted

Preheat oven to 450 degrees. Place crackers into a sandwich bag and crush. Put cracker crumbs in a medium bowl. Add Parmesan and stir to blend. Place each fillet in a buttered individual serving dish. Sprinkle crumb mixture on top of fillets, then top with butter. Bake for 15 to 20 minutes until firm and flaky. Serves 4.

MEAT LOAF

6 slices bread, broken into 2-inch pieces
¼ cup milk
2 pounds lean ground beef
1 medium onion, chopped
1 medium green pepper, chopped
2 eggs
1 teaspoon salt
1 teaspoon pepper

Preheat oven to 350 degrees. Place bread in a medium bowl, pour milk over top, and set aside for bread to absorb all the liquid. Mix together remaining ingredients in a large bowl. Add softened bread and stir to combine. Place mixture in a large loaf pan and bake for 1½ hours. Serves 8.

GREEN BEANS

3 pounds canned green beans with liquid
1 medium onion, chopped
½ cup finely chopped ham

In a large saucepan, mix together all ingredients and bring to a boil. Reduce heat to low and simmer for 30 minutes. Serves 12 to 16.

SMEDLAP'S SMITHY RESTAURANT
Waterville, Ohio

205 FARNSWORTH ROAD
WATERVILLE, OH 43566
419-878-0261

The history of Smedlap's Smithy that is printed on the menu reads like a tale of Paul Bunyan or Pecos Bill. Smedlap Effingtass came to Ohio from Georgia in 1793, leaving the South to escape a lynch mob. Good old Smedlap set up a still, selling the output to the Indians. From that moonshine, he, according to the menu, made enough to build the Commercial Building in Maumee in 1836. (Isn't it actually Levi Beebe who is credited with that venture?) At some point, Smedlap stowed away on a canal barge headed for Waterville, where he met the daughter of the town blacksmith. As the story goes, he settled down, took over for his father-in-law, and became somewhat respectable.

What we actually do know of the structure is that it was built in 1840 and that, through the years, it served as a blacksmith shop, a livery stable, and a horse-drawn hearse business. A picture taken on August 13, 1841, shows the exterior of the building looking very much like it does today. Inside, what was the hayloft during the building's livery days is now a dining room with seating for about fifty. Guests can access this dining room using the stairs near the bar, but many choose to come down via the large playground slide that spirals from the loft to the main floor. The restaurant is full of tools and other items of the period. A yoke, a saw, an ice pick, old wagon wheels, and an anvil are among them. A collection of smoking pipes is displayed at the far end of the restaurant. A playful map is along the same wall. Drawn in the style of nineteenth-century maps, it combines local sites, period advertising, and modern-day features such as Interstate 75.

As I perused the menu, the Thai Cobb Salad caught my eye. It certainly sounded like a new twist on a perennial salad choice. The Warm Chicken Salad, served with mandarin oranges, cashews, and Honey-Ginger Sauce, also sounded appealing. The menu has a lengthy list of sandwiches, such as the Bistro Burger and the Steak Caesar Sandwich. There are pasta dishes, too, including Cajun Chicken Alfredo and Thai Chicken Pasta. The list of entrées boasts several cuts of Prime Rib, along with selections like Raspberry-Roasted Pork Loin, Fried Shrimp, and Barbecued Spareribs, which happened to be an all-you-can-eat special the night I visited. However tempting all these dishes were, I was told that Smedlap's is especially known for its plank cooking. So, of course, that's what I tried. My New York Strip Steak was cooked and served on a one-inch-thick, well-seasoned oak plank. Steamed Carrots, Green Beans, and Duchess Potatoes accompanied the steak. The meat was wonderfully tender and perfectly accented by Bourbon Whiskey Sauce. Other plank choices included Chicken, Orange Roughy, and Salmon. Since Karen couldn't accompany me that day, the chef generously gave me the recipe so she could "walk the plank" at home!

PLANK FISH

2 7-ounce pieces orange roughy
2 plank boards
2 tablespoons butter
salt and pepper to taste
4 Duchess Potatoes (see next column)
½ cup White Wine Mustard Sauce
   (see next column)
2 tablespoons shredded Parmesan cheese

Preheat oven to 350 degrees. Place orange roughy on planks. Rub each piece with 1 tablespoon butter and season with salt and pepper. Place Duchess Potatoes on boards on opposite sides of fish. Bake for approximately 15 minutes until fish is flaky. While fish is cooking, heat White Wine Mustard Sauce. When fish is done, pour sauce over fish and return to oven for 5 minutes. Sprinkle with Parmesan. Serves 2. Note: To cure planks, soak them in vegetable oil for 1 hour, season heavily with salt, and place in a 350-degree oven for 30 minutes. Oak, maple, or cherry wood may be used.

DUCHESS POTATOES

4 large potatoes
2 teaspoons minced garlic
½ stick butter
salt and pepper to taste
parsley for garnish
paprika for garnish

Peel and quarter potatoes and place in a medium saucepan filled with water. Cook approximately 12 minutes until tender. Drain. Place in a large mixing bowl and mash. Combine with garlic, butter, and salt and pepper. Spoon into a pastry bag with a star tip. Pipe out 2 mounds of potatoes for each serving. Garnish with parsley and paprika. Serves 2.

WHITE WINE MUSTARD SAUCE

1 small yellow onion, chopped
1½ teaspoons vegetable oil
¼ teaspoon minced garlic
3 cups white wine
1 cup heavy whipping cream
2 heaping tablespoons Dijon mustard
2 tablespoons fish stock
1 tablespoon cornstarch

In a large pan, sauté onions in oil until translucent. Add garlic. Add wine and cream. Continue cooking until reduced by half. Stir in Dijon. Make a slurry by whisking the fish stock and cornstarch together. Add to sauce to thicken. Yields approximately 2 cups.

GRANVILLE INN

"Great Taste In The Heart Of Granville"

314 EAST BROADWAY
GRANVILLE, OH 43023
WWW.GRANVILLEINN.COM
740-587-3333

The Granville Inn and its land have played a significant role since the town of Granville's 1805 inception. Timothy Spelman, a leader of the settlers who migrated here from Granville, Massachusetts, acquired the block on which the inn stands. An expert carpenter, he constructed possibly the first frame structure in town. The building and the land soon passed to Grove Case. He was a partner in Granville's first distillery, and, as such, he added a brick tavern. I've come across many historic buildings that served dual purposes, but this is the first I've found where a tavern doubled as a bank. I wondered whether Mr. Case or the bank got more of the customer's money!

Mr. Case sold the deep lot to the trustees of the Granville Academy, later called the Granville Female College. In 1838, the college erected a large four-story building that held both classrooms and living quarters for as many as one hundred students. Affiliated with the Congregational and Presbyterian religious philosophies, the Granville Female College was frequently referred to as the "Lower Sem." The "Upper Sem," located at the other end of Broadway, was the rival Young Ladies Institute, first sponsored by the Episcopalians and later by the Baptists. Both schools prospered, and in 1865, Granville Female College principal Dr. William Kerr added a two-story brick building at his own expense. After Kerr's death in 1882, support for the Granville Female College gradually waned. Just as "Upper Sem" became a coordinate part of Denison University in 1898, "Lower Sem" closed its doors. The four-story structure served as a Methodist home for the aged before finally being torn down in 1908.

The current history of the property began in 1924, when coal magnate John Sutphin Jones constructed the Granville Inn out of native sandstone quarried from his nearby estate. Designed on the model of an English country house, the inn was operated by Jones's daughter, Sallie Jones Sexton, until 1976.

My neighbor and I relaxed in the quiet warmth of the wood-paneled dining room. There was no need of a blaze in the large fireplace that anchors one end of the room. In fact, many guests were enjoying lunch on the adjacent patio. The Baby Bleu Salad with Salmon and the quiche de jour—created with spinach, mushrooms, and tomatoes—were duly ordered and quickly delivered. We oohed and aahed over our choices, both of which provided a delicious and quite satisfying midday meal. If I'd been here for dinner, I certainly would have begun with the Tenderloin Crostini—toasted sourdough topped with beef tenderloin, Brie, and leeks. Black Sesame–Crusted Tuna, Roasted Moroccan

Chicken, and Salmon Lyonnaise are but a few of the creative entrée offerings, from which I'd definitely have difficulty choosing.

The last time I was in Granville, Karen was along. During that visit, temperatures hovered around zero and we certainly weren't able to get out and appreciate the town's charm. On this visit, spring gardens were in full bloom, so my neighbor and I sauntered down the sidewalks, thoroughly enraptured by picturesque downtown Granville. It is a town I shall visit frequently, just for sheer want of a pleasant afternoon.

VEAL SCALOPPINE WITH TOMATOES

2½ tablespoons vegetable oil
3 cloves garlic, peeled
1 pound veal scaloppine, thinly sliced and pounded flat
¾ cup all-purpose flour
4 to 5 twists freshly ground pepper
⅓ cup white wine
3 teaspoons tomato paste
½ cup warm water
1 tablespoon butter
½ teaspoon oregano
2 tablespoons capers

In a heavy-bottomed skillet, heat oil over high heat. Sauté garlic until browned. Remove from skillet. Dip both sides of veal in flour, shaking off excess. Sauté very rapidly on both sides in hot oil. Do not overcook; a minute or less is sufficient to brown lightly. Transfer veal to a warm platter. Season with pepper. Tip skillet and draw off most of the fat with a spoon. Turn heat to medium-high, add wine, and scrape and loosen cooking residue from pan. Dilute tomato paste in water and add to pan. Stir. Add butter, stir, and continue cooking for a few minutes until liquids thicken into sauce. Stir oregano and capers into sauce. Cook for another minute, then add veal, turning quickly once or twice in the sauce. Plate, drizzle with sauce, and serve. Serves 4.

POACHED BEEF TENDERLOIN WITH GREEN PEPPERCORN SABAYON

3-pound beef tenderloin, trimmed and tied
salt and pepper to taste
3 quarts beef consommé
1 bouquet garni
3 egg yolks
¼ cup dry white wine
3 green peppercorns, crushed

Season tenderloin well with salt and pepper. Bring consommé to a simmer in a large stockpot. Add tenderloin and bouquet garni. Poach beef until it reaches an internal temperature of 125 to 130 degrees. Remove beef from consommé and keep warm. Combine ⅓ cup consommé with egg yolks in a small pot. Add wine. Cook yolks over medium-low heat, whipping constantly until thick and foamy. Add green peppercorns. Add salt, if desired. Slice tenderloin and serve with sauce. Serves 8 to 10.

BrYan Place

49 NORTH SIXTH STREET
ZANESVILLE, OH 43701
740-450-8008

The community of Zanesville came to be as a result of a business contract. The United States Congress negotiated with Colonel Ebenezer Zane to build a road from Wheeling, West Virginia, to Maysville, Kentucky. In return for his efforts, the road was named Zane Trace. Colonel Zane was also awarded three 640-acre tracts of land and permission to establish ferries where his trace crossed important waterways. The first settlers in the new community were ferrymen Henry Crooks and William McCulloch, who, using planks secured to canoes, began operating ferries across the Muskingum River in 1797.

The first bridge soon followed, its construction beginning in 1813. Built of wooden trestles, stone, logs, and planks, it was of an unusual Y shape, spanning from Main Street in Zanesville to an island at the mouth of Licking Creek, then split to go both north and south across the creek. On November 15, 1814, the *Muskingum Messenger* announced, "This grand and important work is now passable." Foot passengers were charged three cents; horses and mules older than one year were charged four cents; horses with riders

were twelve and a half cents; and coaches with four wheels and a driver drawn by four horses were a full seventy-five cents. Unfortunately, the bridge fell into the river in 1819, and another one had to be built. The bridge has been updated through the years as safety concerns and traffic needs have dictated. Today, the fifth Y bridge maintains Zanesville's claim to a unique architectural fame.

Another interesting structure in downtown Zanesville is its elegant YWCA. Built in 1926, it served in its original capacity until 1993. Across the globe, the YWCA has more than 25 million members and is the oldest and largest women's multicultural organization in the world. Approximately three hundred associations are in operation in the United States today. In the early years, many YWCA buildings also provided housing and shelter for women, including this Zanesville site. It's hard to know how many have danced in the ballroom or climbed the graceful staircase to the sleeping quarters above.

A women's social club was organized in Zanesville as early as 1903 and existed under a variety of names, including the Girl's Club, the Business Women's Club, and the Young Women's Club. A series of revival meetings held in 1917 by evangelist Bob Jones provided the impetus for the fund drive to build a YWCA. An estimated $165,000 was needed to build a new structure. When the cornerstone was finally laid on October 10, 1926, the construction cost of $128,500 came in well under the town's estimate.

Today, the stately building houses Bryan Place. The brick exterior, painted white at some time during its existence, is now returning to its original hue as the white gently fades away. The columned front porch is no doubt as popular a place to sit and enjoy a lovely day in the present time as it was in earlier days. Bryan Place is still a destination where community members gather—for wedding receptions, anniversary celebrations, literacy fundraisers, and myriad other local events. The restaurant is open for Sunday brunch, giving Zanesville residents yet another opportunity to visit. When they come, they can still walk the black and green mosaic tile floors, just as YWCA patrons did long ago.

SPINACH ARTICHOKE DIP

8-ounce package cream cheese, softened
2 cups finely chopped fresh spinach
1 cup shredded mozzarella cheese
½ cup shredded Parmesan cheese
1 cup mayonnaise
1 teaspoon chopped garlic
1 cup chopped artichoke hearts

Preheat oven to 325 degrees. In a large bowl, mix together all ingredients. Place in an ovenproof bowl. Bake approximately 15 minutes until bubbly and golden brown. Serve with tortilla chips or crostini. Serves 3 to 4 as an appetizer.

CAROL'S CHICKEN

4 3-ounce chicken breasts
salt and pepper to taste
½ cup flour
2 tablespoons olive oil
1 cup sliced fresh mushrooms
1 cup chicken stock
½ cup white wine
½ cup red seedless grapes
½ cup artichoke quarters

Pound chicken breasts thin. Add salt and pepper to flour. Dredge chicken in flour. Reserve flour for later use. Heat olive oil in a large sauté pan. Pan-fry coated chicken until lightly browned. Add mushrooms and sauté. Dust chicken and mushrooms with 1 tablespoon of the reserved flour. Combine additional flour with oil to form a roux. Add chicken stock and wine and bring to a boil to thicken. Reduce heat. Add grapes and artichokes and cook until heated through. Can be served alone or over rice or noodles. Serves 2.

AT ROOKWOOD POTTERY
1077 CELESTIAL STREET
CINCINNATI, OH 45202
513-721-5456

We'll have to admit, we were curious about the name when we came across this establishment. It seems the moniker is a tribute to Cincinnati history. In 1818, Elisha Mills opened the first slaughterhouse in Ohio and began packing pork in brine-filled barrels. Salt-cured pork quickly became a staple throughout the United States. Because of its proximity to the Erie Canal and centralized shipping, Buffalo, New York, had been the meat-packing mecca, but by 1829, Cincinnati became the hub, earning it the nickname "Porkopolis." The city continued to be a bustling center for pork production until Chicago and its superior railroad system took the helm during the Civil War. But Cincinnati kept the nickname.

The restaurant that bears this nickname is housed in what was once the Rookwood Pottery building. The world-famous pottery began in the 1870s thanks to Maria Longworth, a prominent Cincinnati socialite. She and other women of her class enjoyed the pastime of painting china. By 1879, Maria organized the first Women's Pottery Club, where women could meet and experiment in the making of pottery. Her father gave her an abandoned schoolhouse to convert for her purposes. Maria chose the name Rookwood because it sounded similar to Wedgwood and to honor her father's contribution, since his estate was named Rookwood after rooks, the crow-like birds that inhabited the grounds.

One of the first female business owners in the United States, Maria hired artist Henry Farny, well known for his American Indian subjects. She also hired top chemists to develop unusual glazes. Rookwood produced pottery according to shape. Each piece was numbered and then recorded in the "shape book." Shape #1, decorated by Maria, was sold to Tiffany in 1880. As accolades grew and international awards were bestowed, the company needed a new site. High atop Mount Adams, a larger factory was constructed next to the incline in 1892. A daily stream of visitors came to watch as Ohio River clay was converted into unique designs and coated in interesting glazes. The distinctive green and gold of the early pieces came naturally from the effect of the Ohio clay.

By the 1920s, Rookwood employed over 225 workers, 114 of them artists. The repertoire had grown to over 7,300 different shapes. Unfortunately, the Depression was a disaster for Rookwood. Pottery was a luxury item that the public could no longer afford. The company managed to eke out an existence until finally closing its doors in 1967.

Rookwood Pottery was reborn as a restaurant in the 1970s. Photos of potters and artisans at work line the walls, and a large display case holds a lovely assortment of the pieces that were once crafted here. Guests can even dine inside one of the authentic kilns. Although the wide variety of offerings on the menu includes sandwiches, salads, pasta dishes, comfort foods, and upscale entrées, pork (not surprisingly) is the main feature. Of course, you can get Ribs, but there are also pork chops served nine different ways. Spiced Apple Chops, Jack Daniels Chops, and Normandy Chops, served in Cream Sauce with walnuts, apples, and raisins, all have guests licking their chops!

BABY BACKS WITH SAUERKRAUT

2 racks baby back ribs
3 cups sauerkraut
2 slices cooked bacon, chopped
salt and pepper to taste

Pan-boil ribs for 4 hours over medium-low heat. In a medium saucepan, stir together sauerkraut, bacon, and salt and pepper. To serve, plate ribs and smother with sauerkraut. Serves 2.

WESTERN PORK CHOPS

4 center-cut boneless pork chops
salt and pepper to taste
1 green bell pepper
1 red bell pepper
1 yellow bell pepper
1 large yellow onion
2 tablespoons butter
2 jalapeño peppers, sliced and seeded

Season pork chops with salt and pepper. Grill 4 minutes on 1 side. Turn and continue cooking until done. Julienne peppers and onions. Melt butter in a medium sauté pan. Sauté peppers and onions until softened. Do not overcook. Plate pork chops. Top with peppers and onions. Garnish with jalapeños. Serves 2.

CHAPTER 6
We've Got the Goods

The Levee House Café

These restaurants certainly do! All were stores during some part of their existence. Today, however, instead of racks of clothing or cases of merchandise, they offer up a wide selection of menu items. Even though the penny candy and the pickle barrel are gone, we met a few people who'd worked in those old emporiums. And we even saw one or two checkerboards ready for a game.

OLD WAREHOUSE RESTAURANT AT

Historic Roscoe Village

400 NORTH WHITEWOMAN STREET
COSHOCTON, OH 43812
WWW.ROSCOEVILLAGE.COM
740-622-4001

In 1816, James Calder laid out a town named Caldersburgh. Fourteen years later, Leander Ransom and Noah Swayne petitioned the state legislature to rename the village Roscoe, in honor of William Roscoe, an English author and abolitionist of the period. The opening of the Ohio & Erie Canal had a strong impact on the community, transforming it from a humble settlement into one of the largest wheat-shipping ports along the 308-mile waterway. Canals continued to operate until the great flood of 1913. But the flood, along with the success of the railroads, marked the passing of the Ohio & Erie Canal's heyday.

The idea for a historical restoration in Roscoe Village was born at the dedication of a mural painted for Coshocton County's sesquicentennial celebration. The artist, Dean Cornwell, had chosen an 1850s canal scene as his subject. Seeing this rendition, local industrialist Edward Montgomery and his wife, Frances, were inspired to return the town to its proud past.

Today, State Route 16 runs where the canal once did. Alongside it is a four-story building that once housed grain, wool, hides, and produce on the lower floors and dry goods on the floors above. It is now an eatery known, appropriately, as the Old Warehouse Restaurant. Arnold Medbery purchased this property in 1838 from Ransom and Swayne and built an establishment he called The Mill Store alongside the canal. The lowest floor was open at the back, so barges could pull up and transfer their cargo easily.

We arrived not by canal barge but by car, driving through the village before parking in front of the restaurant. Just inside the front door is a charming waiting area, complete with a potbelly stove. Downstairs, the massive sandstone blocks of the original foundation are still in place. Antique implements hang on the walls. Many of them have to do with the making of apple butter, which is a big event in this area during the fall.

The main dining room is to the right of the entryway. Its plank flooring and roughhewn beams are original, as are some of the bills of sale and deeds that hang on the walls. You'll also see wagon wheels, feed sacks, and other items of the mid- to late 1800s. Debbie's meal choice, a delicious bowl of Ham and Bean Soup, was in keeping with the time period and the chilly weather outside. At the recommendation of our server, Bill, an Apple Dumpling soon followed, making Debbie feel as if the calendar might just have been turned back. Karen's lunch of Stuffed Pork Loin, served with Mashed Potatoes and Sautéed Vegetables, was every bit as good. We left completely sated, wishing we had more time to spend enveloped in the delightful past of Roscoe Village.

MARINATED SMOTHERED CHICKEN

1 cup olive oil
1 teaspoon minced fresh garlic
¼ teaspoon Italian seasoning
¼ teaspoon onion powder
salt and pepper to taste
4 chicken breasts, boned
1 large onion, chopped
1 large green pepper, chopped
4 ounces mushrooms, sliced
2 tablespoons butter
8 slices provolone cheese

In a large bowl, combine oil, garlic, Italian seasoning, onion powder, and salt and pepper. Marinate chicken in this mixture in refrigerator for at least 6 hours or overnight. Remove chicken and grill to 165 degrees. Discard marinade. Sauté onions, peppers, and mushrooms in butter for about 5 minutes. Top each chicken breast with sautéed vegetables and 2 slices of provolone. Place under broiler until cheese bubbles. Serves 4.

BREAD PUDDING

1 loaf white bread
½ cup raisins
6 eggs
3 cups milk
⅓ teaspoon cinnamon
pinch of ground cloves
½ cup sugar
¼ cup cinnamon sugar
vanilla ice cream

Tear bread into pieces. In a large, shallow bowl, whip together next 6 ingredients until thoroughly combined. Add bread and let sit for at least 2 hours. Preheat oven to 350 degrees. Grease a 16-by-9-by-2-inch baking dish and add mixture. Bake for 20 to 25 minutes. Sprinkle with cinnamon sugar and serve hot with vanilla ice cream. Serves 8 to 10.

THE LEVEE HOUSE CAFÉ

127 OHIO STREET
MARIETTA, OH 45750
740-374-2233

Marietta, established in 1788, was the location of the land-grant office for the Northwest Territory. Consequently, the town was a hub of activity as settlers passed through, full of hope and the promise of a better future, picking up their deeds at a wooden structure that still stands today.

During that time, the Ohio and Muskingum rivers were a major source of transportation and trade. The riverbanks were lined with shops, hotels, taverns, and restaurants. Today, the only original river-front structure that remains is the building that houses The Levee House Café. It was completed around 1826 for Dudley Woodbridge, the first merchant in the Northwest Territory, and was used originally as a dry-goods store. Because of the Flemish-bond brick pattern used in the construction, the building has been credited to Colonel Joseph Barker, whose most famous work is the Blennerhassett Mansion.

The oldest part of The Levee House Café contains the Woodridge Room, a cozy dining room with interesting seating made right in Marietta. The eye-catching black chairs are a special design once made for Chester A. Parsons' Virginia Street Tavern, a place notorious for its bar brawls. Mr. Parsons went through so many chairs that the manufacturer created this special design with no glued joints, so the parts of the chair could easily be put back together after a fight. Other décor in the room has a history as well. The ceiling came from an old clothing store and the light fixtures from a hardware establishment. The marble window sills once served as teller counters in a local bank.

We dined in the main dining room, a sunny addition from 1912 that houses an Underground Railroad display for about nine months of the year. Partner Harley Noland shared his impressive knowledge of local history as we perused the lunch menu. He chose his favorite, Pasta Verde, and offered us a sample before we dug into our individual meals. It was a delightful combination of spinach, chicken, ricotta cheese, and fettuccine. Pasta was the order of the day, as Debbie had the Barbecued Shrimp Pasta, sweet and tangy, while Karen enjoyed one of her favorite flavor combinations in the Chicken and Cucumber Pasta.

Faithful employee Margaret makes desserts on the premises. She'd been off for a couple of days when we visited, so Noland apologized for the selection—eight choices instead of the normal twenty! The kitchen sent out a sampler, and the three of us nibbled on Chocolate Pear Tart, Rum Coconut Custard Pie, Fresh Apple Cheesecake, Pumpkin Pie, Oreo Cheesecake, Chocolate Chip Walnut

Tart, Truffles, and Black Magic Cake, which has been declared "the Best in Ohio" by *Ohio Magazine*. With such dessert choices, entrées made to order, and a lovely river view, The Levee House Café is a treasure for today that allows guests to also treasure its yesterdays.

CHILLED CHERRY SOUP

½ cup raisins
6 thin slices orange
6 thin slices lemon
¼ cup lemon juice
1 stick cinnamon
2 cups water
2 cups sliced peaches
1½ cups sweet or sour cherries, pitted
½ cup sugar
dash of salt
1½ tablespoons cornstarch
whipped cream for garnish

Place raisins, oranges, lemons, lemon juice, cinnamon stick, and water in a large stockpot and bring to a boil. Turn down heat and allow to simmer for 20 minutes. Remove cinnamon stick. Add peaches, cherries, sugar, and salt and bring to a boil. Blend cornstarch with a little water and add it to the fruit. Cook for about 1 minute until clear. Adjust sweetening if necessary. Set aside to cool, then refrigerate. Garnish with whipped cream just before serving. Serves 6.

COCONUT MOUSSE

3 cups plus 6 tablespoons milk, divided
2 cups sugar
pinch of salt
6 egg yolks, beaten
2 tablespoons cornstarch
2½ tablespoons gelatin
1½ cups grated coconut
3 cups heavy cream, whipped
1 tablespoon vanilla
toasted coconut for garnish

Place 3 cups of the milk, sugar, and salt in a saucepan and bring to a boil. Reduce heat to simmer. In a small bowl, blend egg yolks, cornstarch, and 3 tablespoons of the milk. When blended, stream mixture slowly into simmering milk and stir continuously until thick. Remove from heat. Dissolve gelatin in remaining 3 tablespoons milk. Slowly add hot milk mixture and stir well. Place in refrigerator to set. When firm, beat with an electric mixer until smooth. Add coconut, whipped cream, and vanilla and blend well. Spoon into serving glasses and garnish with toasted coconut. Serves 8 to 10.

161 NORTH HIGH STREET
COLUMBUS, OH 43215
WWW.ELEVATORBREWING.COM
614-228-0500

The Elevator Brewery & Draught Haus is housed in the old Columbia Building, a structure built in 1895 for commercial purposes. The Bott Brothers Manufacturing Company moved into the space in 1905 after commissioning the architectural firm of Stribling and Lum to design and build the storefront. Stained-glass arches in the Tiffany style span the front windows, with leaded-glass bands that spell out the names Bott Brothers Billiards and Bott Brothers Cigars. The Bott brothers made and sold billiard tables, bar fixtures, refrigerators, and other equipment for cafés and billiard halls. By 1909, they were conducting the largest and most prosperous business in the city. Although the brothers outfitted many bars throughout Columbus, the only remaining examples of their work are in the Elevator Brewery.

From 1905 until Prohibition in 1919, what was considered one of the finest cafés in the United States operated on these premises. During Prohibition, the establishment served milk shakes, and patrons entertained themselves by playing chess or checkers. Af-

ter Prohibition's repeal, the café reopened as The Clock Restaurant, in honor of the large timepiece just outside the front door. Even today, many Columbus residents refer to the location by that name.

The Elevator Brewery & Draught Haus, owned by Richard Stevens and his son, Ryan, takes its name from their brewery business, which they began several years prior to delving into the restaurant world. At the far end of the restaurant are antique pool tables from the eatery's earlier days. Today, guests may enjoy a game of billiards or step up to the dartboards while waiting for their meal. Hanging on the wall nearby is a picture commissioned by Richard Stevens that depicts what the second story must have looked like in its heyday, when men fought over and bet on what happened at the forty billiard tables lining the room.

Rather than knock around the eight ball, we relaxed in our booth and enjoyed the collection of art on the walls. The senior Mr. Stevens, who has quite an eye, enjoys displaying his acquisitions for the clientele. He chatted with us until lunch was served, promising to return after we'd finished. We both thoroughly enjoyed the Potato and Bacon Soup and the Spinach, Pear, and Almond Salad. The Smoked Chicken Egg Roll, served with Apricot Dipping Sauce, was absolutely the most delicious of its kind that either of us had ever tasted. The eatery is known for its stone cooking, in which tenderloin fillets and Ahi tuna steaks are cooked on heated Finnish Tulikivi stones. The edible result is a unique gastronomic marvel. For those not quite that adventurous, the menu also includes Crab Cakes, Red-Meat Trout, and Blackberry BBQ Ribs.

On our way out, we looked at old photographs and marveled at how like the original the room still is. The ceiling is lovely in its opalescence. Behind the tiger cherry bar built by the Bott brothers, friendly bartenders still serve guests. Even the display cases still house wares. Since the Elevator Brewery's famous Chocolate Stout Cake wasn't available during our visit, we'll drive down High Street on another day and stop at the clock to give it a try.

CHOCOLATE STOUT CAKE

4 sticks unsalted butter
2 cups stout beer
1¼ cups cocoa powder
2 teaspoons salt
2 cups all-purpose flour
2 cups cake flour
4 cups sugar
2½ teaspoons baking soda, sifted
4 extra-large eggs
1 cup sour cream
Chocolate Stout Frosting (see next column)

Preheat oven to 350 degrees. Place butter, stout, and cocoa powder in a medium saucepan and heat until butter just melts. Set aside to cool. Sift together salt, flours, sugar, and baking soda in a large bowl. Set aside. When stout mixture is cool, place in a large mixer bowl. Mix on medium for 1 minute. Add dry ingredients all at once and mix carefully. Beat on high for 1 minute. Add eggs and sour cream, mix carefully, then beat on high for 2 minutes. Cut parchment or wax-paper circles for the bottom of four 8-inch or 9-inch round cake pans. Grease pans. Sift a small amount of additional cocoa powder and use it to coat sides of pans. Tap out excess cocoa. Place a paper circle in bottom of each pan. Divide batter evenly among pans. Bake for 20 to 35 minutes until a toothpick stuck into center of cake comes out clean. Cool cakes completely. Spread Chocolate Stout Frosting between layers and over top and sides to make a 4-layer cake. Serves 12 to 16.

CHOCOLATE STOUT FROSTING

1½ cups heavy cream
½ cup stout beer
6 cups powdered sugar
24 ounces semisweet chocolate
2 sticks unsalted butter
¼ cup Kahlua

In a medium saucepan, combine cream and stout. Stir in sugar and bring to a boil over medium heat, stirring occasionally. Chop chocolate in a food processor. Add butter and pulse to combine. With processor running slowly, add boiling stout mixture. Add Kahlua and process until smooth. Pour into a bowl and allow to cool, stirring occasionally. Whip for 1 to 2 minutes when cool. Yields enough frosting for one 4-layer Chocolate Stout Cake.

COLDWATER CAFE

35 EAST MAIN STREET
TIPP CITY, OH 45371
937-667-0007

The Coldwater Café was a treasure we discovered one day while browsing the picturesque shops along Main Street. The tiny, ten-table café is reminiscent of street-side cafés in Paris, with its French country *décor toile* tablecloths and matching wallpaper. Visitors will note the original plank floor and the exposed bricks. One of the bricks is missing. Proprietress Betty Peachy has replaced it with an egg snuggled in its own small nest. Black-and-white plaid draperies on café rods adorn the windows, and French photographs are hung here and there on the yellow plaster walls.

One of the first things that intrigues guests about the Coldwater Café is that the chairs don't match. Written on the menu is an explanation. It seems that when Betty Peachy opened the café, she invited close friends and family to the very first dinner. The price of admission to this gala event was . . . a chair. So each chair in the dining room has its own story to tell, as do many of the other items. It is interesting to note that the name of the café comes from Betty's late fa-

ther, Joe "Coldwater" Peachy. He grew up in the small mountain community of Belleville, Pennsylvania, where he built his house right next to Coldwater Creek.

The building looks much the same on the outside as it did back in the 1800s. It was erected in 1835 and became a general store under the management of Sidney Chaufee in 1840. By 1875, Albert M. Heckner took over the store. "Wholesale and Retail Dealer in Groceries and Provisions" was how he advertised himself, as was painted along the length of the building. Since those days, the structure has housed a bakery, a confectionary and ice-cream parlor, and a tailor shop. In the 1930s, the first restaurant opened here, operated by Charles Priller. It was followed by a succession of eateries until February 8, 1994, when the Coldwater Café began.

Seated at a round table in a sunny window, we prepared ourselves for a treat. A large selection of sandwiches is on the menu, all served on freshly baked breads. Or guests can choose a salad with a basket of homemade breads on the side. The Chicken Pecan Salad sounded tempting, as did the Black Bean and Rice Salad. We checked out the house specialties served in the evening. We liked the sound of the Lobster Crab Cakes with Remoulade Sauce and the Vegetable Lasagna Pinwheels, and Betty Peachy was kind enough to give us the recipes for them.

It was a difficult choice, but we eventually opted for a Chicken Pecan Salad Sandwich and a Vegetable Pita Sandwich. When they arrived, we promptly halved them so we could sample each. And we couldn't resist trying the Coldwater Café's signature dessert, the English Teacake with Warm Butter Sauce. It was fabulous. We're not going to describe it. You'll just have to visit and try it for yourself!

LOBSTER CRAB CAKES

½ pound jumbo lump crabmeat, picked and flaked
¾ pound lobster meat, cooked and chopped
¾ cup finely chopped red bell pepper
¾ cup finely chopped yellow bell pepper
¾ cup finely chopped green onions
1 cup finely chopped red onion
2¼ cups fresh breadcrumbs, divided
½ cup mayonnaise
9 tablespoons peanut oil, divided
3 cups remoulade sauce

In a medium bowl, stir together crabmeat, lobster, peppers, onions, 1½ cups of the breadcrumbs, and mayonnaise. Form into 18 cakes about 2½ inches in diameter and ½ inch thick. Place remaining breadcrumbs in a shallow bowl. Dredge 6 crab cakes 1 at a time in crumbs and transfer to a plate. In a 12-inch heavy skillet, heat 3 tablespoons of the oil over medium heat until hot but not smoking. Cook crab cakes about 6 minutes until golden brown on both sides and heated through. Clean skillet after each batch. Cook remaining cakes in batches of 6 in 3 tablespoons oil. Serve with remoulade sauce. Serves 9.

VEGETABLE LASAGNA PINWHEELS

12 ounces lasagna noodles
32-ounce can plum tomatoes
2 tablespoons olive oil
2 medium onions, chopped
3 cloves garlic, minced
1 cup chopped zucchini
1 cup chopped broccoli
1 teaspoon oregano
1 teaspoon basil
1 teaspoon garlic powder
1 teaspoon pepper
1 teaspoon dried red pepper, crushed
3 cups low-fat cottage cheese
4 cups marinara sauce
4 tablespoons shredded Parmesan cheese

Prepare lasagna noodles according to package directions, but do not add salt to water. Drain noodles and set aside. Drain and chop tomatoes, reserving liquid. Heat oil in a large skillet and sauté onions and garlic until golden brown. Add zucchini, broccoli, tomatoes, reserved liquid, and spices. Simmer covered for 10 minutes, stirring occasionally. Preheat oven to 350 degrees. Lay 3 noodles side by side, touching each other. Layer cottage cheese and vegetable sauce on top of noodles. Roll up each noodle separately and place in a casserole dish. Continue procedure until all noodles are used. Cover noodles with marinara and top with Parmesan. Bake for 25 minutes. Serve immediately. Serves 3 to 4.

GRAND FINALE

Still Making History!

3 EAST SHARON AVENUE
GLENDALE, OH 45246
WWW.GRANDFINALE.INFO
513-771-5925

When Larry Youse was working in business management and his wife, Cindy, was an advertising art director, friends urged them to open a restaurant. Finally, in the spring of 1975, the two were convinced and went out looking for a location. On their first outing, actually within the first hour of searching, they found the site that was to open on August 6, 1975, as the Grand Finale.

The building they've revitalized had been purchased around the turn of the twentieth century for $750 by J. J. Kelley. He established a saloon, which quickly became a popular stop along the main thoroughfare between Cincinnati and Dayton, now State Route 747. Photos show a horse-drawn Wiedemann beer wagon making deliveries in front of the tavern. Prohibition closed the bar, but Kelley's daughters remained in business by running a grocery store on this street corner in Glendale. Many residents remember stopping in for penny candy after school. Kelley's Corner Grocery remained until 1970.

When the Youses made their discovery in April 1975, canned goods still lined the shelves. Larry and Cindy chose to restore much of what remained, including the tin-tile ceiling. Victorian bric-a-brac, a bounty of fresh flowers, brass lanterns, and antique tables and chairs round out the décor of the main dining areas. Upstairs is a veritable treasure trove of antiques. This is the fun and funky bar area of the restaurant, no doubt called "the Attic" because it is full of an eclectic mix of memorabilia such as antique artwork, prams, skates, bowling pins, and much, much more.

We were seated in an enclosed back-porch area, where French doors and striped awnings give way to year-round patio dining. Hanging plants created a garden feel, and a collection of birdcages added a whimsical touch. Cindy's beautiful artwork is displayed throughout this dining area.

In the late 1970s, five ambitious young people joined the Youses' management team. Today, those same talented professionals are still running the Grand Finale. Virginia Chambers, Joe and Elise Mills, Victoria Raybuck, and Chuck Emmons now proudly share the ownership of this eatery.

When the restaurant first opened, crepes and desserts were the mainstays of the menu. Examples of the crepes include Shrimp Lawrence Crepes, consisting of shrimp and diced asparagus in a mild Paprika Sauce, and Crepes Coq au Vin, filled with chicken breast in White Wine Sauce with toasted almonds. The menu has expanded to include such dishes as Artichoke Fritters, Chicken Ginger, and Veal Morel. Other items that we found particularly tempting were the Herbed Filet

Mignon Brochette and the Shrimp Tango in Green Peppercorn Sauce.

The name Grand Finale was chosen for the restaurant to showcase Larry's luscious award-winning desserts. Chocolate Cordial Pie, Caramel Custard, Red Raspberry and White Chocolate Fudge Pie, and Coconut and Macadamia Nut Fudge Pie are all available for your sweet tooth. We opted for the Limelight Pie, a fresh lime pie in a Hazelnut Crust. What will your grand finale be?

GRAND TRIFLE

4 cups pound cake or yellow cake chunks
1 cup fresh or frozen strawberries in syrup, thawed
½ cup port wine
½ cup cream sherry
8 large scoops vanilla ice cream
1 cup sweetened raspberry purée
1½ to 2 cups heavy cream, whipped
¼ cup slivered almonds, toasted
8 maraschino or chocolate-covered cherries for garnish

In 8 large brandy snifters or a 2-quart clear-glass bowl, layer first 8 ingredients in the order given. Garnish with cherries. Chill at least 1 hour to blend flavors. Serves 8.

STEAK SALAD ANNIE

6-ounce filet mignon, trimmed
¾ cup vinaigrette dressing
3 cloves garlic, finely diced
3 shakes hot sauce
3 cups mixed salad greens
½ cup thinly sliced mushrooms
½ cup cubed Swiss cheese
12 medium Gulf shrimp, cooked and chilled
4 strips crisp bacon, crumbled
1 scallion, finely chopped
1½ teaspoons chopped parsley

Char-grill filet mignon medium-rare. Thinly slice into bite-sized pieces. Combine vinaigrette, garlic, and hot sauce. Marinate meat in this mixture for 30 minutes, stirring occasionally.

Arrange greens in a chilled serving bowl. Top with mushrooms and cheese. Arrange shrimp in a circle, then place filet mignon in center. Sprinkle with bacon, scallions, and parsley. Use reserved marinade to dress salad. Serves 2 as an entrée or 4 as a side salad.

Court GRILL

Circa 1930

112 COURT STREET
POMEROY, OH 45767
WWW.COURTSTREETGRILL.COM
740-992-6840

Former Jefferson Airplane band member Jorma Kaukonen occasionally stops by to play a riff. Other nationally known musicians such as Eddy "the Chief" Clearwater have also performed at the Court Street Grill. Artists on their way from a performance in Pittsburgh to their next show in Cincinnati or Indianapolis frequently play for an evening. The restaurant, in conjunction with the Pomeroy Blues & Jazz Society (known as "PB&J"), sponsors free summer concerts. Through the years, the influence of PB&J has spread, and it now promotes the Big Bend Blues Bash, a multi-day event that is one of the largest blues festivals in Ohio. *Ohio Magazine* has recognized the Pomeroy destination as "The Best Place to Catch the Blues!"

During our first visit to Court Street Grill, we dined with Karin Johnson of the Meigs County Tourism Board and thoroughly enjoyed chatting with her and owner Jackie Welker. Karen tried the soup of the day, Chicken Tortilla, topped with shredded cheddar cheese and a dollop of sour cream. It had just enough zing and was delicious. We sampled the Yamma Damma Doo's, french-fried sweet potatoes glazed with a brown-sugar mixture. Debbie may have finally found a way to get her family to eat sweet potatoes for Thanksgiving! We shared the Court Street Griller, a large grilled ham sandwich topped with melted Swiss, cheddar, and provolone cheeses. It was served with light, crunchy potato chips on the side and a large stack of napkins. The food here is meant to be enjoyed right down to the last drop on your chin. Save those napkins for dinner, too, as the Baby Back Ribs are quite tasty. Other entrées include seafood and steak selections.

After all that food, we certainly didn't have room to try the famous Bungtown Burger, a past winner at the Amsterdam Burger Festival. The name Bungtown comes from the community of Burlingham, just down the road from Pomeroy. According to one story, during Prohibition, many of Burlingham's influential women went around removing the bungs, or corks, from their husbands' stashes of liquor. Word spread, and from that day on, locals have called the area Bungtown. As we sat and enjoyed the casual atmosphere of the restaurant, Jackie said he didn't even know Bungtown wasn't the formal name until someone mentioned Burlingham to him when he was in high school. Another version about the origin of the name Bungtown relates to Burlingham being home to quite a few moonshiners and bootleggers. Local men knew if they wanted to imbibe, all they needed to do was head to Burlingham to get "bunged up." Both stories are just whimsical enough to put a smile on your face.

The restaurant was fashioned from a building constructed in 1864. The space once housed a pharmacy but has been a restaurant of some sort since 1935. Jackie says he and his regulars enjoy the distressed look of the original brick walls, the plank floor, and the once-painted tin ceiling. It's an unpretentious tavern with faithful customers greeted by first name as they walk in.

SUPER SECRET SLAW

½ head cabbage
4 red peppers
4 green peppers
½ pound carrots
½ bunch celery
3 medium onions
1½ cups coarse salt
6¼ cups sugar
1 cup white vinegar

Shred vegetables and mix thoroughly in a large bowl. Add salt and stir. Let stand for at least 4 hours. To strain out remaining salt, place vegetables in a colander and rinse; press and squeeze firmly to remove salt. Return vegetables to bowl. Add sugar and vinegar, mixing thoroughly. Serves 12 generously as a side dish.

YAMMA DAMMA DOO'S

vegetable oil
2 large sweet potatoes, peeled and julienned
2 tablespoons brown sugar
1 tablespoon butter, melted

Heat oil to approximately 350 degrees in a medium pot. Deep-fry sweet potatoes for 3 to 5 minutes. Remove from oil and drain. Sprinkle with brown sugar and drizzle with butter. Serves 2.

CHUM BUCKET

12 ounces beer
1 pound large shrimp, shells on
1 tablespoon pickling spice
1 to 2 teaspoons Cajun seasoning
1 lemon, quartered
¼ cup cocktail sauce
¼ cup drawn butter

In a medium saucepan, bring beer to a boil. Add shrimp and pickling spice. Boil for about 4 minutes; don't overcook shrimp! Drain shrimp, then toss in Cajun seasoning. Serve with lemon quarters, cocktail sauce, and drawn butter. Serves 2 as an entrée or 4 as an appetizer.

80 NORTH PAINT STREET
CHILLICOTHE, OH 45601
740-779-0440

This delightful coffee house is located in the Preservation District of downtown Chillicothe. Surrounded by other historic buildings and just a short walk from Yoctangee Park, it is ideally located for dropping in for a steaming cup of coffee on a sunny morning. Constructed in the 1860s, the building once housed The Dreamland, a silent-movie house that was very popular with local residents at the turn of the twentieth century. Unfortunately, once talkies were in vogue, The Dreamland closed and audiences moved to larger theaters to enjoy their favorite film stars. This space was then occupied by Schlegel's Jewelers. Visitors to the building today can still see the original name in stained glass over the front door. The jewelry store was successful, continuing in business until the early 1970s. The building then remained vacant for two decades.

In the mid-1990s, Bob Etling took over the building and began a complete restoration. The second and third floors have been turned into upscale apartments, while Schlegel's Coffee House is housed on the first floor. This three-story building is typical of stores of its era—long and thin. The first floor, painted in pale colors and complemented by a white tray ceiling, feels cool and spacious. Old-fashioned ice-cream-parlor seating adds charm, as do the many antiques and curios located around the room.

The current owner was careful to restore the ground floor with an eye to the past. Incorporated into the décor are the original Art Deco wall sconces and the old popcorn machine from Chillicothe's Royal Theater. An old theater seat and an automatic ticket taker also remind visitors of the building's illustrious past. Other interesting artifacts include an old coffee percolator, a coffee grinder located in the window display, and an old phone booth. A shiny copper espresso machine is located on a very attractive antique backbar restored to its original 1890s shine. Recovered from the old Miller's Café, located next to Poland Park in Chillicothe, it looks wonderful.

To the right of the backbar is a large pastry case. We stood and examined the goodies, trying to decide among Muffins, Biscotti, Cookies, and a variety of sumptuous Cakes and Tortes. Since Schlegel's advertises "the finest coffees and desserts that Chillicothe has to offer," we were looking forward to our selection. Debbie eventually chose a slice of Caramel Pecan Cheesecake, and Karen, who almost always opts for chocolate on such occasions, chose a slice of Chocolate Truffle Cheesecake. Both selections were yummy. There was a large selection of Coffees, Lattes,

Espressos, Cappuccinos, Teas, and Phosphates from which to choose. Karen picked a Mocha Latte, which was lovely. Debbie opted for the more adventurous Cherry Italian Cream Soda, which also got top marks. It is always a treat to find such a building so lovingly restored. Why don't you treat yourself to an experience you won't forget?

CAFE MOCHA

scant ¼ cup espresso
scant ¼ cup caramel syrup
1 cup chocolate milk
whipped cream as desired

Combine espresso, caramel syrup, and chocolate milk. Steam. Pour into a large mug and top with whipped cream. Serves 1.

PIÑA COLADA ITALIAN CREAM SODA

½ cup very small ice cubes
2 tablespoons coconut syrup
2 tablespoons pineapple syrup
scant ¼ cup half-and-half
1 cup sparkling water
whipped cream as desired

Put ice cubes into a 12-ounce glass. In a mixing cup, combine syrups and half-and-half and stir well. Mix with sparkling water. Pour over ice and top with whipped cream. Serves 1.

My mother and I arrived on a July morning, ready for a hearty breakfast. We shared a Farmer's Omelet, filled with ham, cheese, and potatoes, as well as a bowl of Biscuits and Gravy. We were both stuffed and still left a significant amount of food on our plates. For later in the day, there is a wide variety of sandwiches and burgers on the menu, almost thirty in all, including a Reuben, which would have been my choice. The dinner menu offers appetizers such as Chili Cheese Fries, Cheese-Filled Bread Stix, and Fried Pickle Spears, one of Karen's favorites. Entrée selections range from chicken and chops to steaks and seafood. Each is served with a potato, a choice of a side dish, and dinner rolls. If I lived in the area, I'd be a regular on Friday nights for the Walleye special.

Constructed in the late 1880s, the building that houses Kissner's was home to a dry-goods and grocery store for many years. In 1901, George Wilsnoff opened a tavern here. A few years later, the ornate mahogany-and-cherry backbar, built by the Brunswick-Balke-Collender company, took its place along one of the establishment's long walls. There it sits today, still as magnificent as it was more than

one hundred years ago. Around 1919, the Van Brackel family took over. With Prohibition in full force, they focused on the breakfast and lunch trade, building a thriving business. During the 1920s, the establishment passed into the hands of Bill Widmer, and then J. M. Kissner and Sons on October 30, 1928. They continued the Van Brackels' focus, the establishment becoming known as "the working man's place to eat."

Although Prohibition outlawed the serving of alcoholic beverages, certain customers of good standing were able to get real beer rather than the nonalcoholic variety known as "near beer." Bottles of unmarked home brew and labeled bottles of near beer were cooled in water. After a while, the labels fell off the near beer and floated to the top of the water. The detached labels were then adhered to previously unmarked bottles of home brew so that authorities would be none the wiser.

J. M. Kissner and Sons was hit hard by the Depression, just as other businesses were. It survived by continuing to cater to the working man, allowing anyone who was employed to run a tab, charging meals until payday rolled around each week. From the end of World War II into the early 1950s, the same service was available to migrant workers newly located in the area. Kissner's worked together with local clergy, who often sent folks in to get a hot meal and a little help in getting back on their feet.

Kissner's got a little help of its own from a local police officer back in the 1980s. He was making his rounds through town one evening after the restaurant had closed for the day. As he cruised past, he noticed a glow that wasn't quite right, got out of his car, and peered in the front window for closer inspection. The glare he'd seen happened to be flames reflected in the mirror of the backbar. Had he been just a few minutes later, smoke would have obliterated the glow, and that backbar and Kissner's could easily have been destroyed.

POTATOES MARGARET

5 or 6 medium potatoes
salt and pepper to taste
1 tablespoon dried onion
1 cup sour cream
1 cup milk
1 cup shredded cheese

Cook potatoes until firm but not mushy. Slice. Preheat oven to 350 degrees. Grease a 10-by-6-by-2-inch baking dish. Place half the potatoes in the baking dish and sprinkle with salt and pepper. In a medium bowl, mix together onions, sour cream, and milk. Spread half the mixture over potatoes. Sprinkle with half the shredded cheese. Repeat the layers. Place in oven and bake for 20 to 25 minutes. Serves 6.

CHICKEN AND NOODLES

3 or 4 chicken legs
3 tablespoons chicken base, divided
1½ teaspoons pepper
1 bay leaf
1 stalk celery
16 cups water
1 tablespoon salt
1 tablespoon parsley
2 carrots
1¼ pounds noodles

In a stockpot, combine chicken legs, 1 tablespoon chicken base, pepper, bay leaf, celery, water, salt, parsley, and carrots. Simmer for 2 hours. Strain broth and debone chicken. Return broth and chicken to stockpot. Add remaining chicken base and additional salt to taste. Bring to a boil. Add noodles and continue to boil gently until noodles are tender. Serves 4 to 6.

Mickey Finn's Pub

602 LAGRANGE AT HURON
TOLEDO, OH 43604
WWW.MICKEYFINSPUB.COM
419-246-3466

Mickey Finn's is a very friendly pub. Everyone in the place greeted us when we walked in, even though we had never been there before. We patted the dog and took our seats in one of the high-backed wooden booths. Marveling at the long, curvy bar that extends almost the full length of the pub, we eventually ordered a pint of Old Speckled for my husband, Gordon, and a pint of Blackthorn Cider for me. We both felt right at home immediately and started to relax after our hard day.

The menu here is short, but every item is delicious. A friend had highly recommended the Onion Rings, served with Marinara Sauce, and she was right—they were absolutely wonderful. Gordon really enjoyed his Fish and Chips, and I was equally delighted with my Mickey Finn Burger, served with Donegal Fries. There was only one dessert on the menu, and we just couldn't resist sharing a slice of Baileys Irish Cream Cheesecake. I was sorry that Debbie could not join us on

this occasion. I know she'd have loved it.

This interesting red brick building was constructed sometime in the early 1870s by Ignatius Wernet and John Streicher. We could not discover the purpose for which it was built, but records show that from 1879 to 1933, the ground floor was home to a grocery store, and the floors above housed several apartments. The grocery store was fairly successful. However, when the end of Prohibition came and the owners acquired one of the first liquor licenses in Toledo, everything changed. The grocery store began to sell alcoholic beverages, changed its name to Bouton's Café, and stayed in continuous operation for the next sixty-three years.

In 1996, Mickey Finn purchased the property, not knowing what surprises were in store for him during the massive renovation of the building. One of the first things to go was the old hung ceiling. As it was removed, the original tin ceiling was revealed. Three almost perfectly intact windows were discovered as the old siding was pulled off the outside of the building. Most interesting of all was the discovery—once all the inside paneling had been removed—of a wooden staircase and an unexpected archway leading to the building next door. Great care was taken to recondition the brick walls. Old photographs have been hung on the walls, and fans slowly whirl above. Even the neon Bouton's Café sign still hangs at one of the windows. The final result easily transports guests back to the 1870s.

Through the newly revealed archway is a large room just made for entertainment.

It has a raised stage in one corner, a billiards table in another, and plenty of small tables and chairs. Tricia and Mickey Finn are proud to offer the finest in local and international entertainment. There's something for everyone—from the well-stocked bar and the delicious pub grub to "Gorilla Poker" to Wolfstone, a Celtic rock band from Scotland. Everyone is sure to receive a warm welcome at Mickey Finn's Pub.

GALWAY TURKEY SANDWICH

1 kaiser roll
1 tablespoon mayonnaise
2 slices Swiss cheese
1 small tomato
1 large lettuce leaf
3 slices smoked turkey breast

Cut roll in two. Spread both cut sides with mayonnaise. Place cheese slices on bottom half of roll. Slice tomato and place on top of cheese. Tear lettuce into roll-sized pieces and place on top of tomato. Place turkey slices on top of lettuce. Place top half of roll onto turkey and serve. Serves 1.

SMASHLEY'S MARTINI

4 tablespoons Baileys Irish Cream
2 tablespoons Kahlua
2 tablespoons Frangelico
3 tablespoons vanilla Stolichnaya
splash of half-and-half
4 maraschino cherries

Place all ingredients except cherries into an ice-filled cocktail shaker and shake vigorously for 10 seconds. Place 2 cherries on a cocktail stick at the bottom of each of 2 chilled martini glasses. Pour martini mixture equally into glasses. Serves 2.

CHAPTER 7

It's Tea Time!

Twin Creek Tea Room

The ritual of tea is said to have been begun by Anne, seventh duchess of Bedford. According to legend, she grew tired of her afternoon malaise during the long stretch between meals. One afternoon, she asked for a tray with tea, bread, and butter. She quickly became fond of this repast, and the tradition was born. Author Henry James once said, "There are few hours in life more agreeable than the hour dedicated to the ceremony known as afternoon tea." As most serve tea during the noon meal, you need not wait until the middle of the afternoon to enjoy the establishments in this chapter.

76 SOUTH HIGH STREET
DUBLIN, OH 43017
WWW.BIDDIES.COM
614-764-9359

When Debbie's family lived in Dayton during the mid-1980s, her mother and friends used to make the ninety-minute trek to Biddie's Coach House for lunch once or twice a year. It seems that through the years, people have gone to considerable lengths to get to Biddie's, including the couple who came in a canoe. At the time, the nearby bridge was under construction, leaving historic downtown Dublin difficult to reach from the suburbs of Columbus. Rather than driving miles out of their way, the couple rented a canoe on the opposite bank of the Scioto River and paddled across.

The eatery is housed in what was once Sells Hotel, built in the 1830s as a private home. In the lobby of the restaurant, rough-hewn beams span the ceiling. These were uncovered after a workman's torch sparked some embers that ignited the front of the building and its second story. Fortunately, smoke was spotted by a neighboring business, and help quickly arrived, saving the historic building from catastrophic damage.

The largest dining room is located on the first floor, to the right of the front door. Most of the tables seat two or four, but one table for six occupies "Biddie's Corner," highlighted by a flowery mural. Louise, a friend of owner Mary Marsalka's, painted the ladder-back chairs, which adds to the uniqueness of the décor. Another example of Louise's expertise decorates the walls on the back porch—a mural depicting scenes and buildings from around Dublin. The riders in the picture's hay wagon are likenesses of all the employees at Biddie's when the mural was painted. The dining room to the left of the entry is painted a crisp white, and a variety of quilts cover the tables, giving the room a festive, yet homey, touch.

Sumptuous Victorian Teas are served two days a week or are available for groups with advance reservations. The regular menu boasts traditional favorites such as Ham Loaf, quiche of the season, and Mr. Biddie's—shredded beef served on a roll and accompanied by either soup or salad. With Karen's English background, we opted for tea, of course. Our two-tiered tray was laden with goodies. The savory items included Ham Salad and Egg Salad open-faced sandwiches, Pinwheels filled with Salmon-Dill Spread, and phyllo tart shells heaped with Chicken Salad. All were so delicious that it was difficult to choose. Everything at Biddie's Coach House is homemade, so the desserts were every bit as delectable as the sandwiches. Chocolate Petits Fours, two different types of Profiteroles, and Lemon Bread lightly laced with Cream Cheese were all quite a treat. The Lemon Bread was so good that we took two loaves with us to enjoy with our families.

Named after Mary's mother, who ran the cash register until she was ninety-two, Biddie's Coach House is a rare find. Through the years, many articles about the establishment have been written in area newspapers and magazines. Although the words have varied from writer to writer, the message is the same. Phrases like "down to earth" and "long on charm" echo the hospitality of Mary Marsalka, who treats guests as welcome neighbors and friends.

BIDDIE'S CHILLED STRAWBERRY SOUP

4 cups fresh strawberries, hulled and halved
16-ounce can pears in light syrup
2 tablespoons honey
3 teaspoons lemon juice
fresh mint leaves for garnish
strawberry slices for garnish

Combine strawberries, pears, pear syrup, honey, and lemon juice in a blender or food processor. Cover and blend until mixture is smooth. Transfer mixture to a large bowl. Cover and chill for 4 to 24 hours. Garnish with mint leaves and strawberry slices. Serves 8 to 10 as an appetizer or side dish.

CONFETTI CASSEROLE

2 pounds pork, cubed
1 pound pork sausage
16-ounce package angel hair, linguine, or other noodles
14¾-ounce can cream of chicken soup
1 green pepper, chopped
1 pimento, chopped
1 onion, chopped
16-ounce can whole-kernel corn
½ pound mild cheese, grated
14¾-ounce can sliced mushrooms
2 tablespoons butter, melted
1 cup cracker crumbs

Preheat oven to 350 degrees. Brown pork in a large skillet, simmering until tender. Remove from skillet. Fry sausage, drain, and crumble. Cook noodles according to package directions. Drain. Combine all remaining ingredients except butter and cracker crumbs in a large casserole dish. In a small bowl, combine butter and crumbs. Sprinkle buttered crumbs on top of dish and bake for 1 hour. Serves 8 to 10 generously.

71 NORTH MAIN STREET
WAYNESVILLE, OH 45068
WWW.ANGELOFTHEGARDEN.COM
513-897-7729

Visitors to this address in 1879 found the Wayne Novelty Works Company. At the time, cast-iron novelties were very popular, and none more that the company's dark green frog doorstop, which doubled as a garden ornament. Unfortunately, the popularity of such items was short-lived, and the company closed its doors in 1885. The buildings were taken over by the Reed Broom Factory. Stories still abound about Waynesville's "Great Fire," which started in the Reed stables, where some children reportedly were playing with matches. The fire spread so fast that all but two of the buildings on the west side of the street were completely leveled.

In 1900, Charles Cornell, a relative of Ezra Cornell, the founder of Cornell University, purchased the lot and cleared the site. By 1902, the present Victorian two-story brick house had been erected. After Charles Cornell's death in 1918, the house had two years under the ownership of Samuel Meredith. Mr. Meredith was a buyer for the Miami Val-

ley Leaf Tobacco Company, which was located in nearby Dayton. By 1920, Dr. D. John Witham was using the house as a home and office. The good doctor left a number of fairly grisly objects in the house, including a complete human skeleton found in the attic. The stately old home passed through the hands of many owners. John and Grace Gibson refinished much of the woodwork throughout the house. Today's owner, Pamela McNeily, bought the property with a view to returning it to its former Victorian splendor.

When we arrived for luncheon, our server, Tim, complete with cravat and white gloves, opened the front door. It quickly became obvious that we were in for an elegant treat. Tim seated us in the octagonal front room, which is papered in pink roses. The brass angel wall sconces and the delicate lace tablecloths further enhance the genteel atmosphere. We sipped deliciously refreshing cups of Hot Ginger Tea while admiring the elaborately carved scrollwork in the doorway and the large pocket doors.

Tim gently suggested that we allow Pamela to select which of the many delicious offerings we would try. All the menu items are made from scratch, and accordingly have that wonderful freshly baked taste. We started with the Irish Soda-Bread Scones, served with Lemon Curd. Karen particularly enjoyed the Tomato, Cheese, and Broccoli Quiche, while Debbie preferred the flavorful Potato and Cheese Soup. Though we both tasted a variety of sandwiches, we agreed that the highlight of our visit was the unbelievably good Chocolate Irish Cream Cake. There was a noticeable

Irish flavor to our meal, and we finally realized that it was the month of March, and that Saint Patrick was being honored.

ANGEL HUMMINGBIRD CAKE

3 cups all-purpose flour
2 cups sugar
1 teaspoon cinnamon
1 teaspoon baking soda
3 eggs, beaten
1 cup canola oil
1½ teaspoons vanilla
8-ounce can crushed pineapple with juice
2 cups chopped pecans, divided
2 ripe bananas, mashed
Cream Cheese Frosting (see below)

Preheat oven to 350 degrees. Grease and flour three 8-inch or two 9-inch cake pans. Mix together dry ingredients in a large bowl. Stir in eggs and oil until dry ingredients are moistened. Do not overmix. Add vanilla, pineapple, 1 cup of the pecans, and bananas. Stir well. Pour evenly into cake pans. Bake for 25 to 30 minutes. Cool and cover with Cream Cheese Frosting. Sprinkle remaining pecans on top of cake. Serves 16.

CREAM CHEESE FROSTING

8-ounce package cream cheese, softened
2 sticks butter, softened

3½ cups powdered sugar
2 teaspoons vanilla

Beat cream cheese and butter until smooth. Slowly add powdered sugar and vanilla. Yields approximately 3 cups.

AUTUMN SCONES

2 cups all-purpose flour
½ cup sugar
3 teaspoons baking powder
½ teaspoon baking soda
½ teaspoon salt
½ stick butter
½ cup buttermilk
1 teaspoon vanilla
1 medium apple, peeled, cored, and
   finely chopped
½ cup pecans, finely chopped
2 tablespoons milk
3 tablespoons superfine sugar
½ teaspoon cinnamon

Preheat oven to 425 degrees. In a medium bowl, mix together flour, sugar, baking powder, baking soda, and salt. Cut butter into dry ingredients until crumbly. Add buttermilk, vanilla, apples, and pecans. Mixture will be stiff. Stir together until dough is formed. Divide dough in half. Shape each half into 6 scones. Place scones on baking sheets. Brush tops with milk. Mix together sugar and cinnamon and sprinkle on top of scones. Bake for 15 to 20 minutes until golden brown. Serve warm with butter. Yields 12 scones.

Twin Creek Tea Room

19 EAST DAYTON STREET
WEST ALEXANDRIA, OH 45381
WWW.TWINCREEKTEAROOM.COM
937-839-5094

The lot on which the Twin Creek Tea Room sits was one of the original twenty plots laid out for West Alexandria on what is now the north side of US Route 35. When John M. Davis planned this house, he had to see to many details, including having the bricks made. He contracted with Edgar Derby for the beautiful butternut staircase and the woodwork throughout the house. The home was completed in 1875. John Halderman and J. R. McCleaf were subsequent owners. Benjamin Kennedy and Mr. and Mrs. John Davis bought the property in 1894. After the death of Mr. and Mrs. Davis, the home passed to their daughter, Pauline, a Broadway star who performed under the name Pauline Daigneau. She sold the house in 1936 to Russell and Bess Hall, who enlarged the kitchen in order to open an eatery. The Country Cousin Restaurant operated from the late 1930s until the early 1940s, when it was forced to close due to food shortages brought on by World War II rationing. After the war, Eugene Copp and his mother, Ruth, purchased the home. She lived there with her son and his wife, Verle, helping them raise their family.

Almost three decades later, John and Elfrieda Santo bought the residence, where they lived and operated an antique business called The Red Elephant.

In 1992, Dr. Mark and Carolyn Ulrich purchased the home and converted it to a tearoom and gift shop. Melodie Dill and Pam Morneault oversaw the food operations until 2000, when they retired. As we chatted with Carolyn during our visit, she explained that part of her vision for the venture was to provide her three daughters with summer jobs.

We certainly felt that this attractive home, painted in deep burgundy with accents of hunter and cream, would be a wonderful place to come and spend a few hours each day. Inside, the lovely butternut woodwork blended nicely with the airy rattan chairs in which luncheon guests were seated. The tables were covered in lace with an underlay of green, used during the fall, winter, and very early spring. The rest of the year, pink is used for an accent. Both coordinate beautifully with the hunter and rose floral wall coverings throughout. The ceiling is particularly remarkable, its original plasterwork looking every bit like a wedding cake.

Many delicious sandwiches filled with homemade ingredients are available for the choosing. We both selected the half-sandwich option so we'd have room to taste something else from the menu. Debbie opted for the traditional Chicken Salad and enjoyed the bowl of deliciously creamy Cheddar Chowder that came with it. Karen chose the Vegetable Sandwich and the Vegetable Soup, both of which she found delightful.

After lunch, we just had to poke around in the Ivy Parlor gift shop, housed upstairs. Guests should be sure to leave time to browse. Had we not had other appointments, we certainly could have whiled away the afternoon looking at all the pretty things.

CREAMY BROCCOLI SOUP

1 pound broccoli, broken into florets
2 sticks butter
1 cup flour
4 cups half-and-half
4 cups chicken broth
1 teaspoon salt
1 teaspoon white pepper
1 teaspoon tarragon

Steam broccoli in ½ cup water. Do not drain. Melt butter in a skillet and add flour. Simmer for 2 to 4 minutes. Add half-and-half and broth to skillet and whisk to combine. Raise temperature to almost boiling. Add thickened broth to broccoli. Add seasonings. Heat well but do not boil. Serves 8 to 12.

CHILLED ROYAL CARROT CAKE

2 cups sugar
1 cup oil
4 eggs
2 cups all-purpose flour
1 teaspoon baking soda
1 teaspoon salt
2 teaspoons cinnamon
3 cups grated carrots
½ cup chopped pecans
8-ounce can crushed pineapple, drained
8-ounce package cream cheese, softened
½ stick butter, softened
4 cups powdered sugar
vanilla to taste

Preheat oven to 350 degrees. Cream together sugar and oil. Add eggs and beat until creamy. Add flour, baking soda, salt, and cinnamon. Mix well. Add carrots, pecans, and pineapple. Mix well. Bake in 2 greased 9-inch round cake pans for about 50 minutes. Remove from oven and set aside to cool. In a medium bowl, mix cream cheese and butter thoroughly. Add powdered sugar a little at a time. Add vanilla and mix well. Spread between cooled cake layers and on top. Chill and serve cold. Yields 1 cake.

Olde World B & B and Tea Room

2982 STATE ROUTE 516 NW
DOVER, OH 44622
WWW.OLDEWORLDBB.COM
330-343-1333

The George Stauffer family owned a ninety-acre farm and sold eggs and fruit from its orchard to earn a living. By all appearances, the Stauffers must have been successful, because in 1881 they built a large home constructed of a sandstone foundation, hardwood beams, and sun-baked brick. Both Stauffer children worked on the farm but were college-educated. Gertrude Stauffer lived in her childhood home until her death in the 1960s. At that time, a local investor bought the property in its entirety. The farmland became a strip mine, and the house was rented to a tenant who treated it in such a way that it was condemned for sanitary reasons in the early 1970s.

The house sat empty until August 1992, when it was purchased by the Sigrist family. Growing up on a nearby dairy farm, Jonna Sigrist had dreamed of returning this home to its original grandeur. At the time she bought it, not one windowpane remained in the house. Many animals had taken refuge inside, and overgrowth encroached upon the brick walls. Community members, friends, and neighbors all stopped in to lend a helping hand. Jonna's mother helped with the decorating, as well as the purchasing and refinishing of some of the inn's antique pieces. Her father added the cabin, rebuilt using two mid-1800s buildings. Today, the themed bedrooms for overnight guests, the dining room, and the parlor areas used for serving tea all proclaim that Jonna's wish has been realized.

Upon arriving, we established ourselves at a table in a sunny bay window and spent our first moments gazing across the landscape. The pond and gardens are eye-catching but functional as well, containing herbs and edible flowers that Jonna uses for the kitchen creations. Trying to take it all in, we then turned our attention to the décor. The home still has its beautiful walnut staircase and rich pine four-panel doors, some of which are a full eight feet tall. Across the room from where we were seated was a fireplace surrounded by a lovely mirrored mantelpiece. Throughout the room were numerous Victorian accessories, including a floor lamp with a large, fringed shade.

Our table was beautifully set, and a pot of Earl Grey and a pot of Apricot Tea promptly arrived. To Karen's delight, we were there for the British Traditions Tea, which included Quiche Lorraine, Cucumber Sandwiches, Currant Scones with peaches and Devonshire Cream, the tearoom's Queen of Hearts cookies, Gingerbread, and fresh fruit. The tea ceremony is leisurely, so expect to spend a couple of hours or so treasuring it. Special-event teas are also scheduled with interesting and varied themes. The Little Girls' Fairyland Tea is popular enough to be scheduled once a month, while others, like the Erma Bombeck Tea, are part of a series of teas. With such a charming location, such creatively adorned guest rooms, and such delicious fare, is it any wonder that many of Jonna's guests come back time and again?

EGGS BENEDICT CASSEROLE

2½ cups chopped cooked ham
10 eggs, poached
¼ teaspoon pepper
Mornay Sauce (see below)
1 cup crushed cornflakes or fine
   breadcrumbs
½ stick margarine, melted

Preheat oven to 350 degrees. Put ham in a 9-by-13-inch pan. Place eggs on ham and sprinkle with pepper. Pour Mornay Sauce over eggs. Toss cornflakes and margarine. Sprinkle over sauce in a rectangle around each egg. May be refrigerated no longer than 24 hours before baking. Bake for 45 minutes. Serves 10.

MORNAY SAUCE

½ stick butter
¼ cup flour
½ teaspoon salt
⅛ teaspoon nutmeg
2½ cups milk
1½ cups shredded Gruyère or Swiss cheese
½ cup shredded Parmesan cheese

Heat butter in a saucepan over low heat until melted. Stir in flour, salt, and nutmeg. Cook until bubbly, stirring constantly. Remove from heat. Stir in milk and return to heat. Heat to boiling, stirring constantly. Boil for 1 minute. Add cheeses and stir until smooth. Yields 2 cups.

SPICED RHUBARB BREAD

1½ cups packed brown sugar
⅔ cup vegetable oil
1 egg
1 cup buttermilk
1 teaspoon vanilla extract
1 teaspoon baking soda
2½ cups all-purpose flour
1 teaspoon salt
2 teaspoons ground cinnamon, divided
1½ cups diced fresh or frozen rhubarb
½ cup chopped nuts
½ cup sugar
1 tablespoon butter or margarine, melted

Preheat oven to 350 degrees. In a mixing bowl, beat brown sugar, oil, and egg. Add buttermilk, vanilla, and baking soda and mix well. Mix together flour, salt, and 1 teaspoon of the cinnamon. Stir milk mixture into flour mixture. Fold in rhubarb and nuts. Pour into 2 greased loaf pans. Stir together remaining cinnamon, sugar, and butter to make topping. Sprinkle over loaves. Bake for 1 hour or until bread tests done. Freezes well. Each loaf serves 8 to 10.

Swan House

225 WEST SANDUSKY STREET
FINDLAY, OH 45840
WWW.SWANHOUSETEAROOM.COM
419-429-7926

I sat in the lovely dining room of Swan House and reveled in the beauty of the day, which was equaled by my surroundings. This Italianate home, known as the McConnell-Hosler House, was built in 1865. Its style was popular throughout the country during the Civil War and was the top preference among the nation's elite families. Architectural symmetry is evident on the outside of the structure in the placement of the cornice brackets and windows. Inside, the center halls, both upstairs and down, divide a floor plan identical on either side.

Peter Hosler, the Hancock County treasurer, took ownership of the home in 1880. He went on to found Farmer's National Bank, which evolved into The Ohio Bank and eventually became today's Sky Bank. A subsequent owner, Mrs. E. M. Foresman, established a tearoom in 1929, a precursor of good things to come. During the early 1930s, when the public schools were closed, Kay Potter held art classes here. For a time, the studio space was also used by students learning to tap-dance. The list of various functions for this lovely home expanded in 1933 when doctors E. E. Rakestraw and Hugh Marshall bought it for their medical offices.

By 1998, the structure had been turned into a beauty shop and seven apartments. It was purchased by three enterprising women who intended to restore its original elegance and use it as a gift shop and tearoom. Over the six months of the restoration, many amazing discoveries were made. The tops of the tall, curved windows were found. The ceiling had been lowered twice, obscuring the windows' elegant arches. The front entrance was also returned to its original splendor, as the barrel-vaulted porch and glass fan windows were uncovered. The attic housed yet another treasure. The original louvered shutters were stored there. Upon discovery, they were hand-refinished by one of the owners and her husband.

Karen was unable to travel with me that day. I was fortunate to be seated at a small, round table beside the front windows, where I had ample opportunity to take in the details. Lovely crystal chandeliers shone overhead, and beautiful sideboard pieces were placed throughout the room. Tea started with a warm Blueberry Scone tucked in a linen napkin and served on a silver platter. Everything is made on the premises. The Strawberry Jam, Lemon Curd, and Devonshire Cream that I found in the silver condiment server were all delicious accompaniments. The three-tiered tray that followed was laden with goodies. The French Breakfast Puff, the Spinach

Cheese Bread, and the Raspberry Cake Roll were my personal favorites, although all ten of the items served were luscious. The Cream Puff was particularly unique, fashioned into the shape of a swan.

After dining, I browsed the rooms of lovely gift items. I certainly agree with the ladies of Swan House. Through their labor of love, this is an ugly duckling returned to its rightful place as a lovely swan.

MEDITERRANEAN TURKEY WRAPS

¼ cup mayonnaise
4 large tortilla shells
2 cups shredded romaine lettuce
8 thin slices turkey
½ cup black olives, chopped
½ cup finely chopped roasted red peppers
16 to 20 pepperoni slices
¼ cup crumbled feta cheese

Spread 1 tablespoon mayonnaise over half of a tortilla shell. Place ½ cup lettuce on top of mayonnaise. Add 2 slices turkey. In a small bowl, mix together olives and peppers until evenly combined. Spread 4 tablespoons of olive-pepper mixture over turkey. Layer 4 or 5 pepperoni slices over olive-pepper mixture and top with 1 tablespoon feta. Roll up tightly. Prepare remaining 3 tortillas. Cut on a diagonal before serving. Serves 4.

PARMESAN HERB KNOTS

½ cup vegetable oil
¼ cup grated Parmesan cheese
1½ teaspoons parsley flakes
1½ teaspoons chopped dill
1 tablespoon garlic powder
dash of pepper
1 can refrigerated buttermilk biscuits

Preheat oven to 400 degrees. In a small bowl, mix together oil, Parmesan, parsley, dill, garlic powder, and pepper. Set aside. Cut each biscuit into fourths. Roll each portion into a rope and tie into a loose knot. Place on a greased baking sheet and bake for 5 to 7 minutes until golden brown. Remove from oven and immediately brush generously with oil mixture. Serve warm. Yields 32 knots.

63 WEST MAIN STREET
MADISON, OH 44057
WWW.HISMAJESTYSTEAROOM.COM
440-417-0220

We received a postcard from a friend, and on the back it stated, "His Majesty's Tea Room is a place to be pampered." How right the card was. The owner of this delightful place enthusiastically greeted us. We sat in the dining room to chat. This elegant room simply exudes Victorian charm. The tables are dressed in lace and royal blue tablecloths. The high wooden paneling and the tall sash windows give a light, spacious feel to the room. All around are fine-china knickknacks and gift items, creating an aura of elegance and old-fashioned service.

Originally the Madison Exchange Bank, the structure was completed in 1875 for a total cost of $4,350, including the lot, building, furnishings, and vault. A handsome one-story brick bank with an unusual rounded corner at the main entrance, it would stay in business for the next ninety-four years. The townsfolk have plenty of stories to tell about the bank, the most popular of which concerns an incident that took place on the evening of November 27, 1900, when five bank robbers

broke in. Four of them kept watch while one drilled into the main safe in an attempt to get it open. A local citizen came upon the scene and was captured and locked into the coal shed behind the bank. The Methodist preacher was shot at but escaped to raise the alarm. The robbers eventually got the safe open, only to find it empty. Irate citizens forced the gang to flee into the night empty-handed. Luckily, all the money had been placed in a smaller safe that the would-be robbers totally ignored.

When the bank closed its doors for the last time, the building continued in service as an antique store and then as a clothing consignment shop before it was used as the main office for Redlin Realty. Having reached the age of one hundred, it was nominated for inclusion on the National Register of Historic Places. It has been the site of His Majesty's Tea Room since 1994, and is now under the ownership of Michol Dowling. Locals and visitors alike can enjoy the Old World ambiance inside the building and the refreshing summer breezes on the patio overlooking the town square.

A variety of delicious treats are served here. "Proper Afternoon Tea" consists of a special presentation of sweets and savories on a three-tiered silver server that includes homemade Scones with Lemon Curd and Devon Cream. Instead of full tea, guests may order their favorite items from the menu. There are many interesting sandwiches to choose from, as well as homemade soups, quiches, salads, and baked goodies. Although Karen loves full Afternoon Tea, her favorite menu choice was the Princess Victoria Sandwich, a fresh toma-to-basil-mozzarella panini. Debbie was very taken with the Royal Blue Salad, topped with blue cheese and roasted nuts. But whatever you sample, be sure to try one of the large variety of special teas and chocolates, many of which are flavored with dried fruits, nuts, spices, or even dried flowers!

CLASSIC SHORTBREAD

1 stick butter, softened
⅓ cup powdered sugar
¼ teaspoon vanilla
1 cup flour
vegetable oil spray

Preheat oven to 325 degrees. Using the back of a large spoon, cream butter until it is light. Mix in powdered sugar, then vanilla. Work in flour. Knead dough on an unfloured surface until smooth. Lightly spray a 9-inch round baking pan with vegetable oil. Place ball of dough in center of pan. Working from the center, press dough into pan evenly. Prick dough with a fork and bake for 30 to 35 minutes until lightly browned. Be sure middle is thoroughly cooked. Let shortbread cool in pan for 10 minutes before loosening edges with a knife. Flip pan over onto a cutting board. It may be necessary to tap pan hard against cutting board to extract shortbread. Cut into eighths while still warm. Serves 8.

DEVON CREAM

1 cup heavy whipping cream
½ cup sugar
2 teaspoons vanilla
1¼ cups sour cream

Place first 3 ingredients in a medium bowl and whip until stiff. Fold in sour cream. Refrigerate until ready to use. Yields 2 to 3 cups.

The Sanctuary Tea Room

4086 BROADWAY
GROVE CITY, OH 43123
614-871-8327

Now that I reside in Columbus, Ohio, it is more difficult for Karen and me to travel together. On a rainy spring afternoon, I invited another new Columbus resident, Mona Marple, to accompany me. She proved to be a terrific research companion, asking about old photos hanging in the gift shop. It so happens they're photos of proprietors Debbie Withrow and Marsha Heim in the midst of childhood tea parties. A little foreshadowing, perhaps?

The road from those long-ago tea parties to today's welcoming tearoom was not a smooth one, though. In fact, Debbie went "kicking and screaming" to her first grown-up tea party with some church friends in 2004, and was pleasantly surprised at the end of the experience to have had a good time. A year or so later while vacationing, she and Marsha visited a tearoom that they describe as "spectacular." Inspired, they began to discuss the possibility of creating a similar venture in central Ohio—not immediately, but several years hence, once Marsha retired.

Fate intervened, however, and both Debbie and Marsha lost their jobs within a few weeks of returning from Cape Cod. After the initial shock wore off, the two again tossed around the idea of a tearoom. Still unsure of what their direction should be, they prayed for a sign to enlighten them. That very day, Marsha's niece (and one of Debbie's best friends) told them about a great building for sale. Several days later, a story featured on the Food Network further inspired them. And then, about a week after that, an encounter with a woman whose mother collected teapots—hundreds of them—seemed to reinforce that the tearoom *was* their future.

The Sanctuary Tea Room is situated on land that was once part of the Virginia Military District, set aside by Congress to reward Virginia's Revolutionary War veterans for their service. Hugh Grant, Sr., laid claim to a 405-acre section of the military district. His grandson, Adam, was instrumental in the development of Grove City, including the Beulah Park racetrack (named for his daughter) and this home at 4086 Broadway.

We were seated in the front room, known as the Victorian Room. The terra-cotta walls with crisp white trim create a serene environment. Damask cloths in a variety of warm tones adorn the tables and add richness to the room. Two additional dining rooms sit to the right of the entrance. The first is the Colonial Room, painted a subdued taupe. Here, floral cloths enhance the ambiance. Just beyond is the Fifties Dining Room, an unexpected surprise chock-full of memorabilia and knickknacks!

The appealing menu offers two different Victorian Tea selections that include four tea sandwiches, soup, fruit, scones, and sweets.

Sandwiches, salads, and quiche are also available. Mona opted for the Tuna Salad, served on a croissant. The mixture, full of nutty bits, was uniquely appealing. I chose the Mixed Green Salad, topped with pears, cranberries, walnuts, and feta cheese. Tossed in Blackberry Vinaigrette, it was as tasty as it was attractive. We couldn't visit the tearoom without sampling the scones. We chose the Apple Cinnamon variety, although Blueberry Scones were also available on that occasion. Served with Jam, Lemon Curd, Devonshire Cream, and Lavender Jelly, they were light and delicious. The tearoom's mantra is "Soothe the Soul and Satisfy the Appetite." We certainly did just that.

PATTI'S EGG SALAD

12 hard-boiled eggs
1 cup green olives
1 cup mayonnaise
4 croissants

Chop eggs and olives. Mix with mayonnaise. Chill. Split croissants in half horizontally. Spoon ½ to ¾ cup egg salad onto bottom half of each croissant. Top with remaining halves and serve. Yields 4 sandwiches.

MAMA GRACIE'S BANANA PUDDING

2½ cups milk
5¼-ounce box vanilla pudding
½ cup sour cream
8-ounce container Cool Whip, divided
3 bananas, sliced
1 box vanilla wafers

With a hand-mixer, blend milk and pudding in a medium bowl until thick. Fold in sour cream, ¾ of the Cool Whip, and bananas. Line the bottom of an 8-by-8-inch serving dish with ¼ of the vanilla wafers. Spoon ⅓ of pudding mixture over top. Place a layer of vanilla wafers over pudding layer. Alternate another layer of pudding mixture, another layer of vanilla wafers, and a final layer of pudding mixture. Crush remaining vanilla wafers and sprinkle over top. Chill. Garnish with remaining Cool Whip before serving, if desired. Serves 6 to 8.

ROSEPOINTE COTTAGE

107 CENTER STREET
CHARDON, OH 44024
440-285-8686

As I glanced down the first page of the menu, I decided that I'd have to dine at Rosepointe Cottage on multiple occasions before I would have tried everything that appealed to my palate. The Romaine Mandarin Orange Salad sounded quite refreshing, as did the Spinach and Strawberry Salad. I wavered between the Lobster Citrus Salad and the Cranberry Chicken Salad, served in a puff-pastry shell. There are also traditional tea sandwiches, a Grilled Panini, a Lobster Roll, and an interesting Chicken Caesar Salad Sandwich, as well as a variety of quiches, Welsh Rarebit, Cottage Beef Stew, and a Tuna Melt, for those who want something a tad more substantial. Of course, the sweets and savories of Afternoon Tea, available anytime throughout the day, are always a very popular choice. Guests won't want to miss the Hummingbird Cake. That confection, with its rich Cream Cheese Icing, once won a ribbon at the Geauga County Fair for Rosepointe's owner, Mariann Goodwin.

Special events are scheduled throughout the year, giving guests additional opportunities to enjoy themselves here. Quite well liked are the Holiday Evening High Tea, held in November, and a similar event held in February to celebrate Valentine's Day.

The tearoom is housed in a quaint home painted a cheery blue and trimmed in crisp white. Built in 1839 in the Greek Revival style, it is listed on the National Register of Historic Places and is one of the oldest homes in Chardon. According to the Ohio Historic Inventory, the house was originally the residence of Judge David Aiken. In the years between 1866 and 1901, it served as the parsonage of the Methodist church, the first church in Chardon. It was originally located on the town square but was moved around the corner in 1882 at the time a new church was built at the corner of Main and Center streets.

The original woodwork and the Victorian décor make it just as charming on the inside as it is on the outside. I was seated at a comfortable table bedecked in pink. The rose-colored tablecloth was augmented by a lace overlay, while matching rose napkins and white table service added to the ambiance. Pink floral arrangements, muted Victorian lighting, and lace window treatments finished the look, creating a charming and peaceful setting for tea.

After I visited with Mariann Goodwin, Debbie joined me, and we strolled the streets of this charming community, located not too far east of Cleveland. The town square is a picturesque example of New England–style town planning, with its quintessential central green space surrounded by important community buildings such as the town hall, schools, and churches. The town had its beginnings in 1808, when representatives from the Ohio General Assembly designated an unpopulated wilderness atop a hill as the county seat, surprising the existing residents of other burgeoning communities throughout Geauga County. By 1810, town names were being discussed. Brookfield, Brookville, Marshall, and Chardonia were all discarded before the powers that be settled on Chardon, in honor of the area's previous landholder, Peter Chardon Brooks. The word *chardon* is French for thistle. And the town of that name is a more-than-fitting location for the pleasantries provided at Rosepointe Cottage Tea Room.

AMBROSIA

2 cups drained pineapple chunks, juice
   reserved
11-ounce can Royal Anne cherries, drained
11-ounce can mandarin oranges, drained
2 cups miniature marshmallows
3 egg yolks, beaten
2 tablespoons sugar
2 tablespoons vinegar
1 tablespoon butter
1 cup heavy whipping cream

In a large bowl, mix together fruits and marshmallows. Set aside. In the top of a double boiler, combine egg yolks, sugar, 3 tablespoons of the reserved pineapple juice, vinegar, and butter. Cook over medium-low heat, stirring constantly until mixture thickens slightly. Allow to cool. Pour custard over fruit and mix gently. Whip cream in a chilled stainless-steel bowl. Gently fold whipped cream into fruit mixture. Chill for 24 hours. Serves 6. Note: Rosepointe Cottage Tea Room sometimes substitutes sliced grapes for Royal Anne cherries.

PECAN PIE BARS

2 cups flour
½ cup confectioners' sugar
2 sticks butter
14-ounce can sweetened condensed milk
1 egg
1 teaspoon vanilla
6-ounce package brickle chips (toffee pieces)
1 cup chopped pecans

Preheat oven to 350 degrees. In a medium bowl, combine flour and sugar. Cut in butter until mixture resembles coarse cornmeal. Press mixture firmly on the bottom of a 9-by-13-inch pan. Bake for 15 minutes. Meanwhile, in a medium mixing bowl, beat sweetened condensed milk, egg, and vanilla. Stir in brickle chips and pecans. Spread evenly over prepared crust. Bake for 25 minutes. Allow to cool, then chill thoroughly. Cut into bars. Store in refrigerator or freeze until ready for use. Yields 16 to 24 bars.

AUNT IVY'S TEAHOUSE
62 EAST CHERRY STREET
SUNBURY, OH 43074
740-965-8700

The tan weatherboard cottage that contains Aunt Ivy's Teahouse was built by a Mr. Truman Thomas during the 1840s. Other owners have included the Perfect family, the Landon family, and the Skeels family. John P. Skeels was well known around town, operating a grocery store just east of his house for many years and making deliveries to folks outside of town by horse and buggy. John's great-grandfather Dr. David Skeels came from Connecticut as the first Baptist minister in the area, settling in 1814. John's grandfather laid out the town of Centerville and helped lay out the town of Savanna, just north of Sunbury.

Antique stores abound in this little town, and it's possible that treasure hunters might just find something that belonged to one of the early families. These local shops were the source of some of Aunt Ivy's eclectic mixture of chairs and teacups, which work together to add charm to the décor. Each of the teacups is unique, but Angee Roth can tell the story behind every one. I spotted one that matched the dogwood-patterned dishes that my paternal grandmother used. If she'd been along, Karen just might have spotted a cup and saucer that produced fond memories for her as well.

The featured soup on the day of my visit was a chilled strawberry concoction perfectly suited to the hot summer day. The Chicken Salad was popular amongst the guests. Some chose it served atop a bed of lettuce, surrounded by fresh fruit and melon, and accompanied by a slice of Tea Bread (zucchini on that particular occasion). Others opted for the Chicken Salad Puff, in which the Chicken Salad is presented in a flaky puff pastry. Others were partial to the hot Ham and Cheddar Cheese Croissant. In addition to the à la carte menu items, Afternoon Tea—featuring Mini-Quiches, Scones, filled Croissants, and Tea Bread—is available with advance notice.

The décor, every bit as enjoyable as the food, is in keeping with the history of the home. Both of the front dining rooms have plaster walls painted a rich taupe adorned with intricate stenciling. As an art form, stenciling began its popularity in New England as a method for the less affluent to mimic the rich wallpaper patterns of the day. Moses Eaton and his son, Moses Eaton, Jr., have been credited with many of the most popular stenciling patterns used from the late 1700s to the mid-1800s. Angee and her son, Aaron, used patterns attributed to those artisans.

I just had to ask about the name of the teahouse. In Angee's family, there really was an Aunt Ivy. As a matter of fact, she was Angee's great-great-aunt. Ivy wanted children but had none of her own, so she doted on her first niece, who happened to be Angee's grandmother. When that special niece had her first daughter, she wanted to name her Ivy in honor of her favorite aunt. However, familial pressure being what it is sometimes, Angee's mother was named Margie instead. Through the years, Ivy's life and story have touched Angee, and so she chose to name her teahouse in Aunt Ivy's honor. The teahouse is a family affair in many other ways as well. Angee operates the establishment with Aaron, and I enjoyed chatting with them about their lives and this venture they so obviously love.

CHOCOLATE CHERRY BLISS

16-ounce package brownie mix
1 cup finely chopped almonds
1 stick butter, melted
1½ teaspoons almond extract, divided
4 8-ounce packages cream cheese
16-ounce can chocolate fudge frosting
2 eggs
2 tablespoons flour
1 cup drained maraschino cherries or
    ¾ can cherry pie filling
fudge sauce, if desired

Preheat oven to 350 degrees. Line a springform pan with aluminum foil. In a large bowl, mix together brownie mix, almonds, butter, and ½ teaspoon almond extract. Press into springform pan and set aside. In a food processor, mix cream cheese, frosting, eggs, flour, and remaining 1 teaspoon almond extract. Fold in cherries. Pour into crust. Bake for approximately 50 minutes until firm. Remove from oven. Let stand for at least 30 minutes before removing from pan. Continue to cool. To serve, cut into wedges and spoon fudge sauce over top. Serves 12 to 16.

GINGERBREAD

5 cups flour
2 teaspoons cinnamon
4 teaspoons ground ginger
2 teaspoons ground cloves
1 cup applesauce
1 cup olive oil
1 cup sugar
2 cups molasses
4 eggs
4 teaspoons baking soda
2 cups boiling water

Preheat oven to 350 degrees. In a large bowl, mix together flour, cinnamon, ginger, and cloves. In a separate bowl, combine applesauce, olive oil, sugar, and molasses. Add eggs 1 at a time, stirring after each addition. Gradually add dry ingredients to applesauce mixture. Dissolve baking soda in boiling water. Add to rest of ingredients, mixing well. Pour into a 9-by-13-inch baking pan or 2 loaf pans. Bake for approximately 35 minutes until a toothpick inserted in center comes out clean. Serves 12 to 16.

235 EAST SECOND STREET
XENIA, OH 45385
WWW.EDENHALLMANSIONBED
ANDBREAKFAST.COM
937-376-8000

When I went for tea at Edith Mae's, I took my daughter, Dori, along for an end-of-the-summer treat. We arrived a little early to speak with Tracy Gerhardt, who purchased the home in 2003 along with her husband, Rick, and Sharon Lintz, who operates Edith Mae's. Tracy has her photography business here, using the third-floor space that once housed a ballroom as her studio. On the second floor are three lovely suites available to overnight guests as Eden Hall Bed and Breakfast. There is so much to see—from antique furnishings to original flooring to intricate ceiling medallions—that it's impossible to take it all in on one visit.

The sumptuousness of the items served for tea is a reflection of the opulence of the surroundings in which they're served. Service is relaxing and leisurely here, giving guests time to savor the food while enjoying each other's company. We began with a basket of breads. Our trio included moist Pumpkin

Bread, tasty Raspberry Tarts, and the most luscious miniature Cinnamon Rolls either of us had ever tasted. They truly melted in the mouth. We were still sighing with contentment when our three-tiered tray arrived laden with goodies. Savories included Chicken Salad served on croissants, Egg Salad Triangles, and open-faced Cucumber Sandwiches. Fresh fruit of the season was accompanied by Devonshire Cream. The sinfully good sweets consisted of Sharon's specialty, a lacy Cream-Filled Roll-Up Cookie, as well as a yummy Brownie Torte and an incredibly creative and delicious White Chocolate Teacup filled with Raspberry Mousse. It certainly was hospitality of which the home's original owners would have been proud.

Under Hiram Brown's design expertise, the mansion was constructed in 1840 for Abraham Hivling and his bride. Abraham was the son of John Hivling, a prominent early citizen of Greene County. The family was quite large, consisting of eleven daughters, Abraham, and another son. Eight of the daughters married, and when they did, Mr. Hivling gave each of them a cameo pin, a gold watch and chain, and a new house. When it came Abraham's turn to wed, his father refused to provide the usual gifts, supposedly telling his son that he would have to build his own home. Abraham, a prominent Xenia businessman in his own right, retaliated to this slight by building a house bigger and better than any of his sisters had been given. No expense was spared in the construction of the ninety-four hundred square feet of living space.

Abraham and his family remained here

until 1881, when the house was purchased by John Allen and his wife, a niece of Abraham's. The Allens gave the home to their daughter, Mary Kinney, wife of Colonel Coates Kinney. Colonel Kinney was the noted author of "Ode to Ohio," delivered at the coliseum in Columbus for Ohio's centennial. Another author, Helen Hooven Santmyer, featured the mansion in her book *And Ladies of the Club*. At one time, President William McKinley was welcomed here, just as we were. Regardless of the era, hospitality and gentility are a part of Eden Hall.

APPLE CAKE

2 cups sugar
2 large eggs
1 cup vegetable oil
2½ cups flour
2 teaspoons baking powder
1 teaspoon baking soda
1 teaspoon cinnamon
1 teaspoon salt
1 teaspoon vanilla
1 cup chopped nuts
4 cups diced apples
12-ounce package butterscotch morsels

Preheat oven to 350 degrees. In a large bowl, mix together all ingredients except apples and butterscotch morsels. Mix by hand; *do not* use an electric mixer. Gently fold in apples. Mixture should be stiff. Spread mixture into a 9-by-13-inch pan. Sprinkle butterscotch morsels over top. Bake for 50 minutes. Let cool until just warm or continue cooling until room temperature. Cut into squares. Serves 16.

BUCKEYE BAR SQUARES

2 cups peanut butter
½ cup melted margarine
2¾ cups powdered sugar
1 teaspoon vanilla
12-ounce package chocolate chips
1 tablespoon butter

In a medium bowl, combine first 4 ingredients. Put evenly into a 9-by-13-inch pan. In a microwave-proof container or in the top of a double boiler, melt chocolate chips and 1 tablespoon butter. Pour over top of peanut butter layer, spreading evenly to cover. Chill. Cut into squares or diamonds. Serves 16.

**204 WEST LOVELAND AVENUE
LOVELAND, OH 45140
WWW.MISSANNABELLES.COM
513-774-0827**

The town of Loveland was bustling, in part because of the beautiful weather that day. Folks were basking in the early fall sunshine as they sat at benches and tables around town. Others were enjoying the benefits of the recreational activities that are offered in the area. Loveland is one of the main staging areas for the Little Miami Scenic Trail, which runs from Milford to Yellow Springs along the Little Miami River. Biking, hiking, rollerblading, backpacking, horseback riding, and cross-country skiing are all popular along the trail, depending on the season. Bikers were in abundance on that particular occasion, and all seemed to be enjoying the ambiance of the day and the town as much as I. A phone call to Karen relayed my discoveries and enthusiasm for returning with her along.

Light Tea began with Scones and Muffins, served with Clotted Cream and Jam. This was followed by a tiered tray bearing Tea Breads, Pastries, Finger Sandwiches, and fresh fruit. The experience ended with a palate-cleansing Sorbet. High Tea features all of the above but also includes a more substantial entrée such as Quiche or a cup of Soup, as well as a selection of desserts. Quantities are quite plentiful, as proven by the many to-go boxes that accompanied the ladies as they made their way home.

This is a perfect place to come for tea because visitors can browse and dine at the same locale. As guests near the rich wood-trimmed display windows of what was once Loveland's hardware store, all sorts of interesting items greet the eye. Once inside the inviting front door, two different shops await, crafted from this 1870s structure. To the right is a plethora of tea-related items and other decorative accessories. To the left is a pleasant boutique full of jewelry, accessories, and clothing, including lovely baby items.

The tearoom is to the back of the space, separated by glass-paned doors. Original tin ceilings painted a rich gold set the interior mood. Brass chandeliers provide stately lighting, and cloth-draped chairs add to the richness of the décor. The tables are cloth-covered as well, their patterns as varied as the fashionable hats hanging from the wheat-colored walls. Many of the women enjoying tea on the afternoon that I visited chose to sport a chapeau, and some even donned a boa, too! An antique china cabinet housing an eclectic mixture of floral table-service items furthers the turn-of-the-twentieth-century parlor feel, while soothing music puts the finishing touches on the environs.

No doubt, the wares and the clientele are quite a bit different from when this was

Sparks Hardware, run by William H. Sparks. William's wife, Bessie, worked at the store from 1904 until 1971, missing only fourteen days of work over the span of sixty-seven years. Her dedication to the hardware store was recognized in 1954 when she was honored at the State Convention of Hardware Managers as the only female manager in the entire United States. After all of Bessie's hard work, it's only fitting that the store is now a place to sit, enjoy, and be pampered for just a little while.

VEGETARIAN QUICHE

1 cup Bisquick
2½ cups half-and-half
4 eggs
½ teaspoon oregano
1 teaspoon salt
dash of pepper
¼ teaspoon garlic powder
¾ cup chopped vegetable of choice (asparagus, spinach, tomatoes, or broccoli)
1 cup grated Swiss or cheddar cheese
1 tablespoon chopped onion

Preheat oven to 375 degrees. Grease a 10-inch pie plate. In a large bowl, combine first 7 ingredients with an electric mixer. Fold in remaining ingredients, stirring with a spoon. Pour mixture into pie plate. Bake for approximately 50 minutes until center is firm. Serves 6.

CREAM CHEESE COOKIES

2 sticks butter, softened
3-ounce package cream cheese, softened
1 cup sugar
2 egg yolks
½ teaspoon pure vanilla extract
2½ cups flour, sifted

Using an electric mixer, cream together butter and cream cheese. Add sugar and beat until fluffy. Add egg yolks and vanilla. Add flour ½ cup at a time, stirring to blend after each addition. Chill dough for 30 minutes. Preheat oven to 350 degrees. Grease cookie sheets. Roll dough out to ¼-inch thickness. Cut with cookie cutters. Place cookies on sheets and bake for 10 to 12 minutes. Cool. Yields 4 dozen cookies.

CHAPTER 8
A Cabin in the Woods

The Inn at Cedar Falls

The rough-hewn logs and crude chinking that provided rustic shelter for so many hopeful pioneers as they struggled to make a new life on the frontier have endured. Some are used today as wonderful restaurants. We found new appreciation for the hardships faced by those settlers, and we hope that you enjoy this portal into America's pioneer spirit.

·THE MORGAN HOUSE·

RESTAURANT

5300 GLICK ROAD
DUBLIN, OH 43015
WWW.MORGANHSE.COM
614-889-5703

The taupe clapboard house at the corner of Glick Road and Dublin Road is easily identifiable as The Morgan House Restaurant, even without a sign. When we visited shortly after New Year's, it was still simply decorated for Christmas, with wreaths hung by red ribbons at the windows. In addition to being a restaurant, The Morgan House sells antiques, gifts, and collectibles in such a wide array that guests might easily browse for a couple of hours before or after dining.

Meals are served in two dining rooms. We were seated in the larger of them, at a Shaker-style table situated between the stone fireplace and a Christmas tree decorated with fruit. On the wall opposite the fireplace was a mural of the Ohio countryside. Down the hall, hanging from the Shaker pegboard, were period clothing and implements. We were joined for lunch by Cathy O'Brien, a local personality well known in the food arena. She sampled the Tomato Florentine Soup, which was chock-full of spinach, tomatoes, and other tasty ingredients. She followed that with the Chicken Casserole, as did Karen. It was accompanied by a green salad topped with Poppy Seed Dressing. A wonderful meal! Debbie chose the quiche of the day, which was filled with potatoes, tomatoes, chives, sour cream, and cheddar cheese. Not a morsel remained. We shared a piece of Layered Lemon Pie, which had a crust so flaky that any county-fair participant would have been proud. The layers—one of traditional lemon pie filling and the other of a fluffy cream cheese concoction—combined to make a perfect light dessert. Other items on the menu that tempted the palate were The Morgan House Soup, one of chef Chris Meadows's carefully guarded secrets, and Kendra's Pot Luck, a creamy chicken pot pie topped with puff pastry and baked in a terra-cotta pot.

The other dining room is actually the log cabin that once belonged to the Weaver family. Chris showed us pictures of the family sitting outside the structure, and then embarked on the tale of their home. The cabin was originally situated in Morgan County. On July 22, 1863, General John Hunt Morgan and his Confederate raiders confiscated the house. Morgan slept comfortably inside, while his men camped in a nearby orchard. According to newspaper articles and Morgan County Historical Society documents, Morgan typically chose a log or stone house as his headquarters because those materials were best for stopping bullets. Accounts say that Mrs. Weaver baked bread as Morgan slept. After he awoke and breakfasted on the porch, he kidnapped Mr. Weaver and forced him to be a scout. Eventually, Weaver escaped and John Hunt Morgan was captured, becoming one of the first residents of the Ohio State Penitentiary. Morgan's raiders subsequently helped him to flee, after which he donned civilian clothing and rode a train to Cincinnati amid throngs of Union troops. Fortunately, in the havoc that General Morgan wrought throughout Ohio, he spared this log cabin for all of us to enjoy.

STRAWBERRY CELERY SEED DRESSING

½ white onion
4 fresh strawberries
1½ cups sugar
1 tablespoon dry mustard
1 tablespoon salt
⅔ cup vinegar
2 cups canola oil or virgin olive oil
3 tablespoons celery seed

Cut onion into 4 pieces and place in a blender or food processor. Stem strawberries and place with onions. Purée. Add sugar, mustard, and salt. Mix well. Pour in vinegar and combine. Slowly add oil to mixture. Pour into a storage container. Stir in celery seed until well combined. Dressing will keep up to 3 weeks in refrigerator. Yields approximately 3 cups.

BROCCOLI DILL QUICHE

1 cup biscuit mix
1 cup plus scant ⅓ cup half-and-half
3 eggs
1 cup finely chopped broccoli
9-inch deep-dish pie shell
1 tablespoon chopped fresh dill
2½ cups shredded cheddar cheese

Preheat oven to 375 degrees. Place biscuit mix in a medium mixing bowl and slowly add half-and-half. Whisk briskly. Add eggs and whisk briskly until batter is smooth. Set aside. Place broccoli in pie shell and sprinkle evenly with dill. Sprinkle cheese over broccoli. Pour batter into pie shell and bake for 45 minutes. Serves 6 to 8.

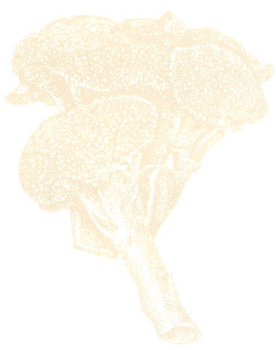

THE INN
at Cedar Falls

21190 STATE ROUTE 374
LOGAN, OH 43138
WWW.INNATCEDARFALLS.COM
740-385-7489

In our search for peace and serenity, we found a treasure in The Inn at Cedar Falls. The inn is comprised of two log cabins built in the early 1800s, surrounded by three of Ohio's most beautiful state parks. Hikers will enjoy the rock formations, caves, and waterfalls in the surrounding Hocking Hills.

We entered the inn through the dining room, with its primitive furnishings and its dried orange slices hanging at the windows. The chinked walls, exposed beams, and uneven floors helped transport us back to the pioneering 1840s. A cross-stitch sampler on the wall and the soft glow of candlelight gave the room a warm, homey feeling.

The central part of the double log house contains the kitchen, where guests can stop by and chat with the chef as she prepares the meals from scratch. The inn has its own organic vegetable and herb gardens, from which seasonal offerings are prepared. To the rear is a delightful sitting room, where we sat next to the fireplace and thumbed through jour-

nals where visitors of all ages had inscribed their thoughts in prose and poetry. Each page related tales of spectacular views, wonderful meals, and a common feeling of being very far from today's modern conveniences. On warm evenings, guests are encouraged to sit outside on the porch and share the breathtaking view. Bird watchers will love spotting the ruby-throated hummingbirds, yellow finches, and pileated woodpeckers.

Two and a half years in the making, The Inn at Cedar Falls was the vision of Anne Castle. Previously a successful businesswoman in the corporate world, she, together with her daughter Ellen Grinsfelder, survived a long struggle against physical, emotional, and financial blocks to create the inn. A short history of the inn is located in each room.

We sipped our drinks and played a game of Chinese checkers until it was time to eat. As we tasted the Wisconsin Cheese Ball and Crackers and polished off a house salad tossed in tangy Maple Balsamic Vinaigrette, we chatted with Debby and Harry Brown, who were also seated at our table. It was their third visit to the inn, and they enthusiastically described their comfortable cabin to us. Debbie chose the lightly breaded Pork Tenderloin with Chardonnay Glaze and Crimson Pear Chutney, while Karen opted for the Pan-Seared Chicken Breast, served over a bed of Grits and finished with Portabello Mushroom Sauce. Both entrées were so wonderful that we barely had room to sample the Cinnamon Raisin Bread Pudding, topped with Caramel Sauce. Good food and good company made for a totally delicious evening.

CHICKEN BREASTS
STUFFED WITH ORANGE,
LEEKS, AND MINT

4 leeks, white part only, cleaned and
   thinly sliced
½ stick butter
½ cup chopped mint
8 chicken breasts, skinned, boned, and
   pounded to ¼-inch thickness
pepper to taste
zest and juice of 2 oranges, divided
2 tablespoons oil
2 cups heavy cream

Preheat oven to 350 degrees. Sauté leeks
in butter until soft and until liquid evaporates.
Remove ⅔ of leeks from pan and mix with
mint in a small bowl. Sprinkle chicken with
pepper and a little orange zest. Spread ½ to 1
tablespoon leek mixture on each breast and
sprinkle with a little more orange zest. Roll
up each breast and tie with string in 2 or 3
places. Brush chicken with oil and place on a
baking sheet. Bake for 30 minutes uncovered.
Do not overcook. Add remaining zest and
juice to remaining leeks and simmer covered
over low heat for 15 minutes. Add cream,
increase heat, and stir about 7 minutes until thickened. Cut each breast crosswise into
5 pieces and spoon sauce on top. Serve immediately. Goes well with rice or risotto and
asparagus. Serves 8.

YAM AND
APPLE CASSEROLE

2 Granny Smith apples
2 16-ounce cans yams, drained and
   patted dry
1 stick butter, melted
½ cup dark corn syrup
⅓ cup plus 2 tablespoons light brown sugar
2 tablespoons dry sherry
¾ teaspoon cinnamon
⅛ teaspoon salt

Preheat oven to 350 degrees. Core, peel,
and slice apples and set aside. In a food processor, purée yams, 6 tablespoons of the melted butter, syrup, brown sugar, sherry, cinnamon, and salt. Spread half of mixture into a
greased 10-inch pie pan or casserole dish. Arrange half of apples on top. Repeat with remaining yam mixture and apples. Brush top
of apples with remaining butter. Bake for approximately 45 minutes until apples are tender. Serves 6 to 8.

The Cabin

28810 LAKE SHORE BOULEVARD
WILLOWICK, OH 44095
440-943-5195

The list of early-bird entrées served Monday through Friday at The Cabin is lengthier than the entire menu at some restaurants. It's a sure indication that there is something here for everyone. The Honey-Roasted Chicken and the Silver Dollar Tenderloin Medallions caught our eye. All the selections are generously served with a salad, a vegetable, a choice of Potato or Wild Rice, and warm bread. The regular menu includes eight appetizer choices and a lengthy list of entrées. Shrimp Scampi, Potato-Crusted Halibut, and Breaded Sea Scallops are among the seafood options. Such favorites as Veal Oscar, New Zealand Rack of Lamb, and Baby Back Ribs are also available. Guests can't go wrong with The Cabin's signature desserts of Apple Cinnamon Napoleon and Crème Brûlée. No wonder patrons were so happy to see this local institution reopen after a devastating fire.

The restaurant burned in June 1993. Just one day before what remained of the building was to be destroyed, longtime friends Joe and Susan Durkoske and Barbara and Marty Belich rescued the structure. The enthusiasm of former patrons and previous employees got the couples through the arduous process of restoring The Cabin to its place as one of Willowick's favorite eateries. Long before the doors once again swung wide, customers were booking parties. Some people even had tailgate parties in the parking lot just to keep up the encouragement. Familiar faces were seen among the staff when the restaurant reopened. The manager and the bartender returned, as did several other employees, including a server with more than twenty years at The Cabin and a member of the kitchen staff who had been there for thirty. It seems that's the kind of allegiance the place elicits.

The Western Reserve land on which The Cabin stands was deeded in 1853. The main part of the original structure, built as a hunting lodge in 1903, was converted to a restaurant in 1933. Owner Andy Anderson was issued the second liquor license in Lake County. When he started the business, there were animal heads on the walls and beer spigots coming out of the walls, serving Wooden Shoe Beer and Genesee Ale. In 1944, Anderson took on partners Bud Handy and Betty Hylkema. Eventually, the restaurant became known for its superb steak and fish dinners. During a 1994 interview, manager Shirley Miller recalled that pike dinners were once so popular and so inexpensive that people would line up around the outside of the cabin waiting to get in. She also remembered fondly that Betty was very concerned about fairness to customers. If she found that someone had been overcharged, she'd try to identify who they were, after which she'd go to great lengths to get the money back to them. If she couldn't, the money was donated to charity.

The current owners have tried to maintain this homey atmosphere. Although oak and pine have replaced the scorched, rough-hewn logs, the old fireplace still stands. People love to come to The Cabin to recall old memories while making new ones.

ARTICHOKE ALOUETTE

12 whole artichoke hearts
2 8-ounce packages cream cheese, softened
2 to 4 tablespoons chopped fresh herbs of
   choice (tarragon, basil, thyme, rosemary,
   etc.)
⅓ cup flour
3 eggs, beaten
½ cup breadcrumbs
4 cups vegetable oil

Cut artichokes in half and make an indentation with thumb in the middle of each. In a small bowl, combine cream cheese with herbs. Scoop approximately 1 tablespoon cream cheese mixture into the indentation in each artichoke half. Roll stuffed artichokes in flour, dip in eggs, and roll in breadcrumbs. Dip in eggs and roll in breadcrumbs again. Heat oil to 375 degrees in a small fryer or a medium saucepan. Fry a few breaded artichokes at a time. Fry approximately 6 to 8 minutes until golden. Serves 4 as an appetizer.

THE CABIN'S TRADITIONAL SCAMPI DINNER

12 4- to 5-ounce scampi or prawns
½ cup clarified butter
¼ teaspoon salt
¼ teaspoon pepper
1 teaspoon garlic salt
½ teaspoon cayenne pepper
⅛ teaspoon onion salt
¼ teaspoon white pepper
½ teaspoon celery seed, crushed
1½ teaspoons paprika
2 tablespoons breadcrumbs

Cut shells of scampi lengthwise along middle of back all the way to tail. Pull scampi out of shells but leave tails attached. Remove black vein that runs length of back. Place cleaned scampi on a large baking sheet lined with aluminum foil. Brush with enough clarified butter to coat. Combine next 7 ingredients. Season scampi lightly with mixture. Sprinkle with paprika, then with breadcrumbs. Place under broiler for 8 to 10 minutes. Serves 3. Note: Three teaspoons Old Bay seasoning may be substituted for salt, pepper, garlic salt, cayenne, onion salt, white pepper, and celery seed.

THE CABIN RESTAURANT AT

MARIO'S INTERNATIONAL
SPA & HOTEL
35 EAST GARFIELD ROAD
AURORA, OH 44202
330-562-9171

The Grey Hotel was built in 1840. It was considered to be quite fashionable, offering excellent overnight accommodations and such amenities as a grand dining room, a bar area, and a "moving" dance floor. At some point, the building was placed on logs and pulled by a team of horses from the southwest corner of State Routes 82 and 306 to its present location at the northeast corner of the intersection. The process took two days. After the move, the building became known as the Aurora House, and its use changed to that of a two-family home. It remained a family dwelling until it was purchased by Mr. and Mrs. Mario Liuzzo in 1977.

As the Liuzzos converted the Aurora House from a home to a spa, they recaptured the early heritage of the Grey Hotel. Guests today use a stone walkway reminiscent of the original flagstone path built to provide ladies clean access to the premises. The foyer area of the spa gives a view of the original stair-case leading to the second floor. Those stairs allow modern-day guests to ascend the long-ago route of those on their way to a memorable evening in the dance hall.

The unique woodwork in the main hallways of the upper and lower levels came from the siding and beams of a barn once located on the property. The Cabin Restaurant, a log cabin dating to the mid-1800s, is one of the three dining options at what is now known as Mario's International Spa & Hotel. The Cabin was constructed as a sugar house on a dairy farm and was later incorporated as the tavern for the Aurora Stage Coach Inn. The rustic restaurant has rough-hewn walls and wide-plank floors. When it expanded several years ago, old barns from Geauga and Portage counties were dismantled and used to enhance the rustic atmosphere.

The Cabin Restaurant serves a wide-ranging menu featuring such items as Bacon-Wrapped Filet Mignon stuffed with Mushroom Duxelle, Crab Cakes served over Parmesan Peppercorn Cream Sauce, and House-Made Sausage, Roasted Red Peppers, and Bowtie Pasta with Italian Pesto. On the night we visited, our favorites were the House Mixed Green Salad, generously topped with mandarin oranges and almonds and coated in delicious Citrus Vinaigrette, and the Lobster and Ricotta Ravioli, served over Basil Cream Sauce. Because the menu items are so delicious and so beautifully presented, it's hard to believe that many of them have significantly fewer calories than you'd expect. The desserts are every bit as wonderful as the entrées. We highly recommend the Amaretto Crème

Brûlée and The Cabin's version of Tiramisu.

That certainly isn't the only recognition that Mario's has received. *Conde Nast* magazine has listed the establishment as one of the ten best spas nationwide. Guests such as David Letterman, Kristi Yamaguchi, Wayne Newton, and Sarah Brightman can attest to the quality of the experience. After eating our way through four states, a little pampering from The Cabin Restaurant and Mario's was good indeed.

LEMON POPPY SEED CAKE

4 cups all-purpose flour
1 cup sugar
1 teaspoon baking soda
5 teaspoons baking powder
⅓ teaspoon salt
½ cup poppy seeds
2 teaspoons lemon zest
⅔ cup oil
2 cups nonfat milk
2 eggs, lightly beaten

Preheat oven to 350 degrees. Combine dry ingredients in a bowl. Combine oil, milk, and eggs in a separate bowl. Lightly mix into dry ingredients. Do not overmix. Pour into a 10-inch tube pan sprayed with nonstick cooking spray. Bake for 50 minutes. Serves 16.

PASTA ALLO ZAFFERANO

16-ounce package pasta of your choice
1 onion, chopped
2 tablespoons olive oil
½ teaspoon saffron
2 tablespoons water
2 tablespoons curry powder
½ cup ricotta cheese
½ cup skim milk
1 cup diced fresh pineapple
½ cup peas, cooked
salt and pepper to taste
fresh mint leaves for garnish

Cook pasta according to package directions. Drain. In a large skillet, sauté onions in olive oil until golden. Mix saffron with water and stir in curry. Add to onions and mix well. Sauté at low heat for 5 minutes. Stir in ricotta and milk. Heat. While stirring, gently add pasta. Place in a serving dish. Sprinkle pineapple and peas over top and toss gently. Season with salt and pepper. Chill. Serve cold, garnished with mint leaves. Serves 10 to 12 as a side dish.

Lake White Club

1166 STATE ROUTE 552
WAVERLY, OH 45690
740-947-5000

Lake White is beautiful, with broad, grassy banks and mature woodlands. The tranquil lake is surrounded by white-walled, red-roofed houses clustered among the trees. Many Canadian geese winter here, and their presence adds to the restful feeling. This area was once Indian country. Originally a forested valley with a gently flowing creek, it attracted many settlers to its fertile ground and abundant timber. Peter Patrick discovered the valley in 1785 but was attacked by an Indian hunting party. He and his companions fled, leaving only Patrick's initials carved into a beech tree next to the stream. Much later, those initials served to give the stream its name—Pee Pee Creek.

Eventually, the Shawnees moved on. By 1799, a pioneer surveyor by the name of John Beasley had recorded some seven hundred acres of this land—including the site of the future Lake White Club—on behalf of John Winston of Virginia. A log cabin was built here in the mid-1820s. It's easy to imagine looking out of the cabin's windows and watching settlers moving west, carried along the Ohio & Erie Canal, now US Route 23. When John Winston died in 1837, his Rich-mond relatives were only too glad to sell the backwoods property for the sum of $1,829. The land subsequently passed through many owners, including the valley's first millionaire, James Emmitt.

In the early 1930s, former Ohio lieutenant governor George D. Nye acquired the property for use by Lake White, Inc. Wayne Wick bought several acres of the original tract, including the site of the log cabin. August 1935 saw the completion of the lake bed. But the occupants of the cabin knew that the lake was going to take many months to fill. Several days later, a terrific storm broke over the Waverly area, and the next morning, lo and behold, the lake was completely filled. It wasn't long before visitors from all over the state stopped by to see it. It was at that time that the kitchen at the log cabin began to serve fried chicken. In 1938, the property officially became the Lake White Club, a popular scenic spot with tourists and locals alike.

Today, visitors can still admire the huge original logs cut from the local woodlands and the fireplace built of large stones removed from Pee Pee Creek. We sat on the porch and enjoyed the view and the atmosphere. We also enjoyed the menu itself, which was sprinkled throughout with amusing quips and notations. Debbie selected the Fried Chicken, and Karen chose the Fisherman's Platter, a mix of deep-fried Scallops, Shrimp, and Oysters. Each came with tomato juice, Coleslaw, and homemade Rolls. Everything was delicious. It's clear that the tradition of home-cooked food and fine service is still in style at the Lake White Club.

CHERRY CREAM PIE

2 tablespoons finely chopped nuts
9-inch piecrust
1 cup whipping cream
16-ounce can sweetened condensed milk
⅓ cup lemon juice
½ teaspoon vanilla
¼ teaspoon almond flavoring
Cherry Glaze (see below)

Preheat oven to 350 degrees. Press nuts into bottom and sides of piecrust and bake for 10 to 12 minutes until golden brown. Set aside to cool. In a medium bowl, whip cream until thick and stiff. Add sweetened condensed milk, lemon juice, vanilla, and almond flavoring and fold gently to combine. Spoon mixture into cooled shell. Top with Cherry Glaze and chill. Serves 8.

CHERRY GLAZE

2 cups canned, pitted sour cherries, drained,
    ⅔ cup juice reserved
¼ cup sugar
1 tablespoon cornstarch
2 to 3 drops red food coloring

Combine all ingredients in a saucepan. Cook over low heat, stirring constantly until thick. Set aside to cool. Yields enough glaze for 1 Cherry Cream Pie.

CHOCOLATE CHEESECAKE

1¼ cups graham cracker crumbs
2 tablespoons sugar
2 tablespoons butter, melted
6 ounces bittersweet baking chocolate
¼ cup rum
2 8-ounce packages cream cheese, softened
¾ cup fine sugar
½ cup sour cream
1 tablespoon vanilla
4 eggs

Line outside of a 9-inch springform pan with foil, shiny side out. Butter inside of pan. In a small bowl, combine graham cracker crumbs, sugar, and butter. Press mixture evenly into bottom of pan. Refrigerate.

Preheat oven to 325 degrees. In a double boiler, melt chocolate with rum. Set aside. In a large bowl, beat cream cheese until light and fluffy. Gradually beat in fine sugar, sour cream, and vanilla. Add eggs and continue to mix well. Place bowl over a saucepan of hot water and stir until mixture is smooth. Place about a third of mixture into another bowl. Combine remaining cream cheese mixture with chocolate mixture. Remove crust from refrigerator and pour chocolate–cream cheese mixture into it. Pour plain cream cheese mixture on top of that, then make swirls in batter with a fork. Bake for 50 minutes. Allow to cool, then refrigerate overnight. Serves 12.

As we entered Ye Olde Trail Tavern, the first things we noticed were the dollar bills lining the wall opposite the bar. Most were signed by the persons to whom they once belonged, including the likes of John Lithgow, Coretta Scott King, Bob Hope, and Cliff Robertson. Rod Serling once tended bar at "The Trail," as locals call it, and taught a writing course in the banquet room upstairs. In addition to the currency, all sorts of other items line the walls, including flasks and steins. We enjoyed identifying the milk jugs, saddle forms, and horseshoes and guessing at the many other things we had no clue about.

Past the bar area and through a low doorway, guests enter the original log cabin. A fireplace at the far end of the room flickers, as it has for many a year. An atrium dining area has been added. For lunch, we moved into the cabin and chose a small booth close to the fire. Other seating is provided at long tables and benches, carved with the names and initials of many who've visited. Pictures of presidents hang on the plaster walls, which appropriately bear the soot of fires from years past. The restaurant is known for its burgers, but after a larger-than-normal breakfast that

morning, neither of us felt we could do one justice. We opted instead to share a bowl of Chili and the Most Excellent Grilled Cheese, made with three different cheeses, tomato, and lettuce. Both were very tasty and satisfying on a bone-chilling day.

Ye Olde Trail Tavern is located in the first home in Yellow Springs, known then as Forest Village. While we were visiting, we thumbed through an old book on the history of Greene County. In it was an account of a gentleman's first visit to the area. It seems that in his travels, he met a man who was planning to settle around here. He later received a letter inviting him to visit what the man portrayed as an up-and-coming village. One day, the gentleman set out on foot from his home in Dayton, arriving at what he thought was the right area by late afternoon. Not seeing the cluster of houses he expected, he asked a passerby where Yellow Springs was. The man pointed to a thicket and said, "Right there. You can't see it for the trees." There in the forest was a lone log cabin, the totality of Yellow Springs.

That log cabin eventually became a stagecoach stop for weary travelers on the Columbus-Cincinnati Trail. Cholera once swept through the town. Forty deaths were attributed to the epidemic, seven of them occurring in the tavern itself. Many others happened in the houses nearby, all of which shared a common well. With today's medical knowledge, one can assume that the single water source was likely the cause of the demise of so many.

Those deaths are thought to be one possible explanation for the female ghost that frequents the restaurant. Those who have seen her describe her either in a blue or a black dress but differ as to the style of her hair. However, all who have seen her share one thing—they have been men with ponytails. Perhaps the ghost is most comfortable with the men's style of her day.

The motto of the tavern is "Many pass through, few pass by." One reason is the variety of soups served, the recipes for which are carefully guarded secrets. Another reason is the well-known burgers. We encourage you to try your favorite flavor combination at Ye Olde Trail Tavern. It's more than a local watering hole.

TAVERN BURGER

⅓ pound ground beef
1 kaiser roll
¼ cup spaghetti sauce, heated
1 slice mozzarella cheese
1 to 2 tablespoons sliced mushrooms,
   sautéed

Form ground beef into a large patty and fry it to desired doneness. Drain. Place burger on bottom half of roll. Top with spaghetti sauce, cheese, and mushrooms. Broil to melt cheese, if desired. Top with other half of bun and serve. Serves 1.

MOST EXCELLENT GRILLED CHEESE

2 tablespoons butter
2 slices whole-wheat bread
1 thick slice cheddar cheese
1 thick slice Swiss cheese
1 thick slice mozzarella cheese
1 leaf lettuce
2 slices tomato

Melt butter in a large skillet or on a griddle. Place both slices of bread in melted butter and grill until crisp. Turn bread over. Place cheddar on 1 slice and Swiss and mozzarella on the other. Grill until bread is browned and cheese is melted. Place lettuce and tomato on 1 side and top with other piece of bread. Cut in half. Serves 1.

CHAPTER 9

Down on the Farm

Bluebird Farm Restaurant

During early United States history, farming wasn't just an occupation but a means of survival. Families had to provide for themselves, as the nearest neighbor could be a mile or two away and the nearest town farther than that. Many settlers were lured from points east by the opportunity of owning something substantial— land. The restaurants in this chapter are the vestiges of a way of life.

Bluebird Farm
Restaurant

190 ALAMO ROAD
CARROLLTON, OH 44615
WWW.BLUEBIRD-FARM.COM
330-627-7980

On the town square of Carrollton sits the McCook House. The McCook family sent two brothers and nine of those brothers' children to battle during the Civil War. One of the Christmas trees at Bluebird Farm Restaurant pays homage to that sacrifice. It is bedecked with ornaments depicting soldiers in Yankee blue and Confederate gray uniforms.

The buildings on the farm predate that conflict. They were constructed in the mid-1800s by Jacob and Louisa Kintner. One barn contains a gift shop, where items are attractively arranged even in the old cattle stalls. Another barn is the home of owner Joyce Hannon. The old farmhouse is now the restaurant. Guests enter through the original kitchen area and head up a flight of stairs to the main dining room. The plank floor is a lovely, mellow chestnut. The cream walls are trimmed with marvelous stencils of buildings, each a structure in town, done by a friend of Joyce's daughter. A corner cupboard and another built-in cupboard contain the restaurant's collection of Blue Bird china. I thought this might have been the inspiration for the restaurant's name, but it seems that the bluebird is the county bird of Carroll County, and the name was chosen for that

reason. The dining room on the third floor is more Victorian in its décor, which includes floral wallpaper and lace curtains over lovely arched windows. Karen wasn't able to make this sojourn, so I dined with Joyce, restaurant manager Ruth Ann, and Amy Rutledge of the Carroll County Visitor's and Convention Bureau. We ate on the enclosed second-story porch, which was a lovely setting after a fresh snowfall.

The restaurant prides itself on its hearty home-style meals. I chose the Chicken Casserole with a side dish of Cranberry Salad, which hit the spot on a wintry day. Other items ordered from our table were Spinach Lasagna Roll-Ups, which looked delicious, and Ham, Broccoli, and Cheddar Quiche, which was extremely appealing. On another visit, I might choose the BLT Chicken Salad, a favorite of many guests. When the dessert tray came, I couldn't make up my mind, so we decided to wait until after we'd toured the other buildings.

Across a short walkway, we visited the gift shop before continuing to the toy museum. Joyce's daughter, Susie, seeking a way to display her collection of antique toys, was the inspiration for the museum. The bear collection alone is unbelievable. You'll also find Madame Alexander dolls, some excellent English dolls, a wide variety of German dolls, and an impressive assortment of Steiff animals. And that's not all. Joyce has an extensive collection of hats that changes with the seasons—felts and velvets for the winter, bonnets and straw hats for the summer. Many are in the restaurant's ladies' room. Mannequins adorned in period dress, antique photos, and an antique curling iron complete the powder room décor. I won't give away what Joyce has done with the upstairs restroom—it's whimsical, clever, and completely unexpected!

After touring, we returned to sate our sweet tooth. My Cherry Macaroon Pie with Coconut-Almond Topping was unique and delicious. Go to Bluebird Farm for lunch or a traditional Sunday dinner and enjoy a down-home meal!

CHICKEN CASSEROLE

10 chicken breasts, boned and skinned
4 cups sour cream
2 15-ounce cans cream of chicken soup
15-ounce can mushroom stems, drained
9-ounce can water chestnuts, drained
6-ounce package commercial stuffing mix

Preheat oven to 350 degrees. Poach chicken in salted water for approximately 10 minutes until tender. Cool and cut into bite-sized pieces. Combine sour cream, soup, mushrooms, and water chestnuts. Add chicken pieces and put in a 9-by-13-inch baking dish. Prepare stuffing mix according to package directions and spread over chicken mixture. Bake uncovered for 45 minutes. May be refrigerated 1 day prior to using. Serves 6 to 8.

CREAM PUFFS

1 cup water
1 stick margarine
1 cup flour
4 eggs
Custard Filling (see below)

Preheat oven to 375 degrees. Combine water and margarine in a medium saucepan. Bring to a boil. Add flour and stir well. Remove from heat. Add eggs 1 at a time, beating well after each addition. Drop mixture by heaping tablespoonfuls onto a greased baking sheet. Bake for 40 to 45 minutes until golden brown. Allow to cool. Put Custard Filling into a pastry tube and pipe into puffs. Yields 12 puffs.

Custard Filling

4½ cups milk, divided
2 cups sugar, divided
½ stick margarine
1 teaspoon vanilla
½ cup cornstarch
2 eggs

Combine 4 cups of the milk and 1½ cups of the sugar. Stir and bring to a boil. Add margarine and vanilla. In a separate bowl, combine cornstarch, remaining sugar, eggs, and remaining milk. Stir until well blended. Add to boiling mixture, stirring constantly until thickened. Set aside to cool. Yields enough filling for 12 Cream Puffs.

Pine Tree Barn

Fine Furniture Interior Design
Beautiful Gifts Gourmet Lunch

THE GRANARY
AT PINE TREE BARN
4374 SHREVE ROAD
WOOSTER, OH 44691
WWW.PINETREEBARN.COM
330-264-1014

The success of Pine Tree Barn—which includes a tree farm, home furnishings and interior design, a gift shop, and a restaurant—is indirectly linked to that of immigrant August Imgard, who arrived from Germany during the 1850s. As his first Christmas in the New World approached, he observed the holiday much as he had in Bavaria—by decorating a Christmas tree. This was very uncommon in America, but by the following Christmas, almost everyone in town followed Imgard's lead, making Wooster one of the first places in America to observe the tradition of Christmas trees.

Over the years, local farmers decided to meet the increasing demand for evergreen trees by growing them commercially. Robert Dush and his wife were one family to do so. Their son, Roger, went through college on money garnered from the tree business. He worked in Chicago for a time before returning to Wooster to open Pine Tree Barn, an expansion of the tree business, with his father. They set up shop in a twenty-five-thousand-square-foot Dutch bank barn. Built in 1868, it once held a significant number of livestock.

Since customers were coming to get trees, the Dushes decided to offer ornaments for sale as well. The family, realizing it was drawing business from a seventy-mile radius, also made food available for customers. At first, the restaurant was tucked into the corner of the barn where the grain bins once were. That area, with its wide-plank flooring and barn walls, is still there. Attractive sage-green bench-style seating extends around the perimeter. Casual side chairs slide up to the linen-covered tables, creating a cozy dining-room atmosphere. Adjacent to this, another dining room has been added overlooking the beautiful grounds and the sparkling lake.

Karen was unable to accompany me that day. I munched on a Lemon Crumb Muffin, a specialty of the house that was featured by Burt Wolf on a cooking segment he filmed here. I toyed with ordering the Gourmet California-Style Thin-Crust Pizza or one of the two quiche selections before deciding on Marie's Pesto Chicken and Pasta. I ended my delightful meal with a piece of Sour Cream Raspberry Pie, made according to a recipe from Roger's mother. The restaurant always has the raspberry and peach varieties of this pie and also offered cherry the day I was there.

The Dushes and their faithful customers proclaim Pine Tree Barn to be in the middle of nowhere. Actually, this luncheon restaurant is just a few miles from Wooster, and it's well worth the trip any day of the week!

LEMON CRUMB MUFFINS

4 cups sugar
6 cups flour
¾ teaspoon baking soda
¾ teaspoon salt
5 fresh lemons
8 eggs
2 cups sour cream
4 sticks butter, melted
2 tablespoons lemon juice
Streusel (see below)
Lemon Glaze (see below)

Preheat oven to 350 degrees. Sift dry ingredients together in a medium bowl. Grate rinds of lemons and set aside. In a separate bowl, whisk eggs, then add sour cream, butter, and lemon juice. Continue to whisk until smooth. Fold lemon rinds into egg mixture. Fold all dry ingredients into egg mixture. Blend well. Spray muffin tins with cooking spray and fill with batter. Top each muffin with 1 tablespoon Streusel and bake for 18 to 20 minutes. Remove muffins from oven and immediately poke each several times with a toothpick. Drizzle top of each muffin with a scant ½ teaspoon Lemon Glaze. Let cool slightly. Remove from muffin tins. Serve warm or allow to cool and store in an airtight container for later use. Batter can be kept up to 1 week in refrigerator. Yields 30 muffins.

Streusel

1¼ cups sugar
1¼ cups flour
⅓ cup butter, softened

Sift sugar and flour together. Add butter. Work into dry ingredients until crumbly.

Lemon Glaze

½ cup sugar
⅓ cup lemon juice

Combine ingredients until all sugar is dissolved.

MARIE'S PESTO CHICKEN AND PASTA

4 4- to 6-ounce boneless chicken breasts
2 tablespoons olive oil
1 pound angel hair pasta
3 tablespoons lemon-infused oil
1 cup julienned red peppers
1 cup julienned green peppers
1 cup diagonally cut green onions
½ cup black olives, halved
1 cup pesto, divided
¼ cup shredded Parmesan cheese

Brush chicken breasts with olive oil. Cook pasta according to package directions. While pasta is cooking, grill chicken until juices run clear. In a large skillet, heat lemon-infused oil and sauté peppers, green onions, and olives al dente. Add ¾ cup pesto to skillet and toss with vegetables. Remove from heat. Place pasta on 4 plates and divide vegetable mixture among them. Place chicken breasts on top. Spoon remaining pesto over chicken and sprinkle with Parmesan. Serve immediately. Serves 4.

12018 US ROUTE 250
MILAN, OH 44846
419-499-4271

Set amid the flat farmland of central Ohio, the property surrounding the Homestead Inn could have inspired the Beatles' tune "Strawberry Fields Forever." Levi Arnold was a strawberry farmer who relocated to this area from Connecticut. He built his large, two-story house in 1883, using several popular styles of the day. An intricate wrought-iron railing surrounds the widow's walk, where Mrs. Arnold is said to have kept watch on the field hands below. According to local legend, the strawberry farm was so successful that the house and its furnishings were paid for with the profits from just one year's crop. When the Lake Shore Electric Railway was completed in 1893, Arnold had a refrigerated rail car designed to ship his strawberries. The fruit was loaded on the train right at the farm, since he also had his own rail siding.

The house and farm remained in the Arnold family for three generations. Interestingly enough, current owners Mr. and Mrs. Robert Berry and Doug Berry have ties to the Arnolds. Doug's great-aunt married

one of the Arnold descendants and lived in the house at the time her children were born. She was in her nineties in 1979 when the Berrys took ownership, and as she walked through the house, she told them bits and pieces about how the rooms had been used and how the home had been decorated. Sure enough, as they began to renovate and restore, color schemes and details she had described revealed themselves. Although the Berrys began their tenure in the late 1970s, the home had been used as a restaurant some twenty years prior to that.

Visible from the Ohio Turnpike, Homestead Inn Restaurant is popular with tourists and locals alike. We arrived from the other direction, coming north on US Route 250. We were immediately drawn to the gnarled trees in the yard and the contrast they provided to the lovely wrought iron of the ornate porch and the patterned slate roof.

Seated at a cozy window table in the main dining room, we marveled at the fabulous beaded gingerbread trim that separates one room from the next. The intricate pattern in shades of black and tan on the inlaid marble fireplace reminded us of those done on Ukrainian Easter eggs. Even the hinges on the ten-foot doors are elaborate. Downstairs, the Rathskeller—the old cellar, built from massive stone blocks—offers a very different dining experience. There, old tools and interesting lighting that gives a candlelight effect decorate the many interesting nooks and crannies.

We shared a cup of Reuben Chowder, delicious on that rainy day. It had a creamy

Swiss cheese broth filled with chunks of sauerkraut, corned beef, and pickle. Karen followed it with the Smothered Crab Burger and Onion Rings, while Debbie enjoyed the Perch Luncheon, served with a Twice-Baked Potato and a dish of Coleslaw. No strawberries were on the menu, though. They just weren't in season.

DEVILED EGGS

12 hard-cooked eggs
½ teaspoon salt
¼ teaspoon pepper
3 tablespoons sugar
1 teaspoon cider vinegar
1 tablespoon prepared mustard
⅓ cup mayonnaise
2 teaspoons celery seed

Shell eggs. Cut in half lengthwise and separate whites from yolks. Place yolks in a bowl and mash with a fork or a pastry blender until they resemble fine crumbs. Add next 6 ingredients, blend until smooth, and then fill whites with yolk mixture. A pastry bag works best for adding filling. Sprinkle with celery seed. Serves 24.

SWEET POTATO BREAD

1 cup cooked and mashed fresh yams
½ cup oil or shortening
⅓ cup water
1¾ cups flour
1½ cups sugar
½ cup chopped walnuts
1 teaspoon baking soda
1 teaspoon grated lemon rind
¾ teaspoon cinnamon
¾ teaspoon nutmeg
½ teaspoon salt
Glaze (see below)

Preheat oven to 350 degrees. Combine first 3 ingredients in a large bowl and beat well. Add all remaining ingredients except Glaze and beat well. Pour into a greased loaf pan and bake for about 1 hour. Brush with Glaze while still warm. Yields 1 loaf.

Glaze

4 tablespoons powdered sugar
1 tablespoon butter
1 tablespoon milk
1 tablespoon lemon juice

Combine all ingredients in a small bowl.

The Sawyer House

Restaurant & Tavern

9470 MENTOR AVENUE
MENTOR, OH 44060
WWW.SAWYERHOUSERESTAURANT.COM
440-358-0100

The stone building on the south side of Mentor Avenue was once part of a group of Sawyer family homes that sat along both sides of the avenue. Daniel Sawyer lived in this house, while his brother Joseph lived on the corner of Mentor Avenue and Chillicothe Road. Another brother, Isaac, lived just across the way. A collage of Sawyer family pictures hangs in the vestibule near the reception desk. Three generations of Sawyers lived in this house. Longtime area residents used to talk about Daniel's son, William, trimming the front hedges. His hard work garnered him much respect, since William had a clubfoot.

The house, marked by a stone over the front entrance, was built in 1843. The construction style, in which native cut stone and cut sandstone were set in a random pattern, is quite unique. Some of the stones are as much as four feet by two and a half feet. This is one of only two or three stone homes more than one hundred years old in Lake County.

Inside, stone walls were visible in the dining room where we were seated and up the steps adjacent to the bar area. The main dining room is more modern than the building's exterior but still has vestiges of the past, including the original cellar door and a wall of weathered barn siding. A large, old-fashioned clock set above a series of booths adorns one of the end walls. Eight ceiling fans turn lazily overhead, operated by an elaborate pulley system. Off the bar area, two additional dining rooms decorated in tones of teal and mauve are located in the downstairs rooms of the Sawyers' original residence.

We were intrigued by the Graham Cracker–Crusted Calamari, served with Curry Coconut Aioli. The Veal Meat Loaf, wrapped in smoked bacon and then char-grilled, also sounded wonderful. Pork Tenderloin is a favorite of Debbie's, so she was tempted by The Sawyer House's version, which comes encrusted with rosemary and walnuts and is served with Sweet and Sour Red Cabbage and Sun-Dried Cherry-Apple Relish. Ultimately, it was the Ravioli, filled with butternut squash and served in Sage Cream Sauce, that got her vote. The portion was just the right size for lunch. Karen had no difficulty in selecting the Crab Cakes, served in four petite mounds with a side of Jicama Slaw. Although we decided to curb our calorie count, the ladies' luncheon next to us gave us an opportunity to observe each of the desserts. The Cheesecake that day was a luscious looking raspberry. The Pecan-Rolled Ice Cream Balls, served with Vanilla and Cinnamon Ice Cream and topped with Kentucky Bourbon Caramel Sauce, was enough for two people. The Double Mousse Parfait, with its layers of creamy white and dark chocolate, looked wonderful. Temptation almost won out when we saw the Chocolate Lucifer Torte, but for once, we refrained!

CRAB-ROLLED HALIBUT

1 cup finely diced mixed red, green, and
  yellow bell peppers
1 tablespoon chopped fresh basil
1 tablespoon chopped fresh thyme
1½ teaspoons chopped fresh rosemary
1½ pounds jumbo lump crabmeat
1 egg
¼ cup mayonnaise
2¾ cups fresh breadcrumbs, divided
2 tablespoons Old Bay seasoning
1 tablespoon granulated garlic
salt and pepper to taste
5 6-ounce halibut steaks
3 eggs, beaten
Orange-Basil Hollandaise (see next column)

Preheat oven to 375 degrees. Sauté peppers until half cooked. Add chopped herbs and cook until vegetables are al dente. Cool. In a medium bowl, mix by hand the crabmeat, pepper mixture, 1 egg, mayonnaise, ¾ cup of the breadcrumbs, Old Bay, garlic, and salt and pepper. Set aside. Lay out a 12-by-12-inch piece of plastic wrap. Place 1 portion of halibut on plastic, then place another piece of plastic on top of fish. Using a meat mallet, pound halibut into a rectangular shape about 6 inches by 10 inches. Pull off top layer of plastic wrap. Put 6 ounces of crabmeat mixture in middle of halibut. Fold short ends of halibut to cover about ¼ of the crabmeat. Firmly but delicately roll up halibut around crabmeat. Repeat with other halibut steaks. Dunk rolled halibut in beaten eggs, then roll in remaining breadcrumbs. In a skillet, sear all sides of halibut until golden brown. Bake until fish is flaky and crabmeat is hot. Slice and place on plates. Drizzle with Orange-Basil Hollandaise. Serves 5.

ORANGE-BASIL HOLLANDAISE

¼ pound fresh basil leaves
2 cups extra-virgin olive oil
1 tablespoon granulated sugar
juice of 3 blood oranges
¼ cup white wine
6 egg yolks
1½ cups clarified butter, warmed
2 teaspoons lemon juice
1 teaspoon cayenne pepper
salt and pepper to taste

Blanch basil and let cool. In a blender, combine basil and olive oil and blend for 5 minutes on high. Strain and set aside. In a small pot or pan over medium heat, combine sugar and orange juice and reduce by half. In a separate stainless-steel bowl, mix wine and egg yolks. Whip over simmering water until yolks form ribbons and triple in volume. Take off heat and gradually add butter, whipping constantly. Add lemon juice, cayenne, and salt and pepper. Set aside in a warm place. Yields approximately 3 cups.

750 MURPHIN RIDGE ROAD
WEST UNION, OH 45693
WWW.MURPHINRIDGEINN.COM
937-544-2263

Turning onto the country lane leading to Murphin Ridge Inn, I immediately felt conspicuous in my red rental car. Amish mothers were out strolling babies, children were playing, and buggies were transporting their inhabitants homeward from the nearby village of Unity. It was quite picturesque. And, as I was soon to find, it was only the beginning of a great evening.

Innkeeper Darryl McKenney greeted me upon my arrival, doing the duties while his wife, Sherry, was out of town. He obviously enjoyed the work, as he mingled among the guests with a refreshing blend of savoir-faire and fun. As Darryl and I explored the property, he hailed guests, built a bonfire, and showed me the original log cabin on the property. The plan is to restore it for conference space. The old smokehouse is now a gift shop. The corncrib still stands, as do a chicken coop and the old well.

Two dinner bells are located at the back of the brick farmhouse, built around 1826. That farmhouse is now the restaurant at Murphin Ridge Inn. The bells were once used to call farm hands to meals, but there is no need of that now, as the cuisine and the ambiance draw customers from quite a distance. Seated at the table next to me were Roy and Joyce Payne, who had driven up from Portsmouth, Ohio. Somehow, during the course of our conversation, Charleston, West Virginia, came up. It turns out that the Paynes, Darryl, and I all have roots there. In fact, Darryl's wife once taught at the high school from which my husband graduated!

Four of the five tables were occupied in the dining room where we were seated. Two of the parties were celebrating birthdays. Darryl serenaded the room with "Happy Birthday"—on the kazoo. Corporate guests were seated across the hall in what is sometimes known as the "Chicken Wing," a room that houses a variety of chicken pictures, antiques, and other bric-a-brac. All the dining rooms are quite elegant in their simplicity. White walls work together with subdued painted woodwork and smooth wooden floors. The Shaker-style dining tables have polished cherry tops that nicely offset the butter yellow place mats and the yellow and rust plaid napkins.

Before being seated, I had glanced at the menu and decided to order the Three Falls Trout, which is sautéed and stuffed with Crab Dressing. The chef, however, suggested that I sample a variety of dishes. A meal here typically starts with soup and a salad. On that evening, the soup was a tasty Vegetable, but I also enjoyed the delicious Creamed Onion. All three of the entrées—April's Chicken, the Three Falls Trout, and e. e.'s Pork Tenderloin—

were fabulous. It was fortunate that I sampled lightly, because dessert soon followed, again in triplicate—West Virginia Bluebarb Crisp (an unusual combination of blueberries and rhubarb), Chocolate Fondue (served with bananas, strawberries, bite-sized pieces of cake, and a Shortbread Spoon), and Lemon Baby Cake (filled with Sweet Cream, surrounded by Lemon Sauce, and topped with Candied Kumquats). Choosing a favorite would have been impossible.

As I left, anxious to tell Karen about what she'd missed, the midwestern sky was a vivid pink. What could have been more perfect after my Murphin Ridge experience than rounding a corner, crossing a covered bridge, and heading off into a glorious sunset?

CREAMED ONION SOUP

6 large sweet onions, thinly sliced
1 stick butter
8 cups chicken stock
2 cups heavy cream
2 cups grated Parmesan cheese
salt and white pepper to taste

In a stockpot, sauté onions in butter until transparent but not brown. Add enough stock to cover by at least 2 inches. Cook until tender. Remove half of mixture from pot and place in a blender. Purée until smooth. Add puréed mixture back into stockpot. Add cream and Parmesan. Heat through but do not boil. Season with salt and white pepper. Thin with additional stock if necessary. Serves 8.

FOGGY BOTTOM PANCAKES

½ cup cornmeal
½ cup whole-wheat flour
½ cup oatmeal
1½ cups white flour
½ tablespoon baking powder
½ tablespoon baking soda
½ tablespoon salt
1 tablespoon sugar
3 eggs
3 cups buttermilk
⅜ cup canola oil
whole milk as required
maple syrup
stewed apples

Combine dry ingredients in a medium bowl. In a separate bowl, combine eggs, buttermilk, and oil. Pour wet ingredients into bowl with dry ingredients and stir to combine. Thin mixture with milk if necessary. Cook pancakes on a hot, oiled griddle. Serve with maple syrup and stewed apples. Yields 8 to 12 pancakes.

BARN RESTAURANT AT
HISTORIC

Sauder Village

STATE ROUTE 2
ARCHBOLD, OH 43502
WWW.SAUDERVILLAGE.COM
419-445-2231

In 1861, a large bank barn was built on the Stutzman farmstead by an Amish crew. The property was passed on to Moses J. Stutzman, then to his daughter and son-in-law, Della and Louis Riegsecker. By the time their children inherited the property, the barn was sadly run-down, an anomaly in a land of pristine farms and outbuildings. As with many of the buildings we see in our travels, it was scheduled for destruction. However, about that same time, a local industrialist and entrepreneur was saving and restoring old buildings as a hobby during his retirement. His intent was to create a living-history village bearing his name.

When Erie Sauder came to look at the old barn, he saw not the gaping holes and rotted siding but the hand-hewn timbers within. Mr. Sauder envisioned a restaurant growing from the remaining bits of woodwork. Soon, the top story of the barn was loaded onto steel beams and dollies for a two-mile trek across frozen fields to proudly take its place in Sauder Village.

The portion of the old barn that Mr. Sauder rescued was once used for hay and straw storage and as a play area for many of Mr. Stutzman's descendants. It was easy to envision the youngsters of prior generations wrestling and playing hide-and-seek here. Many transients also found their way to this barn for a bit of rest. They were called "tramps" and "hobos" by much of society, but the Riegseckers always called them "walkers" and were never surprised to find one curled up in the hay.

At the ripe young age of 115, the barn opened its doors not for livestock but for dinner guests. The granary of yesteryear is now a dining room that seats up to twenty-five. The rope-and-pulley system is still overhead, as are authentic wagon wheel chandeliers designed by Erie Sauder.

The menu is almost as lengthy as the barn's illustrious history. Diners can choose from several appetizers and eight salad selections, including the salad bar. There are no fewer than seventeen sandwich options and thirteen dinner choices. The dinners, such as Roasted Chicken and Butterflied Pork Chops, are served with hot rolls, Apple Butter, and numerous side dishes. The restaurant also offers a daily buffet and family-style dining, a very affordable option for families eating out.

Erie Sauder was certainly a visionary not only in his care of the barn but in his building of the village. Here, professional craftsmen use the skills of their ancestors in plying their trades. Costumed interpreters amid period furnishings tell the story of the pioneer men and women who drained the Great Black

Swamp, transforming it into some of America's most fertile farmland.

HAM LOAF

1 cup finely diced onion
1 cup finely diced celery
2 tablespoons butter
1 sleeve saltines, crushed
4 eggs
1 teaspoon salt
2½ pounds ground ham
1¼ pounds ground beef
1¼ pounds ground sausage
½ cup milk
½ cup water
¼ cup honey
¼ cup mustard

Preheat oven to 350 degrees. Sauté onions and celery in butter until tender and slightly cooked. In a large bowl, combine saltines, eggs, and salt. Stir in onions and celery. Add meats and mix well. Stir in milk and water. Continue mixing until smooth. Place mixture into 2 loaf pans. Bake for approximately 1½ hours. Combine honey and mustard in a small bowl. Spread on top of loaves after baking. Return to oven for 10 minutes. Slice. Serves 20.

PORK LOIN

6-pound pork loin, trimmed
salt to taste
garlic powder to taste
pepper to taste
Apple Chutney (see below)

Preheat oven to 350 degrees. Season pork with salt, garlic powder, and pepper. Place in a baking pan with sides. Bake for 45 minutes to 1 hour. This will cook meat medium-well, leaving it still tender and juicy. Slice pork into ⅜-inch-thick medallions. Arrange medallions on a platter, top with Apple Chutney, and serve. Serves 12.

APPLE CHUTNEY

¼ cup red wine vinegar
½ cup brown sugar
1 teaspoon ground cloves
1 teaspoon nutmeg
½ teaspoon cinnamon
1 teaspoon minced garlic
4 cups peeled and diced apples
¼ cup raisins

Combine first 6 ingredients and cook on low in a large saucepan until well mixed. Add apples and raisins. Cook approximately 4 hours. This is best when made ahead. If made ahead, chutney should be refrigerated, then warmed before use. Yields approximately 2 cups.

CHAPTER 10
Paths to Freedom

Emmitt House

Harriet Beecher Stowe, author of *Uncle Tom's Cabin*, was a Cincinnati resident. The book, which relates the story of an escaping slave and one of the stops she finds on the Underground Railroad, was born out of a visit that Harriet made to Kentucky. She was so moved by the conditions she witnessed in her first experience with slavery that she returned to Ohio to pen the story. The establishments in this chapter are linked by their role as stops on the Underground Railroad, where slaves on the run from authorities in the South could rest before continuing their quest for freedom.

SPREAD EAGLE TAVERN
10150 HISTORIC PLYMOUTH STREET
HANOVERTON, OH 44423
WWW.SPREADEAGLETAVERN.COM
330-223-1583

With one quick turn off US Route 30 onto Historic Plymouth Street, the modern world disappears. It wouldn't have surprised me if my minivan had been transformed into a horse and carriage without a single abracadabra having been uttered. At the end of the block sits the Spread Eagle Tavern. Access to the restaurant is around back, where guests enter through an adorable log cabin. This is the restored stable of the property, rebuilt by owner Pete Johnson from authentic materials of the era. Booth seating has been crafted from old horse stalls, and a cozy nook holds the old blacksmith's fireplace. The tables were handcrafted, as was the cherry paneling on the walls. If you know where to look in a piece of wood near the door, you'll see part of a bullet found by the craftsman as he planed the wood. The slug was buried deep in a tree on his property, which he cut for this specific purpose.

As I toured, I found one dining room as interesting as the next. The one with the large kitchen fireplace is particularly homey. Through that room and into the main part of the old inn is the Hanover Room. One of the photos on the wall is of the daughter of the first owner. According to many reports, her presence is still felt. She was quite a music student in her day and is still credited with playing the piano at odd times and with turning radios on and off inexplicably.

Across the street is Dr. Robertson's house, once a stop on the Underground Railroad. The home was built with a secret room accessible only from an exterior second-story window. Dr. Robertson didn't accept payment for his services to escaping slaves. Instead, they were required to rob graves and bring back the cadavers to further the doctor's study of his profession. Tunnels connected the doctor's house to others on the street, including the Spread Eagle Tavern.

Downstairs in the tavern is Gideon Gaver's Rathskeller, where the old tunnels and crawlspaces are lined with bricks from Mr. Gaver's mansion. Pete Johnson dismantled the home, cleaned the bricks, refired them for strength, and then put them to use in this lovely series of rooms. Upstairs once again, I ordered the Country Pâté, served with gherkins and Lingonberry Sauce. It was delicious but quite a large serving, so I saved half to share with Karen, who was unable to accompany me. That was followed by the excellent Sierra Salad.

As I munched, I contemplated what the politicians might have chosen when they were here. Republicans as far back as Abraham Lincoln have visited. George W. Bush even paid a visit while stumping the campaign trail in 2000. Regardless of guests' political affiliations, the fabulous ambiance and wonderful food of the Spread Eagle Tavern are things everyone can agree upon.

CHICKEN POT PIE

1 stick butter
2 cups diced onion
2 cups diced carrots
2 cups diced celery
1 tablespoon chopped fresh thyme
1 bay leaf
¼ cup flour
8 cups chicken stock
2 cups diced potatoes
2½ pounds chicken breasts, boned and diced
1 cup cream
1 cup frozen peas
salt and pepper to taste
4 sheets puff pastry

Melt butter in a large saucepan. Add onions, carrots, celery, thyme, and bay leaf. Sweat vegetables but do not burn. Add flour and stir. Add chicken stock, potatoes, chicken, cream, and peas. Stir. Simmer for 15 minutes. Add salt and pepper. Cut puff pastry to size required for top of individual pot-pie dishes. Place pastry on a greased cookie sheet and bake as per directions on package. Divide chicken mixture evenly among 8 individual pot-pie dishes and place a baked pastry on top of each. Serve immediately. Serves 8.

SIERRA SALAD

¾ cup olive oil
juice of 1 lime
1 tablespoon poppy seeds
½ teaspoon grated fresh ginger
2 tablespoons vinegar
2 tablespoons soy sauce
8-ounce bag mixed greens
1 cup crumbled feta cheese
1 cup Chinese noodles
1 cup pecans, roasted

In a large mixing bowl, whisk together oil, lime juice, poppy seeds, ginger, vinegar, and soy sauce. Just before serving, whisk once more. Add remaining ingredients and toss gently until all greens are coated. Serves 8.

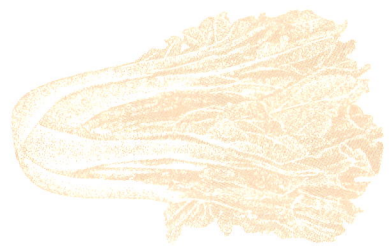

EMMITT HOUSE

1861

123 NORTH MARKET STREET
WAVERLY, OH 45690
WWW.EMMITTHOUSE.COM
740-947-2181

When the Ohio & Erie Canal was completed in 1832, James Emmitt quickly saw its business potential. Over the next twenty years, he made a fortune hauling grain, operating a mill, and building a distillery. Even with all this development, he felt like Waverly's economic growth would be limited as long as the county courthouse was located in Piketon. He and a group of Waverly businessmen agreed to finance the process of petitioning the Ohio General Assembly in an effort to convince it to move the county seat, a goal they later accomplished.

Emmitt was so sure of his eventual success that he commissioned a new hotel to be built along the canal at the corner of Water and Market streets. In the construction of the hotel, Emmitt employed a master carpenter who had come to Pike County in the early 1830s. The superb workmanship of Madison Hemings was unparalleled in the area. Not only is Hemings of interest because of his skill, but also because of his parentage. It was rumored at the time—and never denied—

that he was the son of Thomas Jefferson and a slave by the name of Sally Hemings. Research over the years has further substantiated that lineage.

Upon completion, the Emmitt House quickly developed a reputation as a fine hotel. It was a particular favorite of hardware and dry-goods salesmen, who would display their sample cases in the front room, known as the Drummer's Room.

Today, that room is still known by the same name, though it contains a dining area rather than wares. There are several other dining rooms as well, including The Lounge with its large mural of area sights, The New Room, which is not so new anymore, though the name stuck, and the Bar and Booth area. Through the lobby in the same part of the hotel as the Drummer's Room are The Parlor and The Canal Room, where we were seated. The Canal Room boasts lovely patterned tin walls, in addition to the tin ceiling also visible in the other dining rooms.

Karen chose the Mexican Chicken, served with side dishes of Spanish Rice and tortilla chips topped with melted cheese. It was delicious. Debbie chose the Warm Cashew Chicken Salad, served with a wonderfully moist Carrot Muffin. When it came time for dessert, Karen's eyes were immediately alight when she noticed the Fried Ice Cream on the menu.

Prior to dinner, we'd toured the old hotel from top to bottom. In the basement, we saw the doorway that led to a tunnel stretching under US Route 23. Locals believe it was intended for escaping slaves, allowing them to move between the hotel and Emmitt's office and home down the street. We didn't meet the female ghost that many staff members and the bank employees next door have experienced. Don't let the faces at the upper windows fool you. They're just a touch of whimsy left over from previous owners.

EMMITT HOUSE CHILI

3½ pounds ground beef
1 large onion, chopped
⅓ green pepper, chopped
⅓ red pepper, chopped
2 pounds canned crushed tomatoes
1 packet taco seasoning
2 cups salsa
2½ tablespoons sugar

Brown ground beef in a large pot until slightly pink. Add onions and peppers and cook over medium heat until beef is thoroughly cooked. Drain. Return mixture to pot and add remaining ingredients. Simmer slowly for at least 1 hour, stirring frequently. Serves 10 to 12.

MEAT SAUCE FOR SPAGHETTI

1 medium onion, diced
1 medium clove garlic, minced
2 tablespoons olive oil
1½ pounds ground beef
1 pound sausage
3 cups chopped fresh tomatoes
1½ pounds canned crushed tomatoes
2 cups tomato purée
2½ tablespoons sugar
2 tablespoons chopped fresh parsley
2 tablespoons oregano
1½ tablespoons salt
½ tablespoon pepper
1 bay leaf

In a large pot, cook onions and garlic in olive oil until tender. Add beef and sausage and cook until no pink remains. Remove from heat and drain. Return mixture to pot and add remaining ingredients. Cook over medium heat for about 1 hour. Discard bay leaf. Serves 10.

8092 COLUMBIA ROAD
OLMSTED FALLS, OH 44233
440-235-1223

Clementine's was originated by two very enterprising women, Anne Shier Klintworth and Doris Rundle. They began by managing their own wholesale bakery, creating a large number of cakes and pastries for local hotels and restaurants. However, they wanted to sell their wares directly to the general public and thought that a Victorian tearoom would be ideal. Started as a place that served soup and bread, high tea, and a selection of wonderful teas and coffees, Clementine's was very soon a great success. Gradually, the menu was expanded to include sandwiches and salads, and a Victorian restaurant emerged.

Today, Clementine's is located in the very center of Grand Pacific Junction. This small area is filled with beautiful historic buildings and interesting shops, all linked by brick walkways. The buildings have been lovingly restored by Clint Williams, who owns the local realty company. The largest building is the Grand Pacific Hotel, built in the 1830s. Constructed as a girls' seminary, it was moved across the river to its current location in 1858 and is rumored to have been a stop on the Underground Railroad. Clementine's is located in a late-1800s building that was at one time a livery stable for visitors to the Grand Pacific Hotel.

We sat in the back parlor, known as the Garden Room. This charming room has its original wide-plank floors and an overhanging hayloft above the sliding livery door. It is attractively decorated with tables and chairs and hanging plants. Small rugs and just a hint or two of lace at the windows and on the mantels give the room a warm, cozy feel. The tall loft ladder set against the wall in one corner of the room reminds guests of the original use of the building.

We talked with Doris about her love for this old building as we sipped our choice of teas—traditional Earl Grey Tea with just a hint of bergamot oil for Karen and a refreshing Berry Jubilee Tea for Debbie. Several soups and a large number of salads and sandwiches are on the menu. Debbie enjoyed her Broccoli Quiche, made with Clementine's Hash Brown Potato Crust and served with a large helping of seasonal fresh fruit. Karen chose the Roasted Eggplant Sandwich, which was made with roasted red peppers and Basil Aioli and served with creamy Macaroni Salad. The list of desserts was enormous. We had considerable difficulty in choosing just one to sample. Eventually, we got up from our table and wandered out to the cake case in the shop to see the marvelous selection for ourselves. Finally selecting a Lemon Tart to share, we were not disappointed. The pastry was crumbly, and the lemon filling was tangy and mouth-wateringly good.

There is plenty to see here. Guests enjoy not only the fabulous pastries they can purchase and take home but also the shelves and tables upstairs stocked with fine china and Victoriana. The large glass-fronted case at the bottom of the staircase contains the most delectable homemade chocolates. We bet you won't be able to resist one!

GRANDMA'S STUFFED CABBAGE SOUP

2 cups diced onions
1½ pounds ground beef
3 tablespoons olive oil
½ cup brown sugar
1 small head cabbage, diced
2 14½-ounce cans diced tomatoes
4 cups beef broth
2 28-ounce cans tomato sauce
1 tablespoon lemon juice
2 cups cooked white rice
salt and freshly ground pepper to taste
croutons for garnish

In a large soup pot, sauté onions and ground beef in oil until meat is browned. Do not drain. Add sugar and cabbage and mix well. Add next 4 ingredients and bring to a boil. Reduce heat and simmer for 1 to 1½ hours. Add rice and simmer 10 more minutes. Season with salt and pepper and garnish with croutons. Serves 12.

SAUSAGE AND FENNEL SOUP WITH PASTA

1 pound sweet Italian sausage
1 bulb fennel
¾ cup diced onions
1½ teaspoons minced garlic
3 tablespoons olive oil
14½-ounce can diced tomatoes
14½-ounce can crushed tomatoes
4 cups chicken broth
¾ cup orzo
2 cups fresh spinach, stemmed and torn into small pieces
salt and freshly ground pepper to taste
Asiago cheese for garnish

In a large skillet, sauté sausage until well browned, breaking into small pieces. Drain sausage and set aside. Cut off top of fennel. Wash and dice white part of bulb. Sauté fennel, onions, and garlic in olive oil until onions are soft and translucent. Add diced tomatoes, crushed tomatoes, and chicken broth. Bring to a boil, then reduce heat and simmer for 25 minutes. Add sausage and orzo and cook until orzo is just done. Add spinach and cook another 3 minutes. Season with salt and pepper and garnish with Asiago. Serves 12.

Rider's 1812 Inn

792 MENTOR AVENUE
PAINESVILLE, OH 44077
WWW.RIDERSINN.COM
440-354-8200

The Prime Rib and the Potato Leek Soup are house specialties, made from recipes found in the attic of this structure. The inn, built by Joseph Rider, is situated along US Route 20, which was once the Oregon Trail. Stagecoach stops were located every sixty to seventy miles—the distance a horse could travel in a day. Registers from the inn show that as many as one hundred guests were there in a single day. How this was accomplished in the limited space available is quite a puzzlement until you consider that many of the stagecoach drivers stayed only about four hours, just long enough to bathe, eat, and catch a couple of hours of shuteye on narrow benches upstairs. The rooms for today's guests are much more attractive, spacious, and comfortable.

Mr. Rider came to the area as part of a surveying team for the Connecticut Land Company. He was accompanied by Mr. Moses Cleveland, Mr. Willoughby, and Mr. Paine. Their efforts made Lake County the first planned urban community in the world. We found the history behind this absolutely fascinating. Much of Connecticut was pro-British, the government of the colony technically being a proprietorship of the king. Prior to and during the Revolutionary War, the primary currency was pounds sterling. Of course, after the war, that currency was worthless here, and an alternate way to pay the soldiers was needed. The Connecticut Land Company had investors from other states, and so had acceptable currency. The company purchased property in this area, which it used to pay the soldiers. Within five years of beginning their endeavor, these gentlemen had taken the area from log cabins to clapboard houses and an organized system of streets.

The War of 1812 impacted the area, too. A local army company was commissioned into the navy. The members of that company were attacked at Put-In Bay before they had been trained in naval tactics, so they fought as soldiers would. This caught the British quite by surprise, resulting in an American victory.

Rider's 1812 Inn also figured prominently in the Underground Railroad. Estimates indicate that three thousand slaves went through its basement. Participation in the abolitionist movement in this area was multifaceted. Some chose to help because of their abhorrence of slavery. Others, tired of being undersold by crops from slave states, participated in the Underground Railroad in an attempt to reduce competition for their Ohio crops, farmed with paid labor.

The table in the main dining room at which we were seated was above one of the basement tunnels used for escape. The room was decorated with light blue and cream wainscoting. Karen enjoyed the creamy Lemon Cake and Debbie reveled in the White Chocolate Raspberry Cheesecake as we discovered one historical fact after another. Our favorite piece of information concerned Harvey Johnson. Mr. Johnson was a slave who made his way to freedom via the inn. After the Civil War, he returned to Painesville, where his son and grandson became successful businessmen. Wendell Walker, his great-great-grandson, served as the president of Painesville's city council. Now, that's a success story.

ORANGE ROUGHY STUFFED WITH SMOKED SALMON MOUSSE

4 ounces smoked salmon
1 egg
¼ cup heavy whipping cream
salt and pepper to taste
brandy to taste
2 4- to 6-ounce orange roughy fillets

Purée salmon in a food processor. Add egg and cream. Add salt and pepper and brandy. Blend well. Set aside and chill. Preheat oven to 350 degrees. Grease a baking pan. Spoon mousse equally into center of fillets. Roll and secure. Bake for 8 to 10 minutes. Serves 2.

FROSTED PUMPKIN PECAN DROP COOKIES

2 sticks butter, room temperature
1 egg
1 cup canned pumpkin
1 cup sugar
1 teaspoon cinnamon
½ teaspoon salt
⅛ teaspoon allspice
2 cups all-purpose flour
1 teaspoon baking soda
1 cup pecans
¾ stick butter, melted
1 cup brown sugar
2 cups powdered sugar
1 teaspoon vanilla

Preheat oven to 350 degrees. Cream together butter and egg. When light and fluffy, add pumpkin, sugar, cinnamon, salt, and allspice. Mix in flour, baking soda, and pecans and blend until smooth. Drop by teaspoonfuls onto a baking sheet. You won't need to leave a lot of space between cookies, as they won't spread. Bake for 8 to 10 minutes. Remove from oven and allow to cool. In a small saucepan, cook melted butter and brown sugar until smooth. Blend with powdered sugar and vanilla. Cool slightly before using. Frost cooled cookies. Yields approximately 4 dozen cookies.

Note: Recipes reproduced with permission of Rider's 1812 Inn.

DON'S POMEROY HOUSE

13664 PEARL ROAD
STRONGSVILLE, OH 44136
WWW.DONSPOMEROY.COM
440-572-1111

Ebenezer Pomeroy and his wife, Violatra, introduced "Pomeroy hospitality" when they opened a tavern in 1822. Their son, Alanson, and his wife, Keziah, continued the tradition after Ebenezer met his death, thrown from a wagon when his horse shied.

Alanson was active in community affairs as a Strongsville trustee and justice of the peace. In 1850, three years after building a large manor house, he established the Strongsville General Store adjacent to his home. This area was known as Town Square, because it was here that people met and socialized. Men pulled chairs up to the potbelly stove at the store, waiting for the stagecoach to bring the newspaper, which Alanson's ten-year-old daughter would read.

The citizens of Strongsville were avid supporters of the abolitionist cause. "Pomeroy hospitality" extended to escaping slaves. Harlan Pomeroy recalled seeing his mother carrying trays of food to the cellar. At the time, no explanation was given to the children. Later, Alanson explained to Harlan that slaves were brought from Oberlin by night, hidden in a load of hay. They were then harbored in the cellar until notice was received that a "Freedom Boat" would be leaving. The runaways were loaded again amid the hay and taken to nearby Rocky Road, where they boarded a boat bound for Canada.

The Pomeroys opened their home at every turn, including Sunday afternoons. Many members of the Congregation church traveled too far to go home between the morning and afternoon services. Those families were invited to share Sunday dinner with the Pomeroys before returning to worship.

Members of the family lived in the home until Gertrude, granddaughter of Alanson, moved to Florida in 1963. Left empty, the structure quickly began to decline. In 1966, during preparations for the town's sesquicentennial, the local Women's League developed a plan to open the house for viewing. Donations came from all corners of the community, but the effort failed to raise enough money to save the home. A second open house was held, but by the early 1970s, efforts to prevent its destruction seemed hopeless.

In June 1975, about the same time that the home went on the National Register of Historic Places, Don Strong realized the potential of the property as a restaurant. Restoration began in 1979. It included revitalizing the original interior woodwork around the doors and windows. The stair rail had to be re-created from the example of a single spindle found floating in the flooded basement.

We were seated in deep wing chairs at a cozy table in the main dining room, known as "The Library." Across the room were booth areas, each its own separate nook complete with book-laden shelves. A large fireplace at one end of the room and rich cherry paneling completed the warm ambiance.

Seafood is the house specialty, with

choices changing daily. The Voodoo Shrimp—bacon-wrapped shrimp roasted with Jamaican Curry Marinade—made our mouths water. Never one to pass up mangoes, Karen ordered the Mango Shrimp Salad, which was beautifully presented and equally delicious. The spirit of "Pomeroy hospitality" lives on in this place full of history and excellent food.

SAMBUCA-SEARED DIVER SCALLOPS

¼ cup olive oil
20 scallops
½ cup flour
¼ cup sambuca
Roasted Red Pepper Brie Cream (see below)
fresh greens

Heat olive oil in a sauté pan over medium heat. Dust scallops lightly in flour. Sauté scallops until brown. Pour sambuca into pan to deglaze. On each of 4 plates, place 5 scallops in a pool of Roasted Red Pepper Brie Cream. Garnish with fresh greens or other items of choice. Serves 4 as an appetizer.

ROASTED RED PEPPER BRIE CREAM

2 tablespoons vegetable oil
½ teaspoon minced fresh garlic

1 tablespoon roasted and diced shallots
2 cups heavy cream
½ cup lobster stock
6-ounce wheel Brie with rind
1 tablespoon tomato paste
2 roasted red peppers, chopped
1 tablespoon chopped fresh thyme
salt and pepper to taste

Heat oil in a medium saucepan and lightly brown garlic. Add shallots, cream, and stock. Reduce by half and remove from heat. Stir in Brie, tomato paste, roasted peppers, and thyme. Purée in a blender until smooth. Add salt and pepper. Yields approximately 2 cups.

MANGO SHRIMP SALAD

1 pound 70-110 count shrimp,
    cooked, shelled, and deveined
1 cup mayonnaise
1 cup diced mango
½ cup chopped pecans
⅓ cup raisins
½ bunch scallions, finely diced
2 teaspoons minced cilantro
¼ cup honey
1 tablespoon finely diced red onion
mixed greens

Blot shrimp with a towel to remove excess moisture. Combine all ingredients except greens. Refrigerate. Serve atop mixed greens or as desired. Serves 4.

Dante's PIZZA & PASTA House

261 WEST HIGH AVENUE
NEW PHILADELPHIA, OH 44663
330-339-4444

Local residents remember the house at 261 West High Avenue as the Board of Education Building. Others have known it as the Evans or the Broadhurst Funeral Home. Today, it is Dante's Pizza & Pasta House.

At one time, Augustus Beyer owned the home. At the age of twenty-two, he entered the milling business in Michigan. In 1862, he returned home to New Philadelphia and continued his profession. He purchased River Mills and established a new milling system, the second "All Roller" mill in Ohio. The mill continued successfully for thirty-five years until fire destroyed it in 1897. Beyer rebounded by building the Tuscarawas Electric Power and Light Company on the same site. He received an exclusive contract to furnish electric lights to the communities of Canal Dover (now Dover) and New Philadelphia, which resulted in New Philadelphia's being labeled the "Best Lighted City in Ohio." The first home to receive electricity was that of Beyer himself.

He purchased the home in 1884 from George Dougherty, who had owned the property since 1848. The exact date of construction is unknown, although some records indicate the 1860s. Features of the house discovered during renovation for Dante's Pizza suggest that it was built slightly earlier. A tunnel leads from the basement away from the house, under what is now the parking lot. During the construction of the parking lot, a piece of machinery tipped into a room-sized space when the earth gave way. Dan Drabik, who owns Dante's with his wife, Betty, asked around to see if anyone knew about the room. A few stories circulated about escaping slaves being hidden there. Others had heard about a rock garden in that location with a large rock that pivoted to cover a hole leading to the tunnel.

The history of this home-cum-restaurant so fascinated Betty Drabik that she purchased a 1908 Tuscarawas County atlas. The book contained photos of prominent businessmen and their homes, as well as information about their personal histories. We flipped through it in the most private of the restaurant's three dining rooms. Lace curtains and valences softened the windows. Original wainscoting lined the wall, and a built-in cupboard still stood in the corner. The wooden mantelpiece piqued our curiosity because it's said to have a secret compartment. Karen looked for that compartment, convinced of its location by a directional clue incorporated in the surrounding tile. The other dining rooms were equally attractive. The front one was graced with a beautiful black marble fireplace.

We were treated to several delicious

items and can't wait to go back for more. We started with slices of Italian Sausage Braid and Roasted Vegetable Bread. Both were absolutely fabulous. We brought half of each home to our most appreciative families. We also sampled a delicious Chicken Breast marinated in the unique House Dressing. It, too, was yummy. Wonderfully gracious about our sampling, Betty sent along pieces of the tasty homemade pies being served that day—Caramel Apple and Strawberry Rhubarb. Enjoying them later in the day allowed us to experience Dante's that much longer.

BRUSCHETTA

24 slices Ciabatta or Italian bread
2 tablespoons olive oil
4 cups diced Roma tomatoes
¼ cup finely chopped onion
1 cup chopped parsley
1 tablespoon minced garlic
¼ teaspoon coarsely ground pepper
½ teaspoon salt
2 teaspoons Italian seasoning
2 tablespoons chopped fresh basil
½ cup shredded Romano cheese
20 to 24 slices provolone cheese

Brush bread lightly with olive oil. Toast bread. In a large bowl, combine all remaining ingredients except cheeses. Spoon onto toasted bread. Sprinkle with Romano. Top with provolone and broil just until cheese melts. Yields 2 dozen Bruschetta slices.

ITALIAN VEGETABLE SOUP

1 pound Italian sausage
2 cups chopped onion
3 cloves finely chopped garlic
6 cups beef consommé
6 cups water
1½ cups chopped Roma tomatoes
1 cup prepared spaghetti sauce
¼ teaspoon pepper
1 teaspoon Italian seasoning
4 carrots, pared, sliced, and steamed
1½ cups chopped zucchini
15-ounce can garbanzo beans, drained
8 ounces rotini pasta, cooked and drained

In a large pot, brown sausage, onions, and garlic. Drain fat. Add consommé, water, tomatoes, sauce, pepper, and Italian seasoning. Bring to a boil. Reduce heat and add carrots, zucchini, beans, and pasta. Heat through. Serves 10 to 12.

Brandywine Inn

204 SOUTH MAIN STREET
MONROE, OH 45050
WWW.BRANDYWINEOFMONROE.COM
513-779-4747

The Brandywine Inn was once reputed to be the tallest building for miles around. Today, its white-painted brick exterior and stacked-stone retaining walls invite visitors to step back in time to stagecoach days. Built in 1850 by David Boggs, it was originally a stop on the Great Miami Turnpike, which ran between Cincinnati and Dayton. The ground floor was constructed into a steep hillside, forming a large, cavelike room at one end. Local legend has it that this hidden room was used to harbor slaves escaping from the South. The Red Onion Tavern was also housed on this floor. An enormous picture of an onion was displayed outside to announce the tavern's location to its many patrons—and to slaves who could not read the written signs. There was no access to the inn from the tavern. Overnight guests had to climb the stone stairway at the rear of the building to enter the main doors. This floor housed the dining

rooms and kitchen. Guest rooms were on the third floor. On the top floor, a large hall accommodated visiting lecturers and traveling road shows. Alas, that room no longer exists. In the early 1900s, there was a fire on the top floor. The owner took the opportunity to remove the walls and reroof the building, since it was slowly sinking into the ground, thanks to its heavy, twelve-inch-thick walls.

Today, there are three dining rooms on the second floor. Debbie was unable to accompany me the day I visited. I sat in the farthest original room, which has exposed brick and rough-paneled walls. The doorways are framed with planks of wood from the original floor, complete with square-headed nails. The flickering lamps reflect off the highly polished surfaces, giving a cozy, intimate feel to the room.

The current owners, George and Doris Bernas, wanted to create a haven for fine dining and to make the evening meal the highlight of their guests' day. To that end, the inn serves a prix fixe dinner. The chef changes the menu every week, and the inn boasts that he has not repeated a menu in more than twenty years!

The meal began with a Phyllo Triangle stuffed with wild mushrooms, olives, and goat cheese. It was a tangy and flavorful start to an entirely delicious meal. My waiter, Anthony, was professional and swift, describing each course as it arrived. A tart Cranberry Ice followed, then an entrée of Roasted Pork Loin with Hazelnut Sausage Stuffing. The serving size was restrained, allowing me to finish each course with an expectation of being able to indulge in dessert. Chef George had concocted sweet pastry topped with baked apples, walnuts, and dried cherries and served with homemade Vanilla Ice Cream. I chatted with the charming couple at the next table, who had been eating at the inn once a week for the past eighteen years. Everyone agreed that George and Doris have created a haven of which to be proud.

MAKE-AHEAD TURKEY BREAST

8 cups turkey stock
6-pound whole turkey breast, skinned
1 teaspoon olive oil
½ teaspoon dried thyme
¼ teaspoon salt
¼ teaspoon garlic powder
¼ teaspoon pepper
Herb Stuffing (see next column)

In a large stockpot, bring stock to a boil and add turkey breast. Return to a boil, then reduce heat and simmer for about 1½ hours until turkey reaches 170 degrees. Remove turkey from stock, cover, and refrigerate until needed.

Preheat oven to 250 degrees. Rub surface of turkey with oil, then sprinkle with seasonings. Wrap turkey tightly in foil and bake for about 2 hours until thoroughly heated. To serve, remove turkey breast from bone and slice. Serve with Herb Stuffing. Serves 6.

HERB STUFFING

1 stick butter
1 cup diced onion
1 cup diced celery
16 cups stale bread cubes
2 teaspoons poultry seasoning
1 teaspoon dried thyme
½ teaspoon salt
½ teaspoon garlic powder
½ teaspoon dried tarragon
½ teaspoon dried rubbed sage
¼ teaspoon pepper
2½ cups turkey stock

Preheat oven to 250 degrees. In a large Dutch oven, melt butter over medium-high heat. Add onions and celery and sauté for 3 minutes. Stir in bread cubes and seasonings. Add stock and bake for 1 hour and 55 minutes. This can be baked at same time as Turkey Breast. Serves 6 generously.

SPIRITS BISTRO AT SNOW HILL
11093 STATE ROUTE 73
NEW VIENNA, OH 45159
WWW.SNOWHILLCOUNTRYCLUB.COM
937-987-2491

If you enjoy a good ghost story, then plan to visit Snow Hill during the fall as the staff hosts its "Dinner and a Ghost" events. Another opportunity to experience the phenomenon is via the Haunted Midnight Lantern Ghost Tours. During the lantern tours, participants are actually included in on-site research conducted by Ghost Investigations of Ohio. Shelly Suitor, one of the principal investigators, states that there is no anecdotal information indicating any unusual tragedy, illness, or death that would explain the significant paranormal activities that have been reported. Yet patrons and employees have story after story of unusual occurrences, while photos and film footage taken on site have captured additional activity.

The history of the structure dates back to the 1820s, when Catherine and William Harris came west from Snow Hill, Maryland. Over the course of five years, the couple built Snow Hill as a travel lodge designed to ac-

commodate travelers whose sights were set on locations even farther west than Ohio. The inn was immediately successful and quickly became Clinton County's social hub. Local lore also indicates that the inn became a stop on the Underground Railroad, a possibility reinforced by a tunnel running at one time from Snow Hill's basement to another home located almost a mile away.

Snow Hill continued its service as a popular gathering spot. Catering to golf enthusiasts and the area's elite, a country club was established in 1924. It was used as a private club into the 1980s, when the recession and the draw of exclusive clubs caused a decline in membership. In order to save the business, the golf course was opened to the general public and the dining facility focused on special events.

Ownership changes have inevitably occurred since then, bringing with them significant alterations. The year 2005 saw the opening of Spirits Bistro, a full-service restaurant serving lunch and dinner in the old Harris home, whose brick is now painted a crisp white. Just inside the door is the first of the dining rooms, clad in traditional navy and hunter green, with windows festooned in Federal-style valences. An antique chest of drawers, antique mirrors, two fireplaces, and framed prints of George Washington add to the historic feel. The second dining room is bedecked in raspberry wallpaper and contains both an original fireplace and the original staircase to the second floor. Doors with wrought-iron hardware add to the historic ambiance.

The lunch menu offers a variety of salads and a lengthy list of sandwiches, including a Baked Italian Sub, a French Dip, and my perennial favorite, Pulled Pork Barbecue. The Rum-Fired Shrimp with Southwestern Dressing caught the eye of my daughter, Dori. She was my traveling companion for this visit, since Karen had other commitments back in Pittsburgh. The dinner menu has traditional appeal, offering selections such as Cranberry Barbecue Chicken, Shrimp and Scallop Linguine, Honey Pecan Chicken, and Beef Tips Hunter.

Today, guests at Snow Hill Country Club can enjoy not only a round of golf but also a tasty meal at Spirits Bistro—or a good ghost story. Several guest rooms have been added on the second floor, making Snow Hill a getaway destination.

KEY LIME PIE

2 cups graham cracker crumbs
¼ cup sugar
1 stick butter, melted
4 14-ounce cans sweetened condensed milk
12 egg yolks
1 cup Key lime juice
zest and juice of 2 limes
1 teaspoon vanilla extract

Preheat oven to 325 degrees. Combine graham cracker crumbs, sugar, and butter. Press into the bottom of a lightly greased 10-inch cake pan. In a large bowl, combine remaining ingredients with a hand mixer until smooth. Pour over crust. Bake for 15 to 20 minutes until center is set. Cool thoroughly before serving. Serves 6 to 8.

BOURBON-GLAZED TUNA

¾ cup bourbon
½ cup soy sauce
½ cup water
2 cups granulated sugar
4 8-ounce tuna steaks
¼ cup vegetable oil

Combine bourbon, soy sauce, water, and sugar. Simmer over medium-low heat until mixture is thick enough to coat the back of a spoon or until a candy thermometer reads 220 degrees. Cool and reserve. To prepare tuna, brush steaks with vegetable oil. Grill to desired doneness. Brush steaks with glaze 2 minutes before removing from grill. Serves 4.

CHAPTER 11
On the Road Again

The General Denver Hotel

When the National Road opened the way west, a good team of oxen could make only ten to twelve miles per day before having to stop and rest. No doubt, the human passengers were equally weary. Horses could do slightly better, but the need for frequent lodging along the major thoroughfares was great. Highlighted in this chapter are inns and hotels whose registers over the years have read like a veritable who's who, from drovers and past presidents to modern-day guests. Some still provide overnight accommodations, and all serve meals to sate even the hungriest of travelers.

The Worthington Inn

649 HIGH STREET
WORTHINGTON, OH 43085
WWW.WORTHINGTONINN.COM
614-885-2600

In 1816, a Connecticut gentleman by the name of R. W. Cowles came to this part of Ohio to earn his fortune. Two years later, he married Laura Kilbourne, and together they had nine children. For the mere sum of $250, he purchased three lots in Worthington's downtown area. In 1835, he built an impressive residence on the land. Unfortunately, Cowles enjoyed it for only seven years before passing away. During his tenure as a Worthington resident, he was a prominent businessman, a county commissioner, a justice of the peace, and postmaster.

Ten years after Cowles's death, Theodore Fuller purchased and enlarged the home. Two years later, the structure was again sold, this time to William Bishop. Under Bishop's ownership, the residence operated as an inn known as The Bishop House. For just a dime, guests were served a meal of beef stew or potato soup, along with biscuits or cornbread. For an additional twenty-five cents, they could spend the night. When the property was purchased by Nicholas Van Loon, the name was changed to the Central Hotel. After just three years, the hotel passed into the hands of Robert Lewis. It became known as the Union

Hotel and later as the Hotel Stand.

In 1889, the building returned to the Van Loon family when it was purchased by Nicholas's son, George, who brought back the name his father had used for the inn. It was during his time at the helm that the third story and the mansard roof were added. A fire had damaged part of the original roof, and George Van Loon thought it was a good opportunity to add a third-floor ballroom. William Van Loon, a member of the third generation of the family, took over from his father in 1926. The family retained ownership until 1936. As with many such structures, changes in ownership happened more frequently than needed maintenance. By 1983, time had taken its toll. But the inherent beauty of the building was evident when the process of restoration began.

We came in out of the snow through the side entrance and up a marble staircase that brought us into a casual eating area. The backbar took up one wall, and another wall was highlighted by a lovely stained-glass picture of the inn. Each of the dining rooms has its own unique décor, in keeping with the history of the structure. The room where we were seated looked out over the wide front porch, marked by a colonnade and a spindled balustrade.

Both the lunch and dinner menus are short but extremely interesting. Karen would choose the Chilled Cucumber Soup—served with smoked salmon, dill, and chives—every time, as it is one of her favorite flavor combinations. Debbie had difficulty choosing between the crunchy Red Oak Salad, sprinkled with candied pecans, goat cheese, and apples, and the Thai Beef Salad, accompanied by soba noodles, marinated shiitake mushrooms, spinach, and pine nuts. The Halibut, coated in an almond and coriander crust, is a favorite choice for dinner guests, as is the Beef Worthington in Cabernet and Oyster Mushroom Sauce. Remember to save room for a delicious Coconut Cream and Green Tea Parfait or a selection of wonderful housemade sorbets. For any meal, the Worthington Inn is worth every bite!

MUSSELS IN CHARDONNAY BROTH

1 teaspoon minced garlic
½ cup diced mushrooms
1 tablespoon olive oil
2 tablespoons chopped cilantro
¼ cup chopped scallions
½ cup diced yellow onion
12 mussels, cleaned
3 tablespoons white wine
1½ teaspoons lime juice
1 teaspoon ground saffron
salt and pepper to taste
1 tablespoon butter
chopped parsley for garnish

Sauté garlic and mushrooms in olive oil until light brown. Add next 3 ingredients and heat until onions are translucent. Remove from heat and reserve mushrooms and onions, leaving liquids in pan. Add mussels and

steam until they start to open. Add 2 generous tablespoons mushroom mixture, wine, lime juice, saffron, and salt and pepper. Toss lightly to coat. Whisk in butter to smooth out sauce. Sprinkle with parsley and serve. Serves 4 as an appetizer.

DIVER SCALLOPS

2 to 3 tablespoons olive oil
24 large scallops
salt and pepper to taste
2 shots Absolut vodka
32-ounce bottle Bloody Mary mix
1 tablespoon water
1 tablespoon cornstarch
8 tablespoons crème fraîche for garnish
24 Parmesan chips
1 sprig rosemary

Heat olive oil in a medium sauté pan. Season both sides of scallops with salt and pepper. Sear on both sides about 3 to 5 minutes to cook through. Pour Absolut into a medium saucepan and bring to a boil. Add Bloody Mary mix and reduce by a third. Combine water and cornstarch in a small bowl. Whisk into Bloody Mary mixture to thicken. Season with salt and pepper. Pour ¼ cup sauce onto each of 8 plates. Drizzle plates with crème fraîche. Alternate scallops and Parmesan chips on center of plates and top with fresh rosemary. Serves 8.

THE BUXTON INN
Established 1812

313 EAST BROADWAY
GRANVILLE, OH 43023
WWW.BUXTONINN.COM
740-587-0001

Henry Ford's name appears on the 1938 guest register. Fifty years later, the inn was featured on the back of boxes of Uncle Ben's Rice. The origins of this noteworthy inn extend back to 1801, when a small band of men left Granville, Massachusetts, for the more fertile land of central Ohio. One of the first settlers was Samuel Thrall, who claimed the land on which The Buxton Inn now stands. Eleven years later, the land passed to Orrin Granger, who built an inn for stagecoach travelers. Following Mr. Granger's death in 1815, the inn had a succession of owners until 1861, when James Dilley bought the building. During that time, the inn housed young women who were students at Granville Female Academy across the street. Subsequent to Mr. Dilley's tenure, Major Buxton operated the hostelry, giving it its current name. The major is one of the ghosts said to be seen around the inn. When current owners Audrey and Orville Orr first bought the inn, the staff still set a place at the dinner table for the major. He's also been seen sitting in a rocking chair by the fireplace.

Fred Sweet, son of one of the twentieth-century innkeepers, first wrote about the apparitions in a 1932 alumni bulletin from nearby Denison University. He described the ghost of Orrin Granger, encountered one night in the pantry during Sweet's quest for a piece of apple pie. Many other ghostly experiences involve "the Lady in Blue," Ethel Bounell, who moved from New York City to the inn in 1934. Her spirit was seen walking across the balcony during the Orrs' restoration of the property. A medium from Cincinnati also described a friendly presence dressed in elegant blue that accompanied her from room to room during her visit.

Guests flock to Rooms 7, 8, and 9 in an attempt to experience these prior innkeepers. Quite by chance, we were assigned to Room 9 for the night. We anxiously anticipated what might occur. After checking in, we went downstairs for dinner, starting with the delicious Curried Chicken Soup with toasted almonds and grapes. That was followed by Karen's dinner of Wild Mushroom Stroganoff, filled with five or six different varieties of mushrooms. Debbie went traditional, dining on Ham, Green Beans, and a Baked Sweet Potato. For dessert, we shared a piece of Gingerbread topped with Lemon Sauce, very different from the English variety Karen grew up with, but equally delicious.

Before heading upstairs to settle in for the evening, we looked through the other dining rooms. The largest one, located just off the lobby, is decorated in red and has red plaid draperies hanging at the windows. Down the hall is a more casual room that has oil paintings on the wall and an interesting bar at one end. Downstairs is the tavern, festively decorated with bright quilts on the tables. This is where coach drivers once cooked their own meals at the great open fireplace and slept on beds of straw. We were fortunate to have more comfortable accommodations. As has been the case to date, we slept soundly and well, meeting none of the expected ghostly personalities.

GARLIC VICHYSSOISE

2 to 3 whole heads garlic
4 cups chicken stock
4 potatoes, peeled and quartered
¾ cup chopped celery
1 carrot, chopped
1 cup chopped onions
1 cup half-and-half
1 cup or more heavy cream
chopped garlic chives for garnish

Put garlic and stock into a 2-quart pot and bring to a simmer. Remove garlic when soft, after about 15 minutes. Add vegetables and cook for 10 minutes over medium heat until tender. Allow to cool, then purée in a blender. Taste for garlic flavor. If it's not strong enough, blend in peeled cloves of cooked garlic to taste. Add half-and-half and heavy cream and blend well. Chill. Serve in chilled bowls. Garnish with garlic chives. Serves 8.

PEACH MELBA

12 scoops vanilla ice cream
6 scoops raspberry sherbet
24 fresh peach slices
1½ cups Melba Sauce (see below)
6 generous dabs sweetened whipped cream
almond slivers
6 maraschino cherries

In order, place 2 scoops ice cream, 1 scoop sherbet, 4 peach slices, ¼ cup Melba Sauce, a dab of whipped cream, almond slivers, and a cherry in each of 6 stemmed goblets. Serves 6.

MELBA SAUCE

½ cup currant jelly
1 cup raspberries, sieved, or ½ cup red raspberry jelly
1 teaspoon cornstarch
⅛ teaspoon salt
½ cup sugar
1 tablespoon brandy

Bring currant jelly and raspberry juice or jelly to a boil in a 3-cup saucepan. Separately mix cornstarch, salt, sugar, and brandy. Add to jelly mixture. Cook, whisking well, until mixture is clear and thick. Remove from heat, then chill well. Yields 1½ cups.

THE GOLDEN LAMB
27 SOUTH BROADWAY
LEBANON, OH 45036
WWW.GOLDENLAMB.COM
513-932-5065

When we started the research for this book, the one place everyone mentioned was The Golden Lamb. The history of what is claimed to be Ohio's oldest inn began December 23, 1803, when Jonas Seaman appeared in Warren County Court to request a tavern license for the building where he resided. Seaman's two-story log home was at the very center of the new village named Lebanon, situated at the crossroads of the main north-south and east-west trails. His father had been a tavern keeper in New Jersey, so the nuances of the business were familiar to Jonas. His wife, Martha, was industrious, thrifty, and a good cook. Soon, the tavern gained a reputation as a fine place to stop.

In 1815, a Federal-style two-story brick building replaced the original log cabin, although one of the main-floor dining rooms of today is situated where the log tavern once stood. Additions were made as the inn's pop-ularity grew during the era of coach travel. Since many drivers and other travelers were unable to read, they were simply instructed to go to "the sign of the Golden Lamb."

Since its beginning, the inn has been host to many famous and influential people. Presidents Garfield and McKinley, William Henry Harrison, Benjamin Harrison, Van Buren, John Quincy Adams, Hayes, Grant, Taft, and Harding all stayed here. Mark Twain's slow drawl could be heard as he rehearsed for his performance at the Lebanon Opera House. Had you visited in 1842, you may have been as surprised as innkeeper Calvin Bradley to find that the small, rather disagreeable man sharing his negative opinions about the United States was none other than Charles Dickens. Many of these notables have bedrooms named after them, as do others such as Harriet Beecher Stowe and De Witt Clinton. Each of the eighteen uniquely furnished overnight rooms is open for viewing, provided no guest has checked in.

We enjoyed a quiet lunch in the Dickens Dining Room. Because of the inn's reputation for traditional American fare, Debbie chose the Smothered Steak with Mashed Potatoes. It was filling and good. Karen opted for a more modern choice, the Fresh Fruit Plate. Watermelon, pineapple, strawberries, and oranges were served in a beautifully arranged portion. The Red Raspberry Sorbet that accompanied the fruit was delicious, and the Raisin Nut Bread gave the meal the perfect touch.

We finished with a piece of Sister Lizzie's Shaker Sugar Pie, although we were tempted by the Weary Willie Cobbler because of its story. Weary Willie was a name given to Union soldiers during the Civil War. Legend has it that a tired soldier once stopped at a farmhouse asking for a meal. Food was scarce, and the mistress had little even for her family. All she had managed to scrape together for them to eat that day was a cobbler of cherries and gooseberries. True? That's for you to decide.

BUTTERNUT SQUASH

3 cups diced butternut squash
1 stick butter, divided
¼ cup plus 1 tablespoon brown sugar, divided
¼ teaspoon salt
dash of white pepper
1 unpared Jonathan apple, cored and sliced
½ cup cider or apple juice
¼ cup granulated sugar
1 cup crushed cornflakes
¼ cup chopped pecans

Preheat oven to 350 degrees. Boil squash for 10 minutes. Drain. Add ½ stick butter, 1 tablespoon brown sugar, salt, and white pepper. Heat 1½ tablespoons butter in skillet. Add apples and cider. Sprinkle with granulated sugar. Cover and simmer over low heat about 5 minutes until barely tender. Spread squash and apples in a 3-quart casserole. Mix cornflake crumbs with pecans. Melt remaining butter, combine with remaining brown sugar, and stir into cornflake mixture. Sprinkle over squash. Bake for 30 minutes. Serves 8.

CELERY SEED DRESSING

½ cup sugar
1 teaspoon dry mustard
1 teaspoon salt
1 teaspoon celery seed
¼ teaspoon grated onion
1 cup salad oil
⅓ cup vinegar

Mix together dry ingredients. Add onions. Add a small amount of the oil and mix well. Add vinegar and oil alternately, ending with oil. Yields approximately 2 cups.

SISTER LIZZIE'S SHAKER SUGAR PIE

⅓ cup flour
1 cup brown sugar
9-inch unbaked pie shell
2 cups light cream
1 teaspoon vanilla
2 tablespoons butter
nutmeg

Preheat oven to 350 degrees. Thoroughly mix flour and brown sugar. Spread evenly in bottom of pie shell. Add cream and vanilla. Slice butter into pieces and distribute evenly over top of pie. Sprinkle with nutmeg. Bake for 40 to 45 minutes until firm. Serves 6 to 8.

GUN ROOM RESTAURANT AT

101 FRONT STREET
MARIETTA, OH 45750
WWW.LAFAYETTEHOTEL.COM
740-373-5522

The S. D. H. House Salad was a creation of S. Durward Hoag, whose family owned and operated this hotel from 1918 through 1974. Marietta's version of Cobb salad, it is served with warm Russian Black Bread and the house dressing, Creamy Raspberry Dijon. It was one of the items we decided to share. The other was the Chicken Salad Melt, topped with tomato slices and cheddar cheese, all baked in tender, flaky puff pastry. Both were delicious, as was the side of Potato Salad served with them.

The dining room at The Lafayette Hotel is known as the Gun Room Restaurant because of the private collection of flintlock long rifles that hangs on the walls. These handcrafted relics date from 1795 to 1880. Among the collection is a percussion rifle made by J. J. Henry and his sons, who accompanied Benedict Arnold in 1775.

Other memorabilia pays homage to the influence of riverboats on this establishment. As a matter of fact, the entire dining room looks like a replica of a steamboat. A captain's bell hangs by the entrance, gingerbread trim encircles the room, and black columns fashioned after steamboat smokestacks stand in the archway between the two dining areas. Even the carpet carries the motif, with paddle-wheelers and the Lafayette *L* forming a repeating design.

The Lafayette Hotel, named for the 1825 visit of the Marquis de Lafayette, actually began as the Bellevue Hotel, constructed in 1892. Unfortunately, the Bellevue burned to the ground on April 26, 1916. Two years later, Marietta businessmen rebuilt the hotel, changed its name, and hired Reno G. Hoag as manager at a salary of $150 per month, plus board for his family. It was during his tenure that one of the most interesting stories about the hotel evolved. Residents were suspicious about how a young bellhop working at the hotel could afford shiny new cars. The answer floated up the lobby steps during a flood, as several pint bottles of moonshine bobbed atop the rising water. It seems the enterprising bellhop had been acquiring and storing liquor under the stairs, then selling it to guests at quite a profit! Although Mr. Hoag fired the bellhop, the marketing skills the young man had acquired selling booze came in handy. He went on to employment with Montgomery Ward and worked his way from assistant clerk to executive vice president in just two years!

Tourism is thriving in Marietta, thanks to the town's eleven museums and its strong ties to the Underground Railroad. In fact, some claim that the Underground Railroad began here. Marietta is an official stop for the Delta Queen Steamboat Company. Several times a year, the *Mississippi Queen*, the

Delta Queen, and the *American Queen* dock at the Ohio River levee beside The Lafayette Hotel. When the *Delta Queen* comes to town, it's particularly special, because it's the only time and place where one Historic Hotel of America visits another!

CREAMY BAKED CAULIFLOWER WITH FETA CHEESE

1 head cauliflower
4 cups heavy cream
1 cup crumbled fresh feta cheese
1 teaspoon freshly ground nutmeg
coarse salt and freshly ground pepper
    to taste
¼ cup fresh breadcrumbs

Preheat oven to 350 degrees. Clean cauliflower, cut or break it into large pieces, and place in a small casserole dish. Pour cream over cauliflower. Sprinkle feta evenly over top. Season with nutmeg and salt and pepper. Bake covered for 25 minutes. Uncover, sprinkle with breadcrumbs, and bake uncovered for 8 to 10 minutes more. Serves 8.

ALASKAN SOCKEYE SALMON STRUDEL

2 sticks butter, melted
1 tablespoon chopped fresh parsley
1 tablespoon chopped fresh thyme
1 tablespoon chopped fresh basil
2 pounds sockeye salmon
16 ounces sour cream
2 cloves garlic, minced
½ cup oil-packed sun-dried tomatoes
1 tablespoon chopped fresh oregano
salt and pepper to taste
1 package phyllo dough
1 cup pesto

In a small bowl, combine butter, parsley, thyme, and basil. Set aside. Cut salmon into thin strips. In a food processor, combine sour cream, garlic, tomatoes, and oregano. Season with salt and pepper and continue processing until smooth. Lay out 1 sheet phyllo dough on parchment paper. Brush with butter mixture. Place another layer of phyllo on top and brush with butter mixture. Continue until you have 7 layers. Spread evenly with sour cream mixture, leaving 1 inch on each side. Arrange salmon strips evenly over top and brush generously with pesto. Roll up dough and brush with butter mixture. Refrigerate for at least 1 hour. Preheat oven to 350 degrees. Bake for 20 to 25 minutes until golden brown. Slice and serve immediately. Serves 8. Note: The chef suggests serving Alaskan Sockeye Salmon Strudel with Lobster Cream Sauce.

SHAW'S

RESTAURANT & INN

123 NORTH BROAD STREET
LANCASTER, OH 43130
WWW.SHAWSINN.COM
800-654-2477

Located in a National Register Historic District, Shaw's Restaurant & Inn practically rubs shoulders with history itself. Just down the road, visitors can find the Sherman House, birthplace of Civil War general William Tecumseh Sherman and his younger brother, United States senator John Sherman, the author of the Sherman Antitrust Act. No less popular with tourists is the Georgian Museum, located in the opposite direction. It's a strikingly beautiful restored 1832 mansion complete with furnishings from the period. It would be hard to find a finer collection of nineteenth-century mansions and homes in the Midwest. At the end of a long day of sightseeing, Shaw's is the perfect place to go to be sure of a warm welcome and a delicious meal.

Shaw's was erected at the location of the Pitcher Inn, a popular tavern of the very early 1800s. Rumor has it that the original owner, Rudolph Pitcher, lost the tavern in a poker game in 1806. Hungry travelers in need of a good meal have long made their way here. Indeed, Henry Clay and Daniel Webster could often be found dining on the premises. Current owners Nancy and Bruce Cork have been serving fine food and wine here for long enough to win not only local acclaim but also major accolades including a *Wine Spectator* Award of Excellence.

The menu is short and changes every day, but it always includes a selection of meats, fresh fish, poultry, and pasta. Although we were there for lunch, we checked out the dinner menu and were delighted with the selection. From Ginger-Lime Baked Salmon to Char-Grilled Marinated Elk Chop with Poached Stuffed Pear, it all sounded delicious. We sat in the lower dining room among the local businessmen and the bridge club set. The richly paneled walls with hunt-style sconces and the double valances with pull-back draperies at each of the large windows gave an opulent air to the room. Karen had no difficulty in choosing the Stir-Fried Coconut Curry Chicken with Bok Choy, an extremely creative favorite that came highly recommended. Debbie was intrigued by the Macadamia Nut–Crusted Baked Scrod with Papaya-Basil Sauce.

The inn, one of four hundred North American locations that make up the Select Registry, boasts twenty-two individually decorated suites and guest rooms, many with enormous whirlpools and thematic decorations. Shaw's Restaurant & Inn is definitely making history here in Lancaster, Ohio.

BUTTERMILK-ROASTED LEG OF LAMB

6-pound leg of lamb
3 cloves garlic
1 tablespoon Dijon mustard
½ teaspoon soy sauce
¼ teaspoon pepper
3 tablespoons olive oil
¼ cup buttermilk
½ cup dry white wine
1½ cups beef broth, divided
2 sprigs rosemary
1 tablespoon butter
salt and pepper to taste

Using a knife, pierce holes in top of lamb. Cut 1 clove of garlic into slivers. Insert a sliver of garlic in each hole. Chop remaining 2 cloves of garlic. In a small bowl, mix together garlic, mustard, soy sauce, and ¼ teaspoon pepper. Slowly beat in oil. Slowly add buttermilk. Pour mixture over lamb. Let stand in refrigerator for at least 6 hours, basting often. Preheat oven to 400 degrees. Place lamb on a rack in a roasting pan, reserving buttermilk mixture. Roast lamb for 15 minutes. Combine buttermilk mixture, wine, and ½ cup of the beef broth. Pour around lamb. Add rosemary. Reduce temperature to 300 degrees and continue roasting 15 minutes per pound for medium-rare. Add remaining broth as juices dry up. Remove lamb from pan and set aside. Remove excess fat from sauce. Add butter to finish. Season with salt and pepper. Serve sauce with lamb. Serves 12.

FRENCH BREAD PUDDING

5 eggs
2 cups heavy whipping cream
1 cup sugar
dash of cinnamon
1 tablespoon vanilla
¼ cup raisins
12 1-inch slices French bread
½ stick butter, cubed
Whiskey Sauce (see below)

Preheat oven to 350 degrees. In a large bowl, combine eggs, cream, sugar, cinnamon, vanilla, and raisins. Mix well. Grease bottom of a 9-by-12-inch pan. Pour mixture into pan. Lay slices of bread in mixture and let stand for 5 minutes. Turn bread over and let stand another 10 minutes. Dot with butter. Put pan into a larger pan filled halfway with water. Cover with foil and bake for 40 to 45 minutes, uncovering for the last 10 minutes so top lightly browns. Serve with Whiskey Sauce. Serves 12.

WHISKEY SAUCE

1½ cups sugar
½ cup bourbon
1½ sticks butter
⅓ cup water
1 teaspoon cornstarch

Combine all ingredients in a saucepan. Simmer, stirring constantly, until sauce thickens. Serve warm over French Bread Pudding. Yields 1½ cups.

Hotel Millersburg

est. 1847

35 WEST JACKSON STREET
MILLERSBURG, OH 44654
WWW.HOTELMILLERSBURG.COM
330-674-1457

We arrived at Hotel Millersburg ahead of the normal lunch crowd and took advantage of being the only guests by looking around. The pictures hung on the peach-papered walls depicted scenes from around town. Among those displayed were a picture of the stately courthouse from 1884, one of workmen and horse-drawn wagons, and one from the mid-1920s showing a prosperous downtown. Other photos showed the homes of prominent citizens, including the William T. Hull residence. According to the placard beneath the photo, William McKinley was an overnight guest there in 1895 before making a campaign speech on the courthouse steps the following morning.

Hotel Millersburg was built in 1847. By 1864, the inn was expanded. It soon became the hub of social activity in the town. Over the years, the strain of maintenance began to tell, and the hotel fell into disrepair and ulti-

mately closed. In 1980, Millersburg businessman R. Gene Smith began the slow, tedious process of renovation. Ten years later, local natives Thomas and Cheryl Bird purchased and reopened the hotel, with its handmade bricks and its woodwork painted sage green, burgundy, and gold-toned cream. Other buildings in this section of downtown are also quite interesting. The structure to the left, now a law office, has attractive purple stained-glass transoms. Maxwell's, the building to the right, has lettering on the second-story windows stating, "Trunks and Bags Since 1866." Just down the street is a well-kept emporium.

In the lobby area of the hotel, the owners have maintained the original tin ceiling and oak trim, in keeping with the National Register of Historic Places designation. The formal dining room is available by reservation for up to fifty people. We lunched in the hotel's tavern, a casual room with booths and butcher-block tables. Shortly after we seated ourselves, the restaurant began to fill with business people and local residents. Debbie chose the special of the day, the Open-Faced Roast Beef Sandwich, served with Mashed Potatoes and Applesauce. Karen opted for the Maurice Salad, which contained mixed greens and diced chicken and was served over toasted Sourdough Bread. The tavern offers traditional fare for lunch. Among the nine appetizer choices are Beer-Battered Mushrooms and Potato Skins. There are twelve sandwich options, three of which are highly regarded burger selections. For dinner, five different cuts of beef are advertised. We thought the Pork Tenderloin Medallions with

Apricot Sauce sounded like something one of us might choose.

Holmes County, Ohio, is touted as having the largest Amish settlement in the world. If you're in the area for a bit of sightseeing, Hotel Millersburg will fill you up and allow you to save your pocketbook for some of the crafts that can be found along the country roads.

PORK MEDALLIONS WITH MUSHROOM CAPS

12-ounce pork tenderloin
⅔ cup flour
salt and pepper to taste
3 tablespoons butter
2 cups mushroom caps
¼ cup burgundy wine
¼ cup demi-glace

Slice tenderloin into 6 2-ounce medallions. Mix together flour and salt and pepper in a flat container. Roll medallions in seasoned flour. Melt butter over medium heat in a large sauté pan. Place coated medallions in pan. Brown slightly on both sides. Reduce heat to low. Continue cooking until medallions are almost done, turning once. Drain butter. Add mushroom caps. Deglaze pan with burgundy. Add demi-glace. Reduce liquid by half. Plate medallions and top with mushrooms. Drizzle burgundy reduction over top. Serves 2.

CHICKEN IN MUSHROOM CREAM SAUCE

½ cup flour
¼ teaspoon salt
¼ teaspoon pepper
¼ teaspoon herb of your choice
4 8-ounce chicken breasts
¼ cup clarified butter
½ cup cream sherry
4 ounces mushrooms, sliced
1 green pepper, julienned
2 cups heavy cream

Preheat oven to 350 degrees. In a shallow dish, mix together flour and seasonings. Pound chicken breasts to ½-inch thickness and dredge in seasoned flour. Heat butter in a large, heavy skillet. Brown breasts on 1 side, turn, then place in oven for 15 minutes to finish cooking. Remove skillet from oven and set chicken aside. Drain butter and deglaze pan with sherry. Add mushrooms and peppers and cook about 3 minutes until tender. Add cream, bring to a boil, and reduce sauce to desired thickness. Replace chicken in skillet and warm through. Serves 4.

27 BROADWAY STREET
TOLEDO, OH 43602
419-241-1253

During the War of 1812, Major William Oliver served as a scout. He was stationed at Fort Meigs in nearby Perrysburg, under the command of William Henry Harrison. After the war, he and his Cincinnati partners bought as much land as possible in the Port Lawrence area. Although Oliver built Toledo's first warehouse, he was not immediately successful in his business speculations. He suffered many financial setbacks as he lobbied to have the Lucas County seat moved from Maumee to Toledo.

By 1853, his business ventures had finally succeeded to the point that he commissioned a palace-like hotel to be situated on the highest point of his landholdings. The hotel was to have the finest modern conveniences, including gas lights, running water, and a central courtyard. The courtyard was planned to maximize air circulation and natural sunlight for the 171 rooms.

Eventually, because of its location, the hotel was sold for industrial purposes and

gutted. Riddle Lighting occupied the building from 1919 to 1947, followed by Toledo Wheel and Rim until 1967. Successful Sales next used the structure for display and storage of its novelty items.

Today, what remains of the former luxury hotel are its brick exterior, two ornamental marble mantels, wallpaper, and the black walnut and white ash floor in the lobby. The spacious upstairs dining room of Maumee Bay Brewing Co. occupies what was once the hotel's ballroom. It provides views of the Maumee River and area landmarks. Behind a glass enclosure, the fermenting tanks give diners a glimpse of the brewing process.

I sat in a comfortable booth and enjoyed the simplicity of the dining room's atmosphere. The house brews have been given names that evoke the area. The Buckeye Beer is the lightest on tap. The brewery also creates Glass City Pale Ale and Fallen Timbers Red Ale, among others. I made my dinner choice accordingly, choosing from the list of appetizers the Wings glazed in a dark stout. The serving size was ample enough that I needed to make no other selection. However, the Polynesian Salmon, the Almond-Crusted Pork Medallions, and the Steak and Mushroom Pie were all options that I'll consider on another visit. The desserts were equally appealing, among them Boston Cream Pie, Chocolate Truffle Tart, and Mud Hen Pie, named for the city's minor-league baseball team. It contains Coffee Ice Cream with toffee pieces in a Mint Cookie Crust, all drizzled with Chocolate Sauce and Caramel Sauce. I'll have to try it on my next visit, because it contains an interesting combination of flavors but more calories than I could in good conscience expend on that particular day. Perhaps Karen will be free to come with me next time to share the delicious burden.

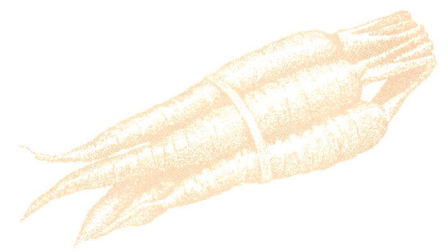

STEAMED MUSSELS

2 pounds mussels, rinsed
½ cup coconut milk
2 tablespoons finely diced red pepper
2 tablespoons chopped cilantro

Place all ingredients in a medium sauté pan. Cover and let steam for 5 minutes. Divide equally between 2 large soup bowls. Serves 2.

ALMOND-CRUSTED PORK MEDALLIONS

16-ounce pork loin
3 tablespoons oil
2 tablespoons dark oyster sauce
¼ cup crushed almonds

Slice pork loin into eight 2-ounce medallions. Heat oil in a large sauté pan. Place medallions in oil and brown on both sides for approximately 4 minutes. When cooked to desired doneness, divide equally between 2 plates. Drizzle with oyster sauce, then sprinkle with almonds. Serves 2.

CHEDDAR BEER SOUP

¼ cup oil
¼ cup diced carrots
¼ cup diced celery
¼ cup diced onion
¾ cup beer
8 cups milk
½ teaspoon thyme
½ teaspoon white pepper
½ tablespoon granulated garlic
½ tablespoon salt
1 small bay leaf
1¼ pounds cheddar cheese, shredded
½ pound provolone cheese, cubed
¼ pound American cheese, shredded

Heat oil in a large pan and sauté carrots, celery, and onions. Whisk in beer, milk, spices, and cheeses. Continue whisking until cheeses melt and mixture is creamy. Serves 10 to 12.

THE GENERAL DENVER HOTEL

81 WEST MAIN STREET
WILMINGTON, OH 45177
WWW.GENERALDENVER.COM
937-383-4141

As in many such communities across the United States during the 1920s, prominent citizens of Wilmington, Ohio, led by Matthew Rombach Denver, had a dream of building a first-class hotel. The town's position between Columbus and Cincinnati seemed ideal for such a venture. During its heyday, the structure contained not only guest rooms and an elegant dining room but also a barbershop, a soda fountain, and a tavern. Not surprisingly, it quickly became a center of business and social life for the community of Wilmington.

Built in 1928, the hotel was named for General James William Denver, considered one of Wilmington's most adventurous citizens. He was a hero of both the Mexican War and the Civil War, a governor of the "Bleeding" Kansas Territory, and a United States legislator serving both California and Colorado. He was also the man for whom Denver, Colorado, was named.

Today, the exterior—with its dark brick, stucco, and cross timbers and its large crest over the entry—provides downtown Wilmington with a decidedly European flair. That feel continues in the small lobby with its simple desk, dark wood, terra-cotta tile floor, and elaborate wall sconces.

To the left of the lobby is the tavern area, its simple bar decorated with memorabilia related to firefighting. Simple burgundy curtains hung at the Gothic-inspired windows as we considered our lunchtime choices. The special of the day was Lasagna, Green Beans, and Garlic Bread, an option that was quite popular with the other guests. We chose another comfort food option—the Cheesy Broccoli Soup, accompanied by the Bacon and Grilled Cheese Sandwich. Both were quite tasty and made a satisfying midday meal.

Dinner and Sunday brunch are served in the more formal dining room, located to the right of the lobby. There, floral carpeting and crisp white linen tablecloths provide a pleasant backdrop for the dining experience. The brunch menu includes traditional fare like Buttermilk Pancakes and Eggs Benedict alongside items with a Western influence, such as Breakfast Burritos, the Fiesta Scramble, and a Denver Breakfast Bake. Entrées such as Grilled Chicken Salad, Turkey Croissants, and Tomato Herb Penne provide alternatives for those wanting something other than breakfast fare.

For dinner, guests can begin with a traditional Shrimp Cocktail or a more casual order of Loaded Nachos. Those looking for light fare may want to try the Black Bean Chili or sample the salad choices. Four pasta choices are available for dinner, including Stuffed

Ravioli and an interesting Southwest Pasta tossed with black beans, corn, red peppers, and Red Cream Sauce. Among the house favorites are the Fire-Roasted Steaks, the Bourbon and Honey Pork Chops, the Chicken Cordon Bleu, and the Tilapia à la Vandervort, topped with a delicious Cucumber Relish.

Innkeepers Mark and Molly Dullea invite guests to slow down, step back in time, and enjoy a visit to The General Denver Hotel. We certainly did.

PURKEY'S PUB STEAK SANDWICH

2 tablespoons sliced onions
2 tablespoons butter, divided
salt and pepper to taste
garlic to taste
1 tablespoon balsamic vinaigrette
2 pieces thinly sliced sourdough bread
2 tablespoons horseradish sauce
¼ cup fresh baby spinach
4 ounces thinly sliced sirloin, grilled
    medium-rare

In a medium sauté pan, sauté onions in 1 tablespoon butter. Season with salt and pepper and garlic. Add balsamic vinaigrette to onions and continue to caramelize. Butter sourdough with remaining butter and grill until toasted. Spread 1 tablespoon horseradish sauce on each slice of bread. Build sandwich with spinach, onions, and sirloin. Serves 1.

DEVILED CRAB TILAPIA

8 4-ounce tilapia fillets
½ stick plus 2 tablespoons butter,
    melted, divided
¼ cup salt, pepper, and garlic blend
1 pound lump crabmeat
½ cup grated Parmesan cheese
½ cup Monterey Jack and cheddar
    cheese blend
½ cup breadcrumbs, divided
1 teaspoon kosher salt
1 teaspoon coarsely ground pepper
1 teaspoon granulated garlic
1 teaspoon thyme
¼ cup diced tomatoes
¼ cup diced onion
¼ cup chopped fresh cilantro

Preheat oven to 450 degrees. Place fillets in a baking pan. Drizzle with 2 tablespoons melted butter. Sprinkle with the salt, pepper, and garlic blend. Combine remaining melted butter, crabmeat, cheeses, ¼ cup breadcrumbs, salt, pepper, granulated garlic, thyme, tomatoes, onions, and cilantro until well blended. Top fillets with equal amounts of crab mixture. Sprinkle evenly with remaining breadcrumbs. Bake for approximately 15 minutes until fillets are flaky and white. Serves 4.

CHAPTER 12

Welcome Home

The White Oak Inn

Home is a concept that each of us has, yet home is completely unique even for members of the same family. Typically, the word evokes feelings of warmth and contentment. At the restaurants in this chapter, all former homes, these same feelings are bestowed upon guests through the service, the ambiance, and the delicious meals served. Even if you're many miles away from your roots, let yourself be welcomed home.

English Ivy

ENGLISH IVY RESTAURANT
104 PARK AVENUE
COSHOCTON, OH 43812
740-622-9201

Just a few blocks from downtown, tucked away in a quiet area of Coshocton, sits the English Ivy Restaurant. It's housed in a Victorian brick home built in 1895 for the Gray family, owners of the Gray Hardware Company in town. In 1906, the home came into the hands of another prominent citizen, Hippolyt Liewor, president of the Coshocton Glass Company. After passing through several other owners during the next ninety-two years, the home was purchased in 1998 by David and Jeanette Hamerdinger and fashioned into the English Ivy Restaurant.

This enjoyable eatery is open for lunch and dinner. In addition, guests can walk in and grab homemade treats such as cookies and brownies. The quality of those baked goods is reflected in the recipe for Raspberry Almond Scones presented here. We lunched with Catherine Howard, an enthusiastic individual from the Coshocton Chamber of Com-

merce. The restaurant was bustling, so we waited briefly in the entryway while our table was being readied. The lovely main staircase has stained handrails and painted spindles, an effect not seen too frequently that coordinates beautifully with the lush wallpaper. As a matter of fact, the woodwork throughout the home exudes a comfortable warmth. The original pocket doors—one of Debbie's favorite features in houses of this era—divide the downstairs dining rooms from the entry. The room to the right of the waiting area has a painted mantelpiece and a burgundy swag border encircling the walls. The delicate lace curtains repeat the lines of the border.

We were seated in the rear dining room just to the left of the tiled fireplace, which added warmth to both the nippy December day and the ambiance of the room. A crystal chandelier hung overhead from the tray ceiling. The room was decorated in shades of burgundy and hunter green.

All the offerings here are made from scratch. Although the menu is short, it was difficult to decide what to pick. Catherine ordered the Broccoli-Cheese Soup, which is always on the menu. She graciously offered us a taste, and it was delicious. Debbie's choice was the Raspberry Salad, a combination of mixed greens tossed with dried cranberries, mandarin oranges, and pecans and served with Raspberry Vinaigrette. Karen opted for the soup and sandwich combination of Mexican Cheddar Vegetable Soup and a Smoked Ham Sandwich topped with Havarti cheese. For dinner, the menu lists Lasagna, Baked Cod, Barbecued Ribs, and Raspberry Chicken among a lengthier list of traditional favorites. Pies and cheesecakes are popular dessert offerings.

Full, and fearing a snowstorm, we asked for some of Jeanette's homemade cookies for the road. Both the Chocolate Chip Cookies and the Peanut Butter Cookies were delicious and let us enjoy the English Ivy Restaurant awhile longer.

RASPBERRY ALMOND SCONES

2 cups unbleached flour
½ cup sugar
2 teaspoons cream of tartar
1 teaspoon baking soda
¾ teaspoon salt
½ cup shortening
2 eggs, slightly beaten
¼ cup buttermilk or sour milk
3 teaspoons red raspberry jam or jelly
2 tablespoons sliced almonds

Preheat oven to 400 degrees. Stir dry ingredients together in a medium bowl. Blend in shortening with a pastry blender until mixture resembles fine breadcrumbs. Add eggs and milk, mixing with a fork. Divide into 2 parts. Turn each part out on a floured surface and form into a ball. Fold 1½ teaspoons of jam into each ball. Top with almonds. Using a rolling pin, flatten each ball into a circle about ½ inch thick. Cut into triangles and place on a greased and floured cookie sheet. Bake for 15 minutes until golden brown. Serve warm and lightly buttered. Yields 16 scones.

SAVORY POTATO-CHEESE SOUP

4 cups peeled and diced potatoes
2 cups chopped onion
1 cup diced celery
5 cups water
15-ounce can cream of celery soup
1 teaspoon dry mustard
1 tablespoon steak sauce
4 cups milk
1 pound Velveeta cheese, diced
2 teaspoons dried parsley
2 cups stewed tomatoes
2 pinches dill

Put first 4 ingredients in a heavy pan. Bring to a boil, cover, and simmer for about 15 minutes. Add remaining ingredients. Cook and stir until cheese is melted and soup is heated through. Serves 8 to 10.

THE ZOAR TAVERN & INN

162 MAIN STREET
ZOAR, OH 44697
WWW.ZOAR-TAVERN-INN.COM
330-874-2170

Religious persecution was a significant cause for many Europeans to emigrate to America. The group of German separatists who exited Wurtemberg in April 1817 was no different. Four months later, they arrived in Philadelphia. Aided by the Quakers there, the group was able to purchase fifty-five hundred acres of land in the Tuscarawas Valley. By spring, the men had constructed enough dwellings to house their families. The name Zoar comes from the biblical story of Lot, who went to Zoar seeking refuge from Sodom.

Since life in the new land was incredibly harsh, the settlers created the Society of Separatists of Zoar. Men and women possessed equal political rights within this society, which managed the goods and services within the community for the mutual benefit of all.

In 1827, the society was contracted to dig seven miles of the Ohio & Erie Canal, which cut across its land. The canal opened the village to commerce. At one point, the Zoarites operated four canal boats. By the mid-1800s, the society had accumulated more

than $1 million in assets. But after the death of its spiritual leader, Joseph Bimeler, the society began to decline. By the late 1800s, the group was no longer commercially viable, thanks largely to increased industrialization. It ultimately disbanded in 1898. In the split, each member equally received land, housing, and goods.

Today, the village is still home to about seventy-five families, who can be seen almost daily at the community post office, since there is no home delivery. The United Church of Christ occupies the meeting house built in 1853. The Ohio Historical Society maintains many of the buildings, including the bakery, the wagon shop, and the blacksmith shop. Others are privately owned and serve as quaint shops. House #23, built as the home of the village doctor, Clemens Breil, was later converted to a tavern where Zoarites could relax. Today, villagers and tourists alike enjoy it as The Zoar Tavern.

We stopped by and tucked ourselves away at a corner table across the room from the high-backed dark wooden booths. Simple muslin curtains and slatted shutters adorn the windows. The menu here is quite varied, ranging from sandwiches such as Pulled Pork BBQ or the popular Chicken Caesar to German selections such as Sauerkraut Balls, Spatzle Soup, Bratwurst, and Jager Schnitzel. There are many other items from which to choose, including pastas, steaks, poultry, and pork chops, along with seven seafood entrées that range from Scrod Almondine to Tempura Shrimp.

The Zoar Country Diner is also part

of the establishment but serves a different menu. Here, comfort food is the focus, beginning with a hearty breakfast. Later in the day, Pot Pies, Meat Loaf, and Stuffed Cabbage are just some of the traditional favorites waiting for guests.

Save room for dessert. We sampled the Oreo Ice Cream Pie and the German Chocolate Cake, both of which were well worth the calories. Our waitress brought out a sample of the Tiramisu as well, which was light and flavorful. It's a good thing we didn't know about the Coconut Cream Pie or the Strawberry Cream Pie. Tasting three desserts borders on gluttony, so we'll just have to save the others for another time.

 SPATZLE SOUP

3 quarts water
3 pounds chicken, cut into large pieces
2 medium onions, chopped
2 cups diced celery
2 cups diced carrots
1 teaspoon salt
¼ teaspoon white pepper
1 batch Spatzle (see below)
5 sprigs fresh parsley, chopped

Bring water to a boil in a large stockpot. Add chicken, vegetables, salt, and white pepper. Bring back to a boil, then reduce heat to medium-low and simmer for approximately 1 hour. Remove chicken. Debone and chop meat. Add uncooked Spatzle to simmering stock. Add chopped chicken and parsley and serve. Serves 12 to 16.

 SPATZLE

3 cups flour
1 cup milk
3 eggs

Thoroughly combine ingredients in a medium bowl. Push dough through a spatzle maker or a colander into chicken stock. Simmer Spatzle for approximately 2 minutes until they float.

CHICKEN SCHNITZEL

¼ cup flour
1 teaspoon salt
¼ teaspoon white pepper
1 egg, beaten
3 tablespoons milk
1 cup breadcrumbs
salt and pepper to taste
4 boneless chicken breasts, pounded to
    ¼-inch thickness
½ stick butter

Combine flour, salt, and white pepper in a small bowl. In another small bowl, beat together egg and milk. In a third bowl, season breadcrumbs with salt and pepper. Lightly coat each chicken breast with seasoned flour. Shake off excess, then dip chicken breasts in egg mixture, then roll them in breadcrumbs. Sauté in butter over medium heat for 5 to 7 minutes per side. Serves 4.

THE DAVENPORT HOUSE

136 WEST BUCKEYE STREET
CLYDE, OH 34310
419-547-4444

Winesburg, Ohio is a very famous novel by Sherwood Anderson. It was one of the first tell-all books ever written, and it caused quite a stir in the small community of Winesburg, where many of the locals recognized the characters, even though the names had been changed. Today, Winesburg is known as Clyde.

Locals still wonder about Miss Irene Davenport, the original owner of The Davenport House, and whether she was a character in that scandalous book. Miss Davenport was a society lady, and as such, she was well taken care of by her wealthy relatives. She never married but did adopt a son, Harkness, whom she named after her wealthy uncle, a colonel in the Union army. The favorite niece of Colonel Harkness, she also had connections with John D. Rockefeller, one of the original seven stockholders who created Standard Oil. Throughout her life, Miss Davenport cashed Standard Oil stipend checks to support herself and her household. There exists some correspondence between Rockefeller and Irene that suggests she often visited him and acted as his hostess at his home in Florida.

A family home for most of its one hundred years, The Davenport House now belongs to Claudia Laurendeau. Claudia explained to us that although she had to extensively renovate the building, she tried very hard to retain its charm and elegance. The high-ceilinged rooms with magnificent crystal chandeliers and Victorian-style globed sconces give the dining rooms a light, fresh feel. Everything is elegant, from the white linens to the tall vases of flowers. We wandered around trying to take in the richness of all the original furnishings that have been retained.

A peek upstairs showed us even more delights. Debbie was extremely fond of the vivid pink, beige, and teal bathroom tiles in one of the luxury bedrooms. On vacation in Italy, the Davenports were so taken with these tiles that they brought them back to Clyde, together with Italian craftsmen to install them. Karen was enamored with the hand-tooled leather wainscoting wrapped around the walls of the stairwell, having never before seen such a fine example.

The lunch menu was interesting. There were a significant number of salad, sandwich, and burger choices besides the main entrées. On the day we visited, the specials were a Barbecued Ham Sandwich and Chicken Pasta Alfredo. We opted for the Hawaiian Chicken with Raspberry Vinaigrette and the Chicken Marsala with Snow Peas and Potato Casserole. Both were delicious, as were the freshly baked Poppy Seed Rolls. Stuffed to the gills, we reluctantly passed on dessert, knowing we'd be back another day. Claudia was proud to tell us that all the food here is homemade using only the finest ingredients. The Davenport House guarantees that you will not eat fresher or more delicious food anywhere.

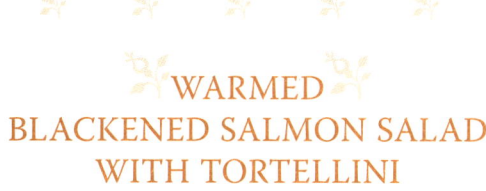

WARMED BLACKENED SALMON SALAD WITH TORTELLINI

2-pound package tricolored cheese tortellini
1¼ cups Italian dressing
6 6-ounce salmon steaks
cooking spray
3 tablespoons olive oil
Jamaican Jerk seasoning to taste
2 heads romaine lettuce, washed
6 Roma tomatoes, quartered
1 medium red onion, thinly sliced
freshly ground black pepper

Cook tortellini according to package directions. Drain. While still warm, toss tortellini with enough Italian dressing to coat liberally. Set aside and keep warm.

Preheat oven to 400 degrees. Place salmon on a foil-covered pan liberally coated with cooking spray. Brush tops of steaks with oil and sprinkle heavily with Jamaican Jerk seasoning. Spray a little olive oil over top of seasoning and place salmon in oven for 8 to 10 minutes.

While steaks are cooking, arrange romaine leaves in spoke fashion on each of 6 plates. Place tomato quarters between leaves. Be sure to leave room in the center for tortellini and salmon.

Change oven setting from bake to broil. Lightly crisp top of salmon. Spoon warm tortellini onto lettuce beds, place salmon in center of plates, top with red onions, and sprinkle with remaining Italian dressing and pepper. Serves 6.

BAKED FUDGE WITH KAHLUA CREAM

2 cups sugar
½ cup flour
¾ cup cocoa
5 eggs, beaten
2 sticks plus 2 tablespoons butter, melted
2 teaspoons vanilla
½ cup chopped pecans
1 cup whipping cream
½ cup powdered sugar
3 tablespoons Kahlua

Preheat oven to 300 degrees. In a large bowl, mix together sugar, flour, and cocoa. Add eggs. Beat in butter and vanilla. Stir in pecans. Pour into 8 custard cups. Set cups in a 9-by-13-by-2-inch pan and add water halfway up. Place in oven and bake for 40 to 45 minutes. While fudge is baking, whip cream in a medium bowl until it starts to thicken. Add sugar and Kahlua and continue to beat until mixture reaches desired consistency. Set aside. Remove Baked Fudge from oven and serve immediately with Kahlua Cream on top. Serves 8.

Lenhardt's

151 WEST MCMILLAN STREET
CINCINNATI, OH 45219
WWW.CHRISTYSANDLENHARDTS.COM
513-281-3600

In 1836, some 5 percent of Cincinnati was German. By 1850, Germans made up more than 77 percent of the population. One such immigrant was Christian Moerlein, who arrived in America from Bavaria in 1841 and headed for Pittsburgh. Not finding work and down to his last fifty cents, he went to Wheeling, West Virginia. Unsuccessful there, he continued to Cincinnati, doing odd jobs along the way. Eventually, he saved enough money to open a blacksmith shop, ultimately employing as many as ten men.

He left that business in 1853 to pursue brewing beer. He and partner Adam Dillman produced a thousand barrels of beer during their first year. The Moerlein Brewery prospered, increasing production to twenty thousand barrels per year in 1860, just seven years after its inception. By 1895, the operation turned out half a million barrels! This growth came in part because Christian Moerlein was one of the first to use pasteurization in making beer, allowing him to export.

Moerlein married in the late 1840s. He and his wife had three children, only one of whom survived to adulthood. He later remarried. That union produced nine children, one of whom was named Elizabeth. Upon her marriage to John Goetz, Jr., in the 1890s, Moerlein commissioned a lovely home as his wedding gift to the couple. That home subsequently was used by a pediatrician. During World War II, the army housed soldiers there. A paddle dated 1953 found on the premises documents the use of the home as a clubhouse for the American Commons Club.

About that time, Anton and Emmi Lenhardt arrived from Yugoslavia. In 1955, Anton and his brother, Kristoff, and their wives opened Lenhardt's Restaurant, a small establishment located at 201½ McMillan Street. They quickly expanded. In 1963, Anton bought the Moerlein estate to house Lenhardt's, which offered Schnitzels, Sauerbraten, and Goulash alongside American foods. In 1977, Anton and Emmi retired and Erika Lenhardt Windholtz and her husband, Joe, took over.

We chatted with Christy Windholtz, the third generation of the Lenhardt family to run the restaurant, as we enjoyed our dinners of Hungarian Goulash with Spatzle and Sauerbraten with a wonderful Potato Pancake. Seated in what once was the music room, we enjoyed the lovely painting of cherubs (purported to be holding hops) on the ceiling. The artwork was uncovered just after the Lenhardts took over the building. A radiator burst, damaging the ceiling. When repairs began, this lovely painting was uncovered. Much of the home's original opulence is still evident, including the ceramic tiles surrounding the fireplaces, said to have been made by the craftsman who taught the Rookwood Pottery people their trade.

When it came time to choose dessert, we had difficulty. How can one select among several varieties of Strudels, Tortes, and other delights? We let Rainy, our server, choose for us. She and Wilma, the gracious hostess, have been with Lenhardt's for more than thirty years. Rainy knew perfectly what we'd enjoy. The Hungarian Cheesecake proved as delicious as it was unusual, and the Linzer Torte was the best we'd ever sampled!

APPLE STRUDEL

6 Granny Smith apples, peeled and sliced
1 cup sugar
¼ cup flour
1½ tablespoons cinnamon
1 sheet puff pastry
1 egg
1 tablespoon water

Preheat oven to 350 degrees. Combine first 4 ingredients in a large bowl to make filling. Prepare puff pastry according to package directions. Visually divide pastry in half lengthwise and place filling in the center of 1 of those halves. Fold remaining pastry over and seal edges. In a small bowl, whisk egg and water together. Brush over pastry. Bake for 1 hour. Cut into 1½-inch slices to serve. Serves 6 to 8.

HUNGARIAN GOULASH

3 large onions, diced
1 green pepper, diced
1 tablespoon shortening
2 pounds stew beef
2 tablespoons paprika
1 cup water
1½ teaspoons salt

Preheat oven to 350 degrees. In a large skillet, sauté onions and peppers in shortening. Add beef and cook until brown. In a small bowl, stir together paprika, water, and salt. Add to meat. Pour into an ovenproof container and bake for 2 hours. Serves 6. Note: Lenhardt's serves this dish over Spatzle.

LIVER DUMPLINGS

1 pound chicken livers
1 onion
6 cloves garlic
1 large egg
4 tablespoons flour
3 tablespoons breadcrumbs
½ teaspoon salt
½ teaspoon pepper

Grind livers, onion, and garlic through a meat grinder into a large bowl. Add egg, flour, breadcrumbs, salt, and pepper. Stir well to blend. Drop dumpling mixture by the teaspoonful into boiling water. Reduce heat and continue to boil for 15 minutes until done. Yields approximately 2 dozen dumplings.

THE GARDEN RESTAURANT

226 EAST PERRY STREET
PORT CLINTON, OH 43452
WWW.GARDENRESTAURANT.COM
419-732-2151

The Garden Restaurant was fashioned out of the dwelling that was once the home of Port Clinton's lighthouse keeper. Following the Battle of Lake Erie in 1813, maritime trade flourished in northern Ohio. This encouraged the government to purchase Lot I, Square 3, from Mr. and Mrs. Ezekial Haines of Cincinnati. Four granite monuments etched with USLHE (United States Light House Engineer) were buried at the corners of that property. It is believed that the entire city of Port Clinton was then platted using those markers.

The United States Lighthouse Service was very specific in its instructions for construction of the lighthouse. It was to be a round, rough-split stone tower forty feet in height. It was to be twenty-two feet in diameter at the base, slimming to ten and a half feet at the lantern deck. Six oil lamps, each with a fourteen-inch silver reflector, made the Port Clinton Lighthouse visible as far as ten miles out on Lake Erie. Austin Smith seems to have had the longest tenure as light keeper. Robert Waterfield and Daniel Finn were also keepers here. Although the United States Lighthouse Service made recommendations to discontinue operations at Port Clinton as early as 1843, service was not officially stopped until 1870.

I was seated in a bright dining room that had the feel of a summer porch. I situated myself so that I could gaze out across Lake Erie. In the park across the street, a small hut caught my eye. That hut was the light keeper's boathouse when the Portage River flowed toward Catawba. At that time, the river cut Catawba off from the mainland, making it an island. After service at the lighthouse was discontinued, local officials decided to change the river's course. It now makes a ninety-degree turn to Lake Erie just across the street from The Garden Restaurant. At the time of the change, two jetties were built and a new lighthouse was constructed. That lighthouse is now in the keeping of a local marina.

With all this maritime history, I chose my meal accordingly, settling on the house specialty, Fish Market Salad. A delicious mixture of greens, fresh fruit, and baby shrimp tossed in Poppy Seed Dressing, it was as refreshing as it was unusual. When it came time to choose dessert, I deferred to the recommendation of my server, having been equally tempted by the Crème de Menthe Parfait, the Almond Cheesecake, the Chocolate Crème Brûlée, and the Upside-Down German Chocolate Cake. The latter is what arrived. Of the two of us, Karen is fonder of chocolate desserts, and after just one bite, I knew she'd be sorry that she wasn't with me to enjoy The Garden Restaurant's unusual version of a longstanding favorite.

The restaurant has a popular dinner theater organized by owner J. Bou-Sliman's wife, Brenda. The couple seated next to me had so enjoyed their dinner here the previous evening that they were back to try the Cajun-Seasoned Salmon and the Chicken Frisco. As their entrées were served, I heard them remark that they'd be back again for dinner and a show.

SEAFOOD PASTA SALAD

½ pound penne pasta
1 cup chopped artificial crabmeat
½ cup salad shrimp
¼ cup sliced black olives
1 cup ranch dressing
¼ cup mild salsa
¼ cup mayonnaise

Cook pasta according to package directions. Let cool. Mix pasta with crabmeat, shrimp, and olives. In a separate bowl, combine ranch dressing, salsa, and mayonnaise. Toss pasta mixture with mayonnaise mixture. Refrigerate for 2 hours to marinate before serving. Serves 4 as a side dish.

THE GARDEN'S TARTAR SAUCE

1 cup mayonnaise
¼ small red onion, finely diced
½ cup pickle relish
2 scant tablespoons Dijon mustard
salt and pepper to taste

In a small bowl, mix together all ingredients thoroughly. Chill until served. Yields approximately 1½ cups.

ALLISTEN MANOR

1307 GARBRY ROAD
PIQUA, OH 45356
WWW.ALLISTENMANOR.COM
937-778-0848

We were seated in a small dining room at a table beside a crackling fire. Over the mantel was an oil painting of the property, looking out from the house across the side porch to the gardens beyond. Our table was covered with an antique tablecloth embroidered with morning glories. The floral motif continued in the wallpaper, printed with hyacinths and roses, and in the floral needlepoint chair seats.

Allisten Manor was named for the first granddaughter of owners Sue and Don Smith. She was born about the time the Smiths acquired the property back in 1982. This was once an eight-room farmhouse built on land granted by President James Madison. Over the years, several prominent Piqua families lived in the house and added a bit here and there. These gradual changes resulted in an evolution in appearance from an 1800s farmhouse to the Colonial mansion of today.

Around the turn of the twentieth century, the property became more of a gentleman's farm than a working farm. It had an orchard, and some truck farming was done. During the 1940s, the estate was known as Jalna, after a series of books by Frenchman Mazo de la Roche. Although quite an avid reader, Debbie had never heard of the books. However, Karen had loved them as a young teen. Jalna is the name of the house in the books, which take readers through stories about the family that builds and lives in the home across several generations.

Allisten Manor serves lunch and dinner by reservation. The Smiths also have a very successful catering business, so the reservations are a must in order for the restaurant to be appropriately staffed. The menu offers a selection of five meals for lunch and four for dinner. Each of the dinner options includes soup or salad, an entrée, and a dessert. The items change seasonally. The evening menu from mid-January to early May includes choices such as Winter Pear Salad and Tomato Dill Soup. Entrées like Chicken Saltimbocca, Grilled Pork Brochette with Zesty Southwestern Salsa, and Tenderloin of Beef Wesley are offered.

Of the five lunches, Karen chose the Cajun Chicken Breast, served with Mixed Vegetables and homemade muffins. That was preceded by a salad, which she chose to dress with Caesar Vinaigrette. It was an unusual twist to a popular flavor combination. Debbie chose the Raspberry Vinaigrette, also very good, to top her salad, which was followed by Broiled Ocean Whitefish and Steamed Vegetables. Having been so very calorie conscious in our entrée selections, we promptly lost our will power and finished our meal with a creamy piece of Cheesecake topped with chopped pecans and Caramel Sauce. It was good to the last bite!

ORANGE CHEESECAKE WITH GRAPES

Crust

¾ cup fine graham cracker crumbs
½ cup all-purpose flour
½ cup finely chopped pecans
¼ cup sugar
1 stick unsalted butter, melted

Preheat oven to 350 degrees. Mix together all ingredients. Press mixture into a standard-sized, ungreased springform pan. Bake for 8 minutes.

Filling

3 8-ounce packages cream cheese, softened
⅔ cup sugar
3 eggs
1½ teaspoons finely shredded orange peel
⅓ cup orange juice

Beat cream cheese and sugar in a mixing bowl until combined. Add eggs, orange peel, and orange juice; mix well. Pour into baked crust. Bake for about 30 minutes until set. Cool.

Glaze

½ cup orange marmalade
⅓ cup white grape juice
3 tablespoons Grand Marnier
2 teaspoons cornstarch
2½ cups seedless grapes, halved

Combine marmalade, grape juice, Grand Marnier, and cornstarch. Cook until bubbling, stirring constantly; cook for 1 additional minute. Cool. Arrange grapes on top of cheesecake. Cover grapes with glaze. Chill cheesecake for a minimum of 6 hours before serving. Serves 12 to 16.

FLAMBÉED SPINACH SALAD

¼ cup brandy
1 cup malt vinegar
1 tablespoon lemon juice
1 tablespoon Worcestershire sauce
½ cup white sugar
⅓ cup light brown sugar
¼ pound bacon, cooked crisp and crumbled
6 cups fresh spinach, washed, stems removed
1 hard-cooked egg, chopped

Heat brandy in a saucepan until warm, then flambé. Add next 6 ingredients and heat until warm. Pour over spinach and toss until spinach begins to wilt. Do not overdo or spinach will cook. Arrange spinach on plates and garnish with egg. Serves 4.

5878 LONGACRE LANE
CHIPPEWA LAKE, OH 44215
WWW.THEOAKSLODGE.COM
330-769-2601

The Oaks Lodge derives its name from the trees around its doorway. At one point, there were five, but time and weather have taken their toll. Only three remain today. These hardy trees, which sit facing the lake, have witnessed the history of this property for quite some time. Some experts have dated them to the days of the Native American mound builders of the area.

During the late 1800s, the Townsend family was closely associated with the railroad. They would come to vacation at Chippewa Lake, transported by their own private railroad car. Ultimately, they purchased the Robb Farm, as well as additional acreage along the east and south shores. Mr. J. F. Townsend remodeled the farmhouse and named it Five Oaks to commemorate the trees standing in a semicircle in front of the home. Townsend added a barn, a carriage house, a boathouse, and formal gardens. A sporting man, he even built a pheasant run. During our visit, we marveled at the portico he added, construct-

ed of a concrete lattice roof supported by thirty-six Doric columns. Lined with hostas in the summer, it is a popular spot for local weddings. The covered terraces set amidst the lovely landscaping are equally popular, both for special events and a simple night out.

The home and family were well known for their hospitality and gracious living. Mr. Townsend entertained friends from all over, including influential men of the time, such as J. Pierpont Morgan. In his travels, Townsend collected stones from around the world, which have been incorporated into the fireplace in today's lounge. The one in the old barroom is interesting, too.

The innovative dinner menu will inspire multiple visits. Starters such as Baked Shrimp and Crab-Stuffed Poblano Peppers, Apricot, Fig, and Sausage-Stuffed Banana Peppers, and Lemon Herbed Ginger Steamed Clams and Mussels quickly caught our attention. We would be happy to sate ourselves with those but wouldn't want to miss entrée concoctions such as the Caramelized Lavender Strip Steak with Roasted Shallots and the Veal Saltimbocca with Vegetable Cannoli. Since the menu changes seasonally, sampling it all is a daunting but tasty challenge.

We were there for Sunday brunch. The salad table offers several choices, including Tossed Salad, Coleslaw, Fruit Salad, and Pasta Salad. In addition to lunch choices, there are quite a few breakfast items, including Omelets made to order. The Pasta Primavera, the Sweet and Sour Chicken, and the Oriental Beef were all delicious. Indecision set in at so many dessert selections, so we took bite-sized samples of several. The Grand Marnier Chocolate Mousse was tasty, as was the German Chocolate Cake. The Coconut Cake was quite good, and so was the Strawberry Swirl Pound Cake. We have no doubt that the other selections—which included Peach Cobbler, Banana Pudding, and Lemon Pound Cake—were every bit as yummy.

CRANBERRY CORNBREAD

2 tablespoons butter
⅓ cup sugar
1 egg
1 cup all-purpose flour
¾ cup yellow cornmeal
4 teaspoons baking powder
¼ teaspoon salt
1 cup milk
1 cup dried cranberries
Ginger Orange Marmalade Glaze
   (see next column)

Preheat oven to 350 degrees. In a medium bowl, cream together butter and sugar. Add egg and beat well. In another bowl, stir together flour, cornmeal, baking powder, and salt. Add flour mixture to butter mixture alternately with milk. Mix well. Fold in cranberries. Spoon into a loaf pan and bake for 35 to 40 minutes, until cornbread is golden brown and a toothpick comes out clean. Cool for 10 minutes. Remove from pan and set on a rack to cool. Drizzle Ginger Orange Marmalade Glaze over top and serve. Serves 6.

GINGER ORANGE MARMALADE GLAZE

4-ounce can mandarin oranges, drained
   and chopped
½ cup fresh orange juice
1 tablespoon grated ginger
1 tablespoon orange zest
2 tablespoons brandy
¾ cup sugar

In a medium, heavy-bottomed saucepan, bring all ingredients to a boil. Reduce heat and simmer for 15 minutes until mixture reaches syrup consistency. Yields approximately 1 cup.

SWEET AND SOUR DRESSING

¾ tablespoon dry mustard
1½ teaspoons celery seed
1½ teaspoons salt
½ cup sugar
1½ tablespoons grated onion
1⅛ cups salad oil
½ cup ketchup
1 tablespoon water
½ cup red wine vinegar

Place all ingredients into a blender. Combine at high speed until creamy. Yields 2½ cups.

29683 WALHONDING ROAD
DANVILLE, OH 43014
WWW.WHITEOAKINN.COM
740-599-6107

Can you imagine a parent *asking* a child to drop out of school? That's what happened in 1916 when George Crise requested that son Paul do so to construct a new family home. George was an entrepreneur and an inventor. Each son he and wife Maude raised inherited that creative ability in slightly different ways. Paul diligently sketched plans as his parents described what they wanted and then set about building the home. George Jr.'s creativity appeared one day during concrete mixing. He'd been assigned the job as a punishment. Rather than doing it by hand, as his father expected, he devised a way to jack up the tractor (a steam engine variety with wheels sixty-six inches high) and use the rear wheel as a drive mechanism to create a cement mixer.

The elder George Crise believed in reusing and recycling. The handrail to the second floor of The White Oak Inn is a single piece of wood brought from the family's original home. As the Sands Hotel in nearby Walhonding was being converted to apartments, George saw another opportunity for thriftiness, purchasing the hotel's old heating system. Believe it or not, those very radiators still heat the inn today!

After completion of the house, George and Maude made it their home for the next twenty years. Following their deaths, their son Lewis and his wife, Thelma, resided there for a lengthy forty-three years. It was Lewis who added the stone light fixture that stands beside today's herb garden. Following in his father's footsteps, Lewis reused the light, which had once stood at the Ralston Hotel in nearby Howard, where it lit the way up an embankment as passengers made their way to the hotel from the railway station.

Today's owners are Yvonne and Ian Martin, Canadians who left the corporate world of Ontario behind and made their way to The White Oak Inn in 1992. The inn functions primarily as a bed-and-breakfast, where ample guest rooms, each with a private bath, showcase antiques that complement the Crises' craftsmanship. Additional guest rooms are uniquely situated in the restored chicken barn, offering a more secluded and romantic environment.

Breakfast is served to overnight guests and might include such delectable offerings as Stuffed French Toast, Broccoli Cheddar Strata, or Belgian Waffles with Pecans and Bananas. At certain times of the year, an overnight stay could land you at The White Oak Inn during one of its special events. Guests throughout the winter months can enjoy the Murder Mystery dinners. During the fall, reservations can be made that include an entertaining rendition of "The Legend of Sleepy Hollow," and Decembers past have included a one-man version of Dickens's *A Christmas Carol.*

For those not staying overnight at the inn, dinner is available by reservation one night per month. Karen was busy with family activities, so I made the trek alone. Upon arrival, I was warmly integrated with the other diners, who included overnight guests, business associates, and neighbors. We began with a creamy Leek and Potato Soup, followed by a light Spinach, Strawberry, and Candied Walnut Salad. Although I chose the Herbed Chicken with Tarragon Sauce, I was interested enough in the other entrée choice, Pork Tenderloin with Peach Barbecue Sauce, to attempt to create it on my own at home. Finishing the evening was a light Lemon Cake topped with fresh berries and whipped cream that brought springtime right to the plate!

MANGO SALSA

2 whole mangoes, peeled and diced into
   ½-inch cubes
2 medium tomatoes, diced into ½-inch cubes
¼ cup minced fresh cilantro
2 teaspoons honey
2 tablespoons cider vinegar
1 tablespoon lime juice
2 teaspoons cumin powder
2 to 3 tablespoons peeled and finely
   chopped fresh ginger

In a medium bowl, mix all ingredients. Cover and chill at least 2 hours before serving. This can be made up to 12 hours ahead. Serves 8 to 12. Note: The chef suggests serving Mango Salsa with salmon or pork tenderloin.

PUMPKIN SOUP

1 cup chopped onion
2 tablespoons butter
4 cups chicken broth, divided
15-ounce can pumpkin
½ teaspoon cinnamon
½ teaspoon ground ginger
¼ teaspoon pepper
1 cup heavy cream
salt to taste

Sauté onions in butter in a medium saucepan until tender. Add 2 cups chicken broth and simmer for about 20 minutes. Using a blender, process until onions are puréed. Return to pan and add remaining 2 cups of chicken broth, pumpkin, cinnamon, ginger, and pepper. Stir well and return to a simmer. Simmer for 5 minutes. Stir in cream and warm through. Do not boil. Add salt, if desired. Serves 6 to 8.

Doc Henderson's Restaurant

318 EAST FIFTH STREET
MARYSVILLE, OH 43040
937-642-6661

We came across Doc Henderson's quite by accident, but what a find it was! We arrived on a gloomy, rainy fall day but felt the sun come out when we stepped inside. The original woodwork gleams throughout the house as it frames large windows and graceful arched doorways. Enormous pocket doors separate the spaces for private dining, but on the day we visited, they were recessed, creating an interior openness. The staff is as sunny as their surroundings, making our experience a truly enjoyable one.

The choices that tempted us included the Baked Brie Salad, the Smoked Salmon Mac and Cheese, the BBQ Meat Loaf Sandwich, the Crab and Corn Cake Sandwich, and Mediterranean Rolls. We enjoyed the daily specials—a Teriyaki Burger with Pineapple Salsa and the Mediterranean Pasta, full of artichokes and feta cheese. We chatted with owner Liz Meeder as we savored our desserts of Buckeye Cheesecake and a Double Chocolate Cream Puff, chosen from a list that included German Apple Cake, Peach Tarts, and Rocky Road Cheesecake.

Liz graciously gave us a tour of Doc

Henderson's old home. As we remarked about the woodwork, she told us that it had taken eighty-two gallons of paint remover to get rid of the layers of paint that had obscured it. The spindles on the staircase are a work of art in their own right, their shape and inlaid wood truly unique.

When David W. Henderson moved to Union County in 1837, only five physicians practiced within the 437 square miles of the county. That number grew to ten by 1840, but the population during that same time tripled. This may have given David his focus as he studied at the Marysville Academy and then went on to attend Ohio Wesleyan University in nearby Delaware, Ohio. In May 1847, at the end of his freshman year, he joined the army, volunteering his services with the Fourth Ohio Regiment protecting Texas during the Mexican War. Upon his return a year later, David began to study medicine under Dr. R. Hills in Delaware, then went on to the Starling Medical College in Columbus, the forerunner of The Ohio State University School of Medicine.

David returned home after graduating in 1852 and set up his medical practice. After ten years in practice, Dr. Henderson enlisted in the army again, leaving his wife and young son, Lutrelle, to serve as the surgeon for the 1,014 men of the Ninety-sixth Ohio Volunteer Infantry as they engaged in the battles of the Civil War. Ill health forced Henderson to return home in April 1863, when he again took up his general medical practice. In 1884, Dr. Henderson had a large brick home constructed on East Fifth Street for Lutrelle, who by that time had also become a physician.

Now, all of us can go to Doc Henderson's for a cure when it's a hunger pang that ails us!

MEDITERRANEAN ROLLS

2 cups sun-dried tomatoes, julienned
2 cups kalamata olives, pitted and chopped
2 cups artichoke hearts, chopped
½ cup pistachios, toasted and cooled
1 cup chiffonade spinach
¾ cup crumbled feta cheese
2 tablespoons balsamic vinegar
1 tablespoon olive oil
salt and pepper to taste
1 package phyllo dough
¼ cup clarified butter, divided
¼ cup breadcrumbs, divided

For filling, mix together first 6 ingredients in a medium bowl. Add vinegar, olive oil, and salt and pepper. Set aside. Preheat oven to 400 degrees. Take 1 sheet of phyllo dough and lay it flat on a clean, dry tabletop. Brush lightly with 1 to 2 teaspoons clarified butter. Sprinkle with breadcrumbs. Lay a second sheet of phyllo on top and brush with butter. Place ¼ cup of filling in an oblong shape across bottom third of sheet, centering the filling in the space. Fold bottom up over filling and continue to roll all the way to end of sheet. Butter the roll and fold edges into center to seal. Place finished roll on a lightly oiled baking pan. Repeat the process until all filling has been used. Place rolls in oven and bake approximately 10 minutes until they turn golden brown. Yields 16 rolls.

PUMPKIN CHEESECAKE

¾ cup graham cracker crumbs
¼ cup crushed gingersnaps
¼ cup sugar
½ stick butter
5 8-ounce packages cream cheese, softened
1¼ cups packed light brown sugar
6 eggs
24 ounces canned pumpkin
¼ teaspoon ground cloves
¾ cup whipping cream

Mix together graham cracker crumbs, gingersnaps, ¼ cup sugar, and butter. Press into bottom of a 10-inch springform pan. Chill. Preheat oven to 350 degrees. Beat cream cheese until smooth. Slowly add brown sugar to incorporate. Add eggs 1 at a time, beating constantly. Fold in pumpkin, cloves, and cream. Mix well. Pour into chilled crust. Wrap bottom and sides of pan in aluminum foil. Place cheesecake in another pan containing 1 inch of hot water. Place in oven and bake for 1 hour and 35 minutes. Turn off oven. Leave cheesecake in oven for another 30 minutes. Remove cheesecake from water bath. Place in refrigerator to cool. Serves 12 to 16.

935 RIVER ROAD
GRANVILLE, OH 43023
740-587-7266

The Bancroft family was prominent in the founding of Granville, Massachusetts, and subsequently the development of Granville, Ohio. The 1866 *Atlas of Licking County* has a picture of a house called Spring Valley Place and identifies it as the home of Dr. William Bancroft. Today, it's home to River Road Coffeehouse. Originally, the house sat along Lancaster Road just south of Raccoon Creek, but it was in the way of progress in the early 1960s, when a four-lane bypass, an interchange, and a gas station were constructed. Rather than being destroyed, the residence was relocated to its present site.

The coffeehouse is an eclectic mix of old and new that I know Karen would have enjoyed. Outside, the beige paint dousing the clapboard siding contrasts pleasantly with the crisp white trim and dark green shutters. On the sunny front porch, where customers bask on warm spring days, an old barrel is topped not with a checkerboard but with a modern glass tabletop. Inside, track lighting, brightly colored rugs on the wide-plank floor, and contemporary seating mix with simple tables,

an old fireplace, and painted rough-hewn walls to create a destination that appeals to college students, senior citizens, and everyone in between.

The father-son team of Mark and David Forman runs this popular spot. My neighbor Elody Krieger and I discovered the Formans and their establishment quite by accident as we drove home to Columbus after a research expedition. Mark quite generously spent some time with us, even though we had dropped in unannounced. He explained that he has always loved coffee and at one time frequented an establishment on Case Western University's campus. That coffee shop was nestled in an old house, and he found the combined comforts of the home and a morning cup of coffee quite appealing. In the back of his mind, he thought one day he might trade in the world of medical administration for that of espresso and cappuccino.

What the Formans most desire is to be known for their focus on coffee and specialty drinks. Each customer receives an order made just for them by specially trained baristas, not by preprogrammed machines. The tea is also custom-blended, purchased locally from a woman in Granville. Elody sampled one of the eight gourmet varieties and was intrigued not only by the blend of flavors but also by the teabag itself. In addition to the hot drinks, a variety of iced and blended drinks are served. The chilled variety are created with a special cold-brewed espresso that is milder than the hot-brewed type. The afternoon we visited, several folks were enjoying those on the deck that overlooks Lake Hudson.

Regular customers scurry in each morning hopeful of getting not only their morning brew but also a traditionally made Bagel. Mark told us that his supply is usually gone by 9:30 A.M. Popular at lunch is the Pineapple Almond Chicken Salad, served on a toasted croissant. The coffeehouse also bakes Scones, Muffins, Danish, and Coffeecakes. The choices are delicious, yet limited. This is a purposeful decision. The Formans want everything they serve to be of quality, and they want the art of coffee making to be their primary focus.

ICED COFFEE

- Obtain 1 pound of high-quality coffee from your local coffeehouse. Remember to make sure that it has been roasted in the last 7 to 14 days.
- Have it ground on a coarse setting.
- Pour the coffee into a filter bag, tie it with a string, and place it in a 1-gallon container in a dark place.
- Add cold water and let sit for 24 hours.
- Drain the cold brew into a closed container and refrigerate.
- Make iced coffee by adding 2 shots (3 ounces) of cold brew to 9 ounces of cold water, then adding 3 ounces of ice.
- Feel free to vary the ratio to suit your own preference.
- Note: If you can't find a filter bag at a local store, strain the final product through a standard paper coffee filter.

PERFECT HOME-BREWED COFFEE

- Buy high-quality coffee roasted in the last 7 to 14 days. If your coffeehouse can't tell you the date it was roasted, don't buy it!
- Make sure the coffee is packaged in a container that has a special valve lock that lets air out but doesn't allow air or light in.
- Never buy coffee stored in barrels or clear glass or plastic containers.
- Store coffee in a dark location away from foods or items with any odors.
- Grind the coffee just before brewing, preferably with a burr-type grinder.
- Match the grind to the brewing system used. Use auto/drip for drip-through brewers, coarse for French press brewers.
- Use the proper amount of coffee, about ½ ounce for every 8 to 10 ounces of water, or 1 coffee scoop for every 6 ounces of water.
- Heat water to just shy of boiling, between 195 and 198 degrees.
- Use a brewing method that allows 4 to 4½ minutes of contact between water and coffee. Most automatic drip coffee makers conform to this standard.
- Use a thermal carafe or air pot for brewed coffee to assure that an external heatplate-does not come into contact with the coffee

87 WEST STREET
CHAGRIN FALLS, OH 44022
WWW.GAMEKEEPERS.COM
440-247-7744

The history of Gamekeeper's Taverne includes some of the most intriguing information we've come across in a while. Its story begins around 1861 with the construction of two cottages in the town of Chagrin Falls. Skip ahead to 1927, when Arthur Crane purchased those cottages and joined them with a ten-thousand-square-foot addition. The newly created building became famous as Crane's Canary Cottage, a restaurant that saw visits from notables such as Duncan Hines, Will Rogers, Charles Lindbergh, and John D. Rockefeller. Mr. Crane's name wasn't recognized by either of us, but we sure recognized his product! He's the candy maker who created Life Savers. We also recognized the name of his son, early-twentieth-century poet Hart Crane.

Arthur Crane passed away in 1932, and his wife subsequently remarried. She and her new husband continued to operate the cottage as he pursued his hobby of antique collecting. Parts of his collection from around the world

are still on display at Gamekeeper's Taverne and the adjoining Inn of Chagrin Falls. Alas, rationing during World War II forced Crane's Canary Cottage to close its doors. Had it not, who knows what other interesting history it might have created.

Following the war, the site reopened as a ladies' tearoom. Later, it became a restaurant known as The Artist's Palate before being transformed into Gamekeeper's Taverne in 1976. Inside, the cozy fireside dining is comfortable and charming. Dark paneling lines the walls, adorned with outdoorsy items. Framed prints of wild animals hang side by side with hunting and fishing gear. We were particularly drawn to the bar's elevated eating area, accessed by a staircase spiraling to the second story.

As cozy as the interior is, it is the tavern's courtyard dining that has received extensive accolades. Year after year, Gamekeeper's Taverne has been given the honor of "Best Outdoor Dining Experience" by both *Cleveland Magazine* and *Northern Ohio Live*. In 2005, it was voted the Cleveland area's "Best Outdoor Restaurant" by AOL via online polling. Since we visited in August, we took advantage of the lovely courtyard. The brick patio nestled behind the tavern is a haven where guests can relax for a drink or a meal.

There were so many menu items that piqued our interest that we couldn't try them all. What's more, they were very unique. Where else can you find Blackened Shrimp Quesadillas, Lobster Nachos, Lamb Chops with Walnut-Crusted Goat Cheese Cake, and Antelope Burgers all on the same menu?

And that's just quoting from the list of "Little Plates." Since we've tried antelope before (not to mention ostrich and bison), we opted to sample the Elk Strip Loin, served with a crisp Potato Croquette on the side. We also shared the Chicken Waldorf Salad. It was a satisfying combination of mesclun greens, dried cherries, toasted walnuts, and chicken, accompanied by unusual Cinnamon Crackle Flatbread.

Next door, the atmosphere and lodging choices available to guests at the inn are as comfortable and as welcoming as the restaurant. The quaint town of Chagrin Falls is a triple threat—fun shopping, relaxing accommodations, and terrific dining. We'll be back!

WALNUT-CRUSTED TILAPIA

2 5-ounce boneless tilapia fillets
2 pinches kosher salt
2 pinches pepper
¼ cup crushed walnuts
¼ cup mixed apple and cranberry preserves

Par-cook tilapia on both sides. Combine salt, pepper, and walnuts. Coat fillets with walnut mixture. Place under broiler for approximately 5 minutes until cooked and flaky. Warm preserves and ladle over fish. Serves 2. Note: The chef recommends serving this dish with a side of rice.

GRILLED CHICKEN AND PENNE

6 to 8 ounces penne pasta
1 tablespoon olive oil
2 tablespoons minced garlic
1½ cups diced tomatoes
2 4-ounce chicken breasts, grilled
¾ cup diced roasted red peppers
2 tablespoons diced scallions, cut at
   a 45-degree angle
⅓ cup grated Romano cheese, divided
¼ cup basil butter
salt and pepper to taste
¼ cup veal stock
¼ cup chopped spinach

Cook pasta according to package directions. While cooking, heat olive oil in a large skillet. Sauté garlic in olive oil until lightly browned. Add tomatoes to keep garlic from burning. Cut chicken into very thin slices. Add chicken, red peppers, scallions, and most of Romano to tomato mixture, reserving approximately 2 tablespoons for garnish. Add basil butter and salt and pepper. Add veal stock as needed to adjust moisture. Drain pasta and toss with tomato and chicken mixture. Remove from heat. Stir in spinach. Sprinkle with remaining Romano and serve. Serves 2.

PUNDERSON MANOR

RESORT AND CONFERENCE CENTER

Operated by **Xanterra** *Parks & Resorts® for ODNR*

11755 KINSMAN ROAD
NEWBURY, OH 44065
WWW.PUNDERSONMANORRESORT.COM
440-564-9144

Punderson Lake dates to the Ice Age, as retreating glaciers left behind a number of glacial lakes across northeastern Ohio. With its ninety acres of surface area, Punderson Lake is one of the largest, and with its depth of eighty-five feet, it is the deepest. Seated at one of the large windows overlooking the lake, we enjoyed breakfast on a late summer morning, a serene experience that invited anyone partaking to linger over Omelets, French Toast, or Pancakes. Outdoors, Adirondack chairs across the flagstone patio and cushioned settees pulled up to cozy firepits proffered other opportunities for guests to relax and take in nature's bounty.

The lake is the namesake of surveyor Lemuel Punderson, who came to the area in 1806 from Connecticut. At the foot of the lake, Punderson constructed three homes—one for himself and one for each of his two sons. Obviously well built, those homes still stand today. With mill irons from Pittsburgh and millstones from Burton, a gristmill was erected and subsequently operated for more than one hundred years.

Beginning in 1902, W. B. Cleveland began acquiring the land bordering Punderson

Lake. By 1908, he also attained rights to the lake itself. During the late 1920s, ownership transferred to Karl Long, a Detroit industrialist. Long spent $250,000 to build a sprawling manor house containing twenty-nine rooms and fourteen baths, to serve as a summer home. Unfortunately, Long lost his fortune during the Depression and died just prior to the home's completion. His widow abandoned the project, and the property reverted to ownership by Mr. Cleveland's widow and brother-in-law, Dr. D. C. Coppedge. In 1948, the state of Ohio purchased 505 acres of this tract, including the lake and the unfinished mansion. After the Division of Parks was created within the newly formed Department of Natural Resources in 1949, the Punderson area was transferred to its jurisdiction, ultimately opening as a park in 1956 and growing to its current thousand acres by the late 1980s.

Today, the manor is both a hotel and a conference center housing dining rooms that serve breakfast, lunch, and dinner. The dinner menu reflects the Tudor-style manor in which it's served. Baked Stuffed Haddock, Veal Chops with Whole-Grain Mustard Demi-Glace, and Medallions of Beef with Stilton all appear on the roster. A bite of any of those would transport Karen across the Atlantic to her native England.

Considering that no one actually ever took up residence in the manor house, it is home to a surprising number of supernatural activities. Park rangers, Punderson employees, and overnight guests have described loud knocking on doors that, when opened, revealed no one there, cold blasts of air accompanied by female laughter, televisions and lights being turned off and on at will, and footsteps belonging to no one apparent. Numerous investigations have confirmed these occurrences but have revealed few clues to their origins, since there is no record of any deaths here. As usual, we had no unusual experiences. Maybe next time we'll have to visit late at night instead of early in the day!

BUBBLE AND SQUEAK

4 medium to large potatoes
¼ head cabbage, finely shredded
2 tablespoons butter, divided
salt and pepper to taste
¼ to ⅓ cup milk

Scrub potatoes clean. Cut into quarters and place in a pot of water, making sure all potatoes are covered. Add a dash of salt to water. Boil potatoes over medium-high heat until soft but not mushy. While potatoes are cooking, steam cabbage until soft. Drain potatoes and cabbage separately. Place potatoes into a deep bowl and add 1 tablespoon butter and salt and pepper. Mash using a potato masher or electric mixer. Add milk a little at a time until desired consistency is reached. Do not add too much milk, as it will make potatoes too thin to handle. Stir cabbage into potatoes. Melt remaining 1 tablespoon butter in a medium skillet. Form potato mixture into balls or patties. Sauté in melted butter until brown on both sides. Serves 4 to 6.

PORK IN MUSTARD CREAM

6-ounce pork loin
¼ cup flour
2 tablespoons butter
scant ¾ cup heavy whipping cream
¼ cup Dijon mustard
salt to taste

Slice pork into medallions. Dredge medallions in flour. Melt butter in a large sauté pan. Cook medallions in pan until lightly browned. Add cream and reduce by half. Add mustard and salt, gently stirring to combine. Heat through to allow flavors to mix. Remove medallions to 2 plates. Spoon sauce over top. Serves 2.

Restaurant Index

Recipe Index

Also by Debbie Nunley & Karen Jane Elliott

A Taste of Maryland History
ISBN 10: 0-89587-313-3
ISBN 13: 978-0-89587-313-2
$19.95 paperback

A Taste of Pennsylvania History
ISBN 10: 0-89587-193-9
ISBN 13: 978-0-89587-193-0
$18.95 paperback

A Taste of Virginia History
ISBN 10: 0-89587-293-5
ISBN 13: 978-0-89587-293-7
$20.95 paperback

John F. Blair, Publisher - 1.800..222.9796 - www.blairpub.com